Princeton University

AND NEIGHBORING INSTITUTIONS

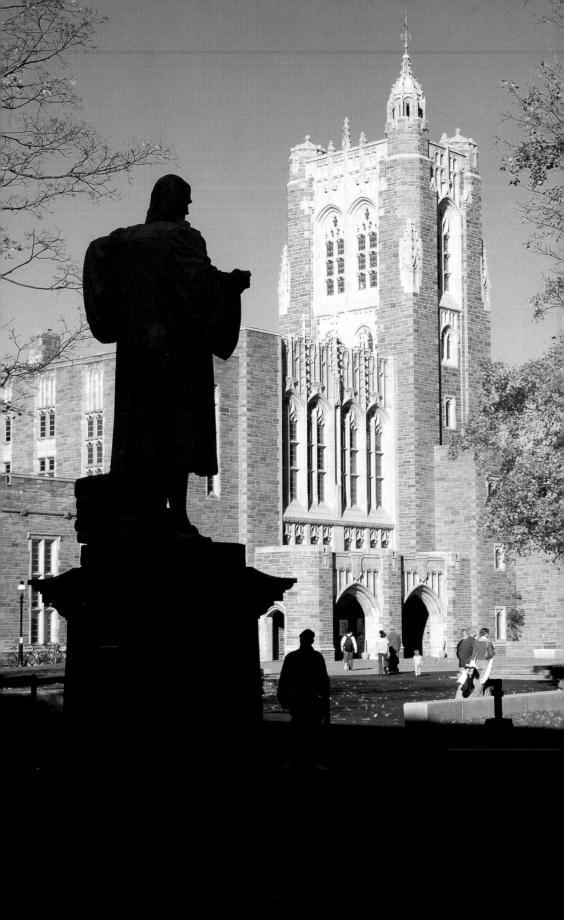

THE CAMPUS GUIDE

Princeton University

AND NEIGHBORING INSTITUTIONS

SECOND EDITION

AN ARCHITECTURAL TOUR BY
Robert Spencer Barnett

FIRST EDITION BY RAYMOND P. RHINEHART

PRINCIPAL PHOTOGRAPHY BY ROBERT SPENCER BARNETT,
WITH ADDITIONAL PHOTOGRAPHY BY
WALTER SMALLING JR.

FOREWORD BY CHRISTOPHER L. EISGRUBER
PREFACE BY SHIRLEY M. TILGHMAN
INTRODUCTION BY RON McCOY

PRINCETON ARCHITECTURAL PRESS
NEW YORK

PUBLISHED BY
Princeton Architectural Press
37 East 7th Street
New York, New York 10003
www.papress.com

First edition text by Raymond P. Rhinehart

SERIES EDITOR: Jan Cigliano Hartman
PROJECT EDITOR: Meredith Baber
DESIGNER: Benjamin English
MAPMAKER: Tom Gastel

SPECIAL THANKS TO: Nicola Bednarek Brower, Janet Behning, Erin Cain,
Tom Cho, Barbara Darko, Jan Haux, Mia Johnson, Valerie Kamen,
Stephanie Leke, Diane Levinson, Jennifer Lippert, Sara McKay,
Jaime Nelson, Rob Shaeffer, Sara Stemen, Kaymar Thomas, Paul Wagner,
Joseph Weston, and Janet Wong of Princeton Architectural Press
—Kevin C. Lippert, publisher

LIBRARY OF CONGRESS CATALOGING-IN-PUBLICATION DATA
Barnett, Robert Spencer.
Princeton University : an architectural tour / by Robert Spencer Barnett ;
principal photography by Robert Spencer Barnett, with additional
photography by Walter Smalling Jr. and Christopher Lillja ; preface by
Shirley M. Tilghman ; foreword by Christopher L. Eisgruber ; introduction
by Ron McCoy.—Revised and updated.
     pages   cm—(The campus guide)
Includes bibliographical references and index.
ISBN 978-1-61689-234-0 (alk. paper)
1. Princeton University—Guidebooks. 2. Princeton University—Buildings.
3. Princeton University—Tours. 4. Princeton University—Pictorial works.
I. Title.
LD4611.B37 2015
378.749'65—dc23   2014044925

Contents

This book is a resource for those interested in learning more about the campus of Princeton University and its neighboring institutions. Whether used for walking tours, an armchair guide, or both, the visitor-reader will benefit from the geographical, chronological, and thematic organization of the text, maps, and images. As part of the Campus Guide series, the book can also be used for comparative purposes.

There are eleven walks on the campus of Princeton University, including Landscape Walks, the Princeton University Art Museum collection highlights (Walk Six) and the Graduate College (Walk Ten). There are three additional walks, featuring the Princeton Theological Seminary (Walk Eleven), the Institute for Advanced Study (Walk Twelve), and Downtown Princeton (Walk Thirteen). The walks feature individual buildings from the eighteenth century to the present, landscapes—greens, courtyards, walkways, gardens, woodlands, and wetlands—and works of art. On the university campus, exterior sculptures and some interior paintings and sculptures are part of the John B. Putnam Jr. Memorial Collection, unless noted otherwise. Campus Art at Princeton—a website for mobile devices—is available at artmuseum.princeton.edu/campus-art.

For each walk, an illustrated, aerial perspective map orients the visitor-reader to the featured buildings and environs; north is located at the bottom of these maps. An essay for each walk introduces historical and contemporary issues associated with the featured buildings, landscapes, and artworks. Landscape walks include plans, text, and images of connective landscapes that contribute to the character of the university campus; north is at the top of these plans. Dates given in parentheses are for graduation years of alumni or an individual's tenure in an official position.

While the walking tours are oriented toward the grounds and building exteriors—except for the Art Museum collections—certain university buildings are open to the public, including, in addition to the Art Museum, the University Chapel, the Frist Campus Center, the University Store (114–116 Nassau Street and 36 University Place), and athletic, exhibition, and performance spaces, during scheduled events. For current visitor information and scheduled events, please refer to the contact information below.

Princeton University
www.princeton.edu/main/visiting
(609) 258-3000

Princeton Theological Seminary
www.ptsem.edu
(609) 921-8300

Institute for Advanced Study
www.ias.edu
(609) 734-8000

Historical Society of Princeton
www.princetonhistory.org
(609) 921-6939

**Princeton Regional Convention
& Visitors Bureau**
www.visitprinceton.org
(609) 924-1776

Graduate College window tracery with golf course in distance

During my years as Princeton's provost I always enjoyed listening as Orange
Key tour groups assembled outside my office window on the first floor of Nassau
Hall. The student leading the tour invariably pointed out the cannonball scar
on the building's west wing—a vestige of the Revolutionary Army's efforts to
flush out the British during the Battle of Princeton. Hearing that tale brought a
smile to my face, not just because it reminded me that I sat within an American
landmark, but because I knew that the small dimple in Nassau Hall's facade was
connecting visitors to Princeton's traditions and this country's history.

This magical place—captured so thoroughly and beautifully in this
guide—has inspired students, alumni, faculty, staff, and visitors since the university, then known as the College of New Jersey, moved to Princeton in 1756.
This book will enable you to trace the remarkable evolution of our campus, and
that of our neighboring institutions and town, from the colonial period to the
modern day.

An intense love for our campus is one of the strongest bonds shared by
Princeton students and alumni. I experienced those ties from the moment I first
stepped foot here. Pictures in campus brochures had impressed me as a high
school student in Oregon, enough to apply for admission sight unseen! But
when I arrived for my freshman year in the fall of 1979, Old Nassau's graceful
buildings and inviting courtyards took my breath away.

Cuyler Hall, a Collegiate Gothic residence hall built in 1912, was my home
as a freshman. I marveled at the magnificent stonework, the stunning craftsmanship, and the palpable sense of tradition that I felt walking the grounds of my
new dormitory. How lucky I was to be in such a place! I experienced a sense of
wonder as I passed through the majestic Blair Arch on my way to meals in what
was then known as the Commons (now dining and common room space for
Rockefeller and Mathey colleges).

Like so many other Princetonians, I quickly grew attached to many of the
glorious and welcoming spaces around campus. I loved walking across Firestone
Plaza—flanked by the venerable Chapel, East Pyne, and Chancellor Green—and
into Firestone Library. Exploring the stacks and inhabiting the reading rooms
of our world-class "library-laboratory" connected me to the academic soul of the
university. The same can be said for Jadwin Hall, where I spent so many hours
as a physics concentrator, puzzling through problem sets and seeking to glimpse
fundamental truths about the natural world.

Now, some thirty years after my graduation and more than a decade after
my return to Princeton as a faculty member, I continue to feel a mixture of affection and awe when I stroll through the campus. While so much of the campus
remains as it was decades ago, so too have there been vibrant transformations.
Some of the paths around Fine Tower, where I once took walks to clear my head
as I drafted papers and prepared for exams, have given way to the brilliantly bold

Butler College 1976 Garden

Lewis Library that houses our science collections. Other recent additions to the campus—from the Gothic Revival Whitman College to the shimmering psychology complex linking Peretsman-Scully Hall and the Princeton Neuroscience Institute—have enabled Princeton to enhance the vitality of student life and extend the frontiers of learning.

Today I feel very fortunate to call this campus my home and to play a role in its stewardship. And I hope you will find this guide to be a valuable companion as you traverse the paths, examine the architectural marvels, and soak in the spirit of the campus that we Princetonians lovingly call "The Best Old Place of All."

Christopher L. Eisgruber
President of the University
Laurance S. Rockefeller Professor of Public Affairs in the
Woodrow Wilson School and the University Center for Human Values

After almost thirty years of daily interaction, I have not become inured to the beauty of Princeton's campus. Its unique combination of breathtaking vistas and intimate spaces; of manicured greens and verdant woodlands; of Georgian, Victorian, Collegiate Gothic, modern, and postmodern architecture never ceases to delight. Cradled in five hundred acres is the work of some of the world's most iconic architects, including Pritzker Prize winners Frank Gehry, Rafael Moneo, I. M. Pei, and Robert Venturi, as well as monuments to giants of former times: Benjamin Latrobe, architect of the U.S. Capitol; John Notman, who popularized Italianate design in America; and Beatrix Farrand, the celebrated landscape architect. To turn a corner is to be surprised—by a whimsical gargoyle, a shimmering curtain wall of glass, a profusion of magnolias, or an arch that appears to epitomize all arches until the next one is encountered. This "revelation of the unexpected," to quote Princeton's first supervising architect, Ralph Adams Cram, is a physical metaphor for what occurs in our classrooms and laboratories: an opening of minds.

At their best, these revelations are informed by the insights of those who have made it their work to study them. And so, while all visitors to Princeton can expect to have their senses stimulated by the natural and man-made beauty that surrounds them, their experience will be greatly enriched by seeking out a guide, none better than this volume. The architectural tour it promises is actually thirteen tours—or walks—that tell the story not only of our university but also of two sister institutions, the Princeton Theological Seminary and the Institute for Advanced Study, as well as the town of Princeton's historic center. Each campus walk, organized around architectural epochs, disciplinary neighborhoods, or facets of university life, reveals one part of an interlocking puzzle that may at first appear to lack coherence but is, in fact, a synthesis of form and function spanning more than two and a half centuries.

The perspectives offered by this volume range from panoramic to precise. We move, for example, from the broad meaning of Princeton's adoption of

Holder-Campbell-Blair archways

Collegiate Gothic architecture at the close of the nineteenth century—"to achieve the credibility of a great modern university, Princeton reached back into history and dressed itself in Gothic stones"—to the intricacies of Cuyler Hall: "If a spider could spin stone webs, the ceiling inside Pitney archway would be the result, with rosettes, leaves, coats of arms, and shields caught like so many flies." We are introduced to unique juxtapositions, like that abutting Scudder Plaza: "Here stand four episodes of twentieth-century architecture: the Collegiate Gothic former Frick Laboratory on the north; an austere Cold War

Washington Road woodlands at Streicker Bridge

brick-box-cum-cylinder in Corwin Hall; and postmodern Bendheim and Fisher Halls on the east; and a flamboyant recollection of the Parthenon in Robertson Hall on the south." But, on other occasions, we are guided to places that evoke a single moment in time, like the sequestered grounds of the Graduate College.

Finally—and most importantly—we are reminded that Princeton's campus is a work in progress; that the innovations of today will be, a century or more from now, the beloved remnants of the past. Our responsibility passed from generation to generation is twofold: to care for the campus and to enjoy it, and that can only happen if we see the campus as the remarkable expression of human aspiration and natural beauty that it clearly is. Happily, no one who walks its paths with this volume in hand can fail to do so.

Shirley M. Tilghman
President of the University (2001–13)
Professor of Molecular Biology and Public Affairs

At its best the American college campus is the ideal form of community, where scale of space, landscape, and architecture exist together with a special sense of purpose and meaning. Whether the size of a small village or a small city, all of the campus parts work together and reflect the identity of a single institution. The result is a continuous record of both the enduring values of the institution and the changing nature of higher education. The campus is a different kind of place than the city, where both the vitality and the cacophony of relatively disconnected institutions, industries, and communities simultaneously evolve and compete for identity. The college campus therefore provides a special opportunity to experience architecture in an ideal setting.

At Princeton traces of the past and aspirations for the future are particularly moving. The campus has a serene beauty and timeless sense of place that is vividly captured in the specific qualities of material, craft, and landscape. The Princeton campus presents an image of unity, yet it is remarkably diverse. The historic campus is more eclectic than it seems—there are eleven distinct styles among the eighteen extant buildings built prior to the Collegiate Gothic era— and the modern campus is more unified than apparent. This balance reflects a deep institutional commitment to the importance of campus planning and the creative potential of each generation of architects and landscape architects.

This guide is organized as a collection of walks through which the Princeton campus and neighboring institutions can be understood and experienced. While this is a convenient tool for organizing a campus visit, one should remain open to the beauty of the Princeton campus as a compelling totality. The native woodland setting and the gently sloping site of the campus anticipate a sense of place that is precisely defined by a particular interplay of landscape and the presence of buildings.

Interspersed among the eleven university walks are four distinct eras of campus architecture and planning. The first is the colonial campus, established with the construction of Nassau Hall and Maclean House in 1756 and expanded in the early part of the nineteenth century to include Stanhope Hall (Geologic Hall), West College, and the symmetrical twins of these buildings: Philosophical Hall and East College (both replaced by new buildings in the late nineteenth century). In this era the American campus consciously broke from European precedents and established the campus as a place apart: an idealized and self-contained community free of the vices and distractions of the city.

As American campus planning evolved, so did Princeton's colonial campus and, under the influence of new plans such as those at Union College and the University of Virginia, Princeton took the form of a small but more complex academic community. Whig and Clio Halls (both constructed in 1892) defined the southern boundary of the campus, creating a "back campus" (now called Cannon Green) to complement the historic "front campus" north of Nassau

McCosh–Dickinson–Chapel courtyard

Hall. This historic campus is experienced as a quiet and gentle field with classical buildings occupying balanced positions within the extended horizon of lawns and the tall canopy of trees.

The second distinct phase of campus planning, created under the leadership of President James McCosh (1868–88), is defined by the landscape and planning principles of the English landscape park. Two buildings of the McCosh era, the Victorian Chancellor Green and Collegiate Gothic East Pyne, are situated to maintain the symmetry of the colonial campus. The remaining buildings of this era are Alexander, Witherspoon, Edwards, Dod, and Brown Halls. These buildings make no attempt to create a space like their classically oriented predecessors. Instead they are arranged with picturesque variety along a strong diagonal pathway that extends from Witherspoon to Brown and continues through campus to the McCosh Health Center.

Collegiate Gothic architecture, the third generation of campus architecture, has become the defining style of Princeton. Officially begun with the construction of Blair Hall in 1898, the principles of this style shaped the identity of the campus under the leadership of Supervising Architect Ralph Adams Cram and through the work of a generation of Philadelphia architects, most notably the firms of Cope and Stewardson, and Day and Klauder. This style stretches from Washington Road to the Graduate College and from Nassau Street to

McCosh Walk

Goheen Walk, and was used through the 1948 construction of Firestone Library. Unlike the open landscapes of the earlier campus, the Collegiate Gothic campus is composed of enclosed and semienclosed courtyards, linked lawns, and a magical rhythm of episodic vistas and emerging spaces. Cram saw the style as one that would unify the campus into a single academic community. Collegiate Gothic also imbues the campus with an intimate sense of form, material beauty, and craft, complementing the natural setting and the campus landscapes.

The modern campus began with the interiors of Firestone Library and continues through the current generation of growth. For a brief period, from 1948 to 1980, a generation of architects found it difficult to reconcile innovation with memory, and fell short of the ideal of creating a unique and coherent place. As a consequence the campus suffered because of the creation of buildings that are either too generic or too isolated. Through several significant projects the architectural firm Venturi, Rauch and Scott Brown reintroduced to Princeton—and to modern architecture—the importance of the relationship between the part and the whole.

The current generation of architects, landscape architects, and planners are reimagining the character of the campus at its edges and transforming parts in between. Shapiro Walk, Tilghman Walk, the Natural Sciences Neighborhood, Lakeside Graduate Housing, the Andlinger Center for Energy and the Environment, and the Lewis Center for the Arts are all informed and inspired by a sense of place that defines Princeton. Each is a reflection of this generation's values with respect to art, material, technology, and sustainability. And each is a contribution to the physical record of the aspirations of a unique academic community and the expression of that community in the form of a campus.

Ron McCoy
University Architect

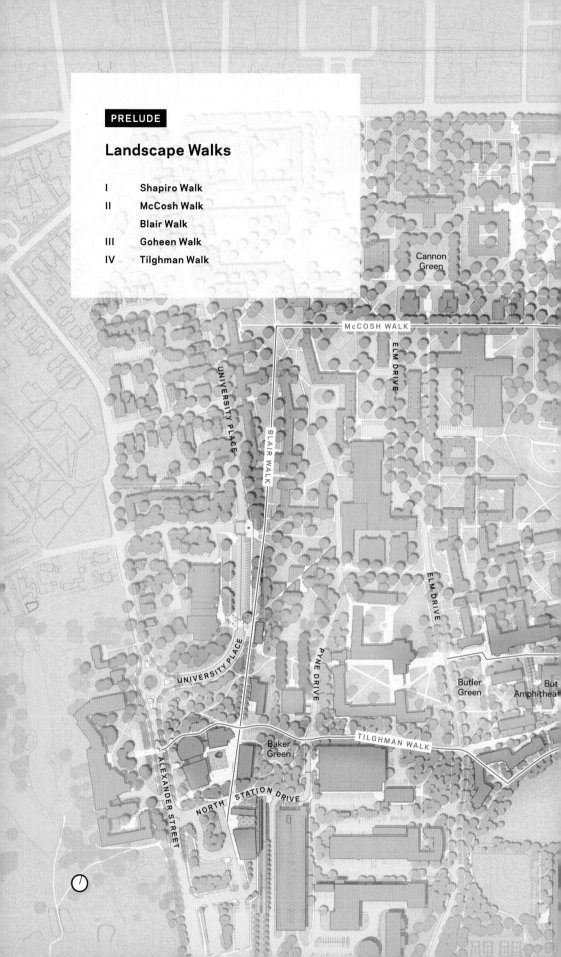

PRELUDE

Landscape Walks

Cannon
Green

McCOSH WALK

ELM DRIVE

UNIVERSITY PLACE

BLAIR WALK

ELM DRIVE

UNIVERSITY PLACE

PYNE DRIVE

Butler
Green

But
Amphithea

TILGHMAN WALK

Baker
Green

ALEXANDER STREET

NORTH STATION DRIVE

WILLIAM STREET

OLDEN STREET

SHAPIRO WALK

Scudder
Plaza

WASHINGTON ROAD

PROSPECT AVENUE

IVY LANE

GOHEEN WALK

Jadwin
Plaza

WASHINGTON ROAD

Poe / Pardee Field

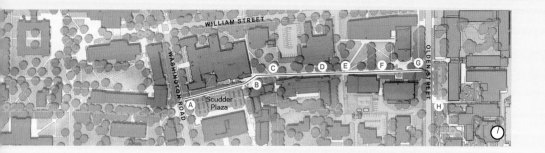

I   Shapiro Walk

Landscape: Michael Vergason, 2000; Landscape: Quennell Rothschild &
Partners, 2001–5; Landscape: Michael Van Valkenburgh Associates, 2009

Shapiro Walk, an eastward continuation of McCosh Walk that extends from Washington Road to Olden Street, is named for the eighteenth president of the university, Harold T. Shapiro, and his wife, Vivian. During Shapiro's tenure (1988–2001) the university celebrated its 250th anniversary, the endowment quadrupled, the undergraduate student body increased by 10 percent, and plans for a campus center and other student life and academic initiatives were realized. The walk links the Woodrow Wilson School of Public and International Affairs (WWS), where Shapiro is professor of economics and public affairs, and the School of Engineering and Applied Science (SEAS). While president, Shapiro oversaw the construction of six new buildings for WWS and SEAS.

In the early 1990s the pedestrian connection between WWS and SEAS was tenuous at best. A narrow asphalt walk, squeezed tight against the chain-link fences of eating club parking lots and crossed by Charlton Street (a service drive at the time), provided nothing campus-like in the passage. In 1997 university architects sketched out plans for a broad tree-lined walk between Scudder Plaza and Olden Street, along with a new social sciences building (Wallace Hall) on the site of a former club parking lot. In 2000 landscape architect Michael Vergason finalized the resulting walk design, using gray concrete pavers bordered by orange-red brick pavers. Charlton Street was given similar treatment, converting it to a pedestrian-friendly lane shared with vehicles. Vergason's plan included an allée of honey locust trees along the walk's western half and wisteria vines at Wallace Hall's entry trellis. The walk's eastern half was built the following year, concurrent with the construction of Friend Center and an addition to the Princeton University Press. Quennell Rothschild & Partners' (QRP) design contributed the dawn redwood that stands west of the press building, the hollies screening the parking lot, and a small Zen-like garden across the walk, tucked between Mudd Library and Wallace Hall. These much-needed landscape improvements, along with the new buildings, began to unify the neighborhood and to extend the pattern of buildings and grounds characteristic of the historic campus. The plantings along Shapiro Walk were intended to match the quality of plantings in campus areas west of Washington Road but to do so in a slightly

different way. Along Shapiro Walk, the plantings are more garden-like, with increased
emphasis on perennials, flowering shrubs,
and ground cover, rather than the canopy
trees that characterize other campus walks.

Shapiro Walk begins at Washington
Road and heads east along a sloping walk
lined with magnolia trees and Scudder
Plaza Ⓐ on the right, and the south walls
of 20 Washington Road (formerly Frick
Laboratory) on the left. It continues under
20 Washington's entrance bridge to a plaza
adjacent to Corwin and Wallace Halls Ⓑ
at the base of stairs leading down from
Scudder Plaza. To the north the walk opens
to a campus green planted with London plane
and black tupelo trees. Crossing this green
and leading to a passage between Corwin
and Wallace Halls is a pathway Ⓒ that
connects William Street to the north with
Prospect Avenue to the south. Continuing
east between Wallace Hall and Princeton
University Press Ⓓ, the walk is bordered by
parrotia trees with beds of fothergilla and
clethra designed by Michael Van Valkenburgh
Associates (MVVA). Just beyond Charlton
Street, flanking the walk, QRP designed a

pair of granite benches and a dedication
plaque honoring the Shapiros Ⓔ set in the
pavement. An inscription on the benches
reads in part, "A place to pause and reflect in
the company of friends, ideas and dreams."
From here another campus green opens
Ⓕ, defined by the press, Friend Center,
Computer Science, and Sherrerd Hall.
MVVA planted witch hazel and liriope along
Sherrerd's facade and a Himalayan pine east
of the press. As with many open campus
greens, the spatial experience of the walk
is enhanced by diagonal paths leading to
building entries, lawns, and shade trees.

The projecting bay of the Computer
Science Building and the forecourt of
Mudd Library define the approach to Olden
Street Ⓖ. The Olden Street frontage of
the Computer Science Building is graced
with a gravel path lined with honey locust
trees and park benches. New pathways and
landscapes Ⓗ designed in conjunction with
the Andlinger Center for Energy and the
Environment buildings will provide continuity
with Shapiro Walk and guide one's view to the
entrance of Andlinger and access into public
spaces within the expanded E-Quad.

Shapiro Walk at Charlton Street

Cannon
Green

F E McCosh Walk D C B A Scudder
Plaza

WASHINGTON ROAD

ELM DRIVE

UNIVERSITY PLACE

Blair Walk

G

H

PINE DRIVE

I

J

Baker
Green

K

ALEXANDER STREET

NORTH STATION DRIVE

L

II McCosh Walk

*Renovation: Princeton University Office
of the University Architect, 2014–17*

Blair Walk

*Landscape: Beatrix Jones Farrand,
1912–43; Restoration: Michael
Van Valkenburgh Associates, 2008*

Pair of Tigers

*Bruce Moore, 1968; cast bronze
Princeton University, gift of Hugh
Trumbull Adams, Class of 1935*

McCosh Walk, named for James McCosh, extends in a straight line west from Washington Road to Lockhart Arch on University Place. Believed to be Princeton's first named walk, it is labeled on the 1906 campus map, bordering the south side of the newly completed McCosh Hall. It connects Scudder Plaza on the east to the residential courtyard below Blair Hall on the west. This courtyard was once the terminus of the train spur to campus from Princeton

Junction. When the terminus was moved south near the intersection of Alexander Street and University Place in 1917, new dormitories and a landscaped pathway named Blair Walk were built on the vacated railroad right-of-way. Together McCosh and Blair Walks engage a significant portion of the university's heritage.

During his tenure President McCosh initiated a program to beautify the campus grounds by stabilizing footpaths and planting trees, lawns, and gardens. Beatrix Farrand further developed landscape improvements to McCosh and Blair Walks. Her work is evidenced by the beds of rhododendrons along McCosh and the magnolias, yews, and pines along Blair.

Michael Van Valkenburgh observed that Princeton pathways follow three trajectories: level and generally straight east–west pathways; sloping north–south pathways that often jog around buildings; and mostly sloping diagonal pathways that slice between and through buildings. McCosh and Blair are examples of the first two types and intersect several diagonals of the third type along their length.

A walk starting on Scudder Plaza and ending at the Lewis Center for the Arts provides a pleasant downhill route to experience a sequence of campus arts venues and the various landscapes that connect them. Several arts venues are not featured on this walk: the Lewis Center's visual arts studios and James M. Stewart (Class of 1932) film theater at 185 Nassau Street; the university's primary concert hall, Richardson Auditorium in Alexander Hall; and a recital hall, Taplin Auditorium in Fine Hall.

After crossing Washington Road, the space between McCosh Hall and Marx Hall frames the eastern terminus of McCosh Walk Ⓐ. Here the Class of 1970 plaza features a circular raised planter edged in green granite. American elm and beech trees line the walk to frame a view ahead and provide the walk's signature high shade canopy. To the right a short path leads through an arch to McCosh-Dickinson-Chapel courtyard. To the left is 1879 Green, with the Frist Campus Center arcade and north facade terminating the vista to the south. The north wing of the T-shaped School of Architecture flanks McCosh Walk paralleling McCosh Hall.

Students exploit the well-traveled nature of this section of McCosh Walk by hanging banners (usually painted bedsheets) announcing their organizations' events over the walkway. Beyond the architecture building to the left, the front lawn of Prospect House, known as Sherrerd Green, can be glimpsed through the rhododendrons lining the walk. Stone gateposts at the entrance drive to Prospect House Ⓑ are remnants of a gated enclosure that secured the grounds when Prospect was a private residence for the Potter family and, later, the president's home. An iconic photograph from 1890 depicts McCosh standing on the walk at this location sheltered by rows of mature American elm trees. Judging by the size of the elms, they were likely planted before his presidency, when the east half of the walk was still a drive from Washington Road to the Potter family's front gate— now Prospect's gate. Some time later, the western half of the walk was extended to Little Hall and also planted with elms. Many of the original elms were lost to Dutch elm disease, and in the 1960s American beech trees were introduced to fill in the gaps.

On the left a diagonal path across a lawn leads to the main entrance of

President McCosh, ca. 1890–1900

McCormick Hall and the Art Museum. On the right is an intimate landscaped courtyard between Murray and Dodge Halls featuring a tribute to the spirit of Woodstock given by the Class of 1969. Just beyond the library wing of McCormick Hall Ⓒ another diagonal path leads from Firestone Library to Dillon Gym (an arch and stair between Dillon and Little Hall continues the path toward the train station). Here McCosh Walk begins a downward slope. New accessible entrances to Whig Hall and Clio Hall are located along this segment. Looking right between Whig and Clio Halls, steps rise to a view of Nassau Hall framed by a pair of stalking tigers Ⓓ by Bruce Moore. Moore was a student of Alexander Phimister Proctor, the artist who created the tigers in front of Nassau Hall. While Proctor's tigers are naturalistically rendered, Moore's are larger, stylized representations. The tigers arrived on campus in the same year as Princeton's first female undergraduates and quickly became symbols of Princeton's coeducation. Looking left—perpendicular to McCosh Walk along a central

axis that begins at Nassau Hall's cupola—is a broad, tree-lined path between Dod and McCormick Halls. This path, designed by university architects in 1997, is the only realized portion of a central mall concept proposed by Ralph Adams Cram in his 1909 master plan.

McCosh Walk crosses Elm Drive before continuing its descent. Elm Drive—which provides access for service, shuttle bus, and emergency vehicles—is the only north–south campus roadway between Nassau Street and Faculty Road. A diagonal pathway from Rockefeller and Mathey Colleges to Frist Campus Center also crosses Elm Drive at this point. Next is Tiger Gate, an opening in the wall between Buyers Hall and Little Hall Ⓔ. Stone pedestals, surmounted by carved tigers clutching shields, provide a gateway to the expansive green lawn of Blair Hall courtyard, on axis with Lockhart Hall's arch. A compass pattern embedded in the pavement Ⓕ marks the intersection of McCosh Walk and Blair Walk. To the right, up a broad flight of steps, is Blair Arch, once the ceremonial entrance to campus for those arriving by train. Blair Walk continues south to the left. Working closely with the architects for the new dormitories on the vacated railroad right-of-way, Farrand used varied planting strategies to enhance the walking experience. In Blair's large informal court, trees were planted sparingly and away from the walk to preserve the vista. The upper banks of Blair Hall were planted with ground-hugging shrubs that complement the architecture without obscuring it. Farther south, Blair Walk passes through the first of two pairs of converging dormitory wings to enter a domestically scaled courtyard Ⓖ defined by four undergraduate dormitories built in the 1920s. The courtyard provides access to dormitory entryways and communal space and is enhanced by wall

"Pair of Tigers"

Blair Courtyard looking south

plantings, lawns, and shade trees designed by Farrand. A three-arched passageway between Henry and Foulke Halls is graced with climbing wisteria vines, a Farrand trademark, and at the northeast corner, delicate tamarisk trees are espaliered against stone walls. Beyond Dodge Gate, at the court's south end, the vista opens south toward the Arts Neighborhood and Transit Center. Here Farrand's landscape changes character to a more formal allée of clipped evergreen yews, pruned in a "haystack" profile and backed by low stone walls. The broad center walk is paved in random-pattern bluestone. This portion of Blair Walk (H) passes by Pyne Hall and white pines on the left before reaching the intersection of College Road and University Place. On the right, Farrand's grove of saucer magnolias shelters the allée from University Place. A crosswalk leads to College Road and the main entrance of the McCarter Theatre Center on the west side of University Place. As Blair Walk passes Spelman Halls it merges with a diagonal path from Dillon Gym (I). Here, a view of Whitman College opens

to the left. The main entrance of the Berlind Theatre building is across University Place, accessed via a crosswalk.

As University Place curves south toward the intersection with Alexander Street, Blair Walk continues its linear path toward the arts plaza and the transit plaza. On the left, the two stone-clad, slate-roofed former train station buildings—repurposed as a cafe and restaurant—provide outdoor dining in favorable weather. Formal rows of saucer magnolias line the passing walk, continuing Farrand's palette. Tilghman Walk intersects Blair Walk just south of the former station buildings (J). To the right is a lawn densely planted with a variety of native trees. The arts plaza (K) is framed by three buildings devoted to the arts. It features paving stones—some tightly jointed, some interspersed with grass—and a shallow pool with aquatic plants, shade trees, and views into rehearsal spaces below. Like the prototypical Princeton three-sided courtyard, the arts plaza is open on the south end to the transit plaza beyond (L).

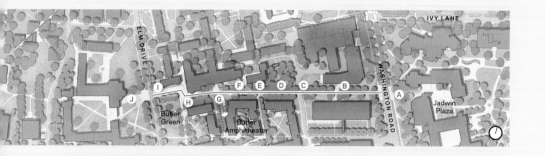

Goheen Walk

Venturi, Scott Brown and Associates, 1986–95; Landscape: Princeton University Office of Physical Planning, 1998–2004; Landscape: Michael Van Valkenburgh Associates, 2008–9; Landscape: Office of University Architect, 2005–14

Pair of Lions

Cast by J. L. Mott Ironworks, A. Schiffelman, before 1889
Zinc covered in bronze lacquer and gold paint
Princeton University, gift of the Class of 1879

Goheen Walk, named for Robert F. Goheen, the sixteenth president of the university, extends from Washington Road on the east to Elm Drive on the west. It connects the central segments of the Natural Sciences Neighborhood to the residential colleges. During Goheen's administration (1957-72) the university first admitted women undergraduate students, expanded the faculty by 40 percent, quadrupled the annual budget, and almost doubled the size of the physical plant. Goheen oversaw construction of the Jadwin-Fine complex and the original Butler College and Wilson College buildings, which are located to the south and north of Goheen Walk.

Similar to several other campus walks, Goheen Walk began as Maple Road, which crossed Washington Road and connected the former Brokaw Athletic Field (now the site of Whitman College) to the former

Palmer Stadium. It opened in 1910, flanked by athletic fields, and was lined with maple trees soon after. In the early 1960s the construction of Faculty Road, farther south, provided an alternative route that allowed the tree-lined road to be converted to a more pedestrian scale and function. Construction of Wu Hall (1983), Thomas Laboratory (1986), and Schultz Laboratory (1993) improved the walk at both ends, with bluestone paving at Thomas and Schultz and red asphalt hexagonal pavers at Wu. The early 1990s brought new concrete pavers to the middle stretch of the walk, with additional improvements in 1998 when the walk was dedicated to President Goheen.

Starting at the east end of the walk Ⓐ the entrance stair and covered entry to McDonnell Hall provide westward views of Goheen Walk and terminate the eastward vista from the walk. The maple allée Ⓑ

defines the walk as it progresses west between Schultz and Thomas. Beyond the laboratory buildings the walk crosses Guyot Lane ⓒ, a walkway and service drive that connects Tilghman Walk to the south with Frist Campus Center to the north. At this juncture a grove of mature saucer magnolia trees graces an open space on the north side of the walk ⓓ. Proceeding west, the facades of Scully Hall and Butler College on the south and Wilson College on the north define the walkway. Between Scully Hall and 1976 Hall of Butler College ⓔ, a walk leads south to Scully's arch, framing a view of Poe and Pardee Fields beyond and connecting with Tilghman Walk. A few steps farther west on Goheen Walk is President Goheen's granite dedication plaque ⓕ set in the pavement. Looking north, a walkway passes between two gilded lions as it leads toward 1927-Clapp Hall. This pair of bronzed lions flanked the entrance to Nassau Hall until 1911, when they were replaced by the tigers that guard the building today. The lions are located in the Wilson College complex, appropriately so, considering that they once overlooked Prospect Avenue from 1879 Hall, where Woodrow Wilson occupied an office as university president.

Farther west the new entrance pavilion to Wilcox Hall asserts its presence on the north side of the walk and serves as the focal point ⓖ for Lourie-Love Walk, which connects to Tilghman Walk at its south end. The pavilion was given a foreground on Goheen Walk with the addition of a raised entry plaza paved in bluestone, and embraced by low, stone seat-walls. It adjoins an existing terrace south of Wilcox, used for outdoor dining. A cluster of arborvitae trees announces the north entrance to Lourie-Love Walk, which is lined by tightly spaced katsura trees. Two small courts designed by Michael Van Valkenburgh Associates, one story below this walk, serve as light wells for Butler's below-grade common level. The court floors are fashioned from slabs of locust tree wood, set flush with the ground. Stewartia trees and ferns enliven the views from inside Butler.

Back on Goheen Walk, just west of Wilcox's cobblestone bike park, the bay window of Wu Hall punctuates the walk and points to the Butler College sundial and tiger monument ⓗ on the south side. Here Goheen Walk opens onto Butler Green ⓘ, a broad expanse of open lawn framed by mature zelkova trees along Elm Drive, and a scattering of evergreens, ginkgo, and parrotia trees along its east edge. The western extent of Goheen Walk ends with a flourish—the Collegiate Gothic facade of Whitman College ⓙ across the drive.

Goheen Walk looking west

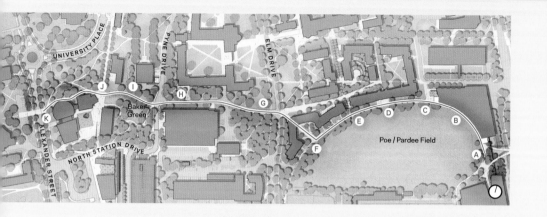

IV Tilghman Walk

Landscape: Quennell Rothschild & Partners, 2004; Landscape: Michael Van Valkenburgh Associates, 2012–17

Upon Shirley M. Tilghman's retirement as university president, the trustees named a major east–west walkway in her honor. The walk is aptly named, as it connects three neighborhoods developed during her tenure: natural sciences (see Walk Nine), residential colleges (see Walk Eight), and arts (see Walk Seven). Tilghman Walk extends through the southern part of the campus from Washington Road to Alexander Street.

The walk starts at Streicker Bridge Ⓐ, which joins the eastern and western sectors of the Natural Sciences Neighborhood. Tilghman's administration planned and constructed four first-class facilities in this neighborhood, for genomics, chemistry, psychology, and neuroscience, as well as a multidisciplinary science library.

The first section of the walk passes through the contemporary cloister of Icahn Laboratory Ⓑ. At the time she was elected president, Tilghman was the founding director of the Lewis-Sigler Institute for Integrative Genomics, housed in Icahn. Patterns of shadow and light created by

sunlight on the exterior louvers, and the activity within the atrium cafe and conference rooms enliven this part of the walk. The walk emerges from the cloister onto a small plaza Ⓒ paved with exposed aggregate and planted with shade trees. Guyot Lane, a walkway leading to Guyot Hall and Frist Campus Center, extends from the north side of this plaza.

Beyond the plaza the path around the Ellipse extends in front of Scully and Bloomberg Halls. Shrubs and benches set amid beds of ground cover define the north side of the walkway and regularly spaced oak trees define the south edge along the fields. The fields were filled and leveled in 1946 with earth excavated during construction of Firestone Library. They are now used for recreation and summer camp sports. The walk is paved in bluestone slabs bordered by red-orange precast concrete pavers and bluestone curbs. A tower defines a portal to Scully Hall Ⓓ, where a tree-lined walk leads north through a quadrangle to Goheen Walk. Farther west a grove of giant arborvitae between Scully and Bloomberg announces Lourie–Love Walk (E), which traverses Butler College to connect with Goheen Walk at the Wilcox Hall terrace. On axis with Bloomberg Hall's archway (F), Tilghman Walk leaves the ellipse, heads northwest through the arch, and continues west toward Elm Drive and Whitman College. Significant residential buildings in this neighborhood—Bloomberg Hall, Butler College, and Whitman College—were constructed during Tilghman's administration.

Crossing Elm Drive the walk heads west through a reconstructed woodland (G) between Whitman College, 200 Elm Drive, and Baker Rink. While this segment, also known as Baker Lane, functions as a service drive, campus planners designed the plantings and paving materials to preserve the pedestrian-friendly nature of the walk. Older shade trees on the Baker Rink side are complemented by maturing trees and understory plantings on the Whitman College side. A short bluestone walk (H) framed by redbuds, pines, and cryptomerias leads to the entrance of the Princeton Writing Program in Whitman College.

Beyond Baker Rink, west of Pyne Drive, the walk will enter the radically transformed southwestern precinct of the main campus. The Lewis Center for the Arts, one of Tilghman's highest-priority capital projects, will replace surface parking lots, service buildings, and train track barriers. From Pyne Drive the walk will enter Baker Green (I) and its network of meandering paths and varied topography created by Michael Van Valkenburgh Associates. Here the grade will rise to a grassy hillside that provides a seating area for outdoor performances. Underneath this constructed hill there will be a service tunnel that connects Pyne Drive to the Lewis Center loading dock. Tilghman Walk will cross Blair Walk (J) at Lewis Center's arts plaza, where one will find a reflecting pool and resting place. The walk will then curve around the north facade of the Lewis Center building, past groves of shade trees on the right, and toward the walk's terminus at Alexander Street (K). There, a signalized crosswalk will lead to the main entrance of Forbes College with views of the golf course and the Graduate College beyond.

Tilghman Walk looking west along Ellipse

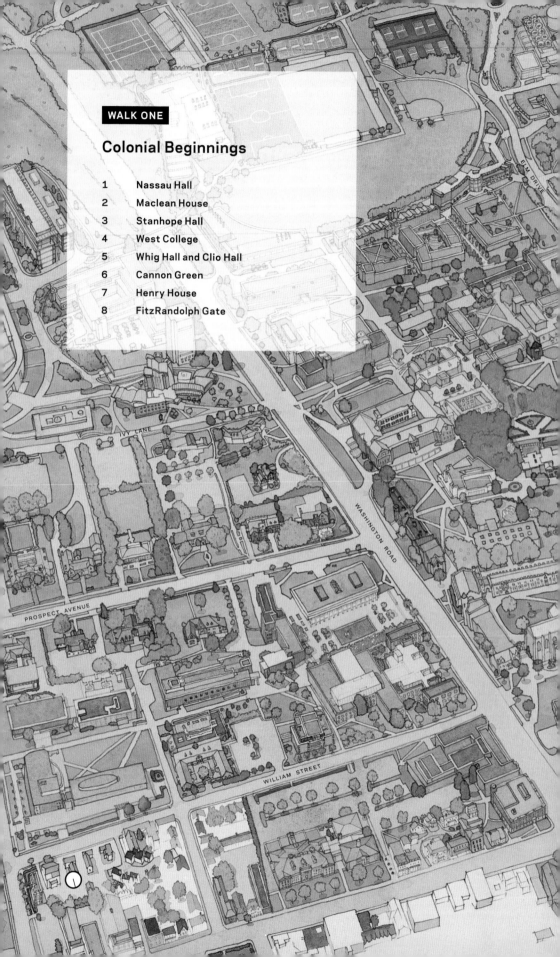

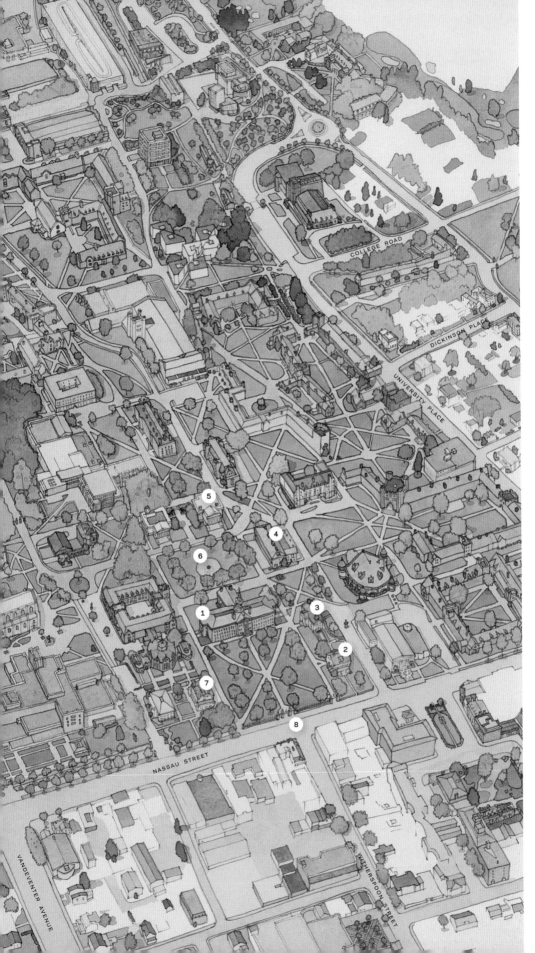

Colonial Beginnings

THE BEGINNINGS

Meeting in Newark in 1753, the trustees of the College of New Jersey were at a fateful crossroads. The college, which had been founded in Elizabeth in 1746 and moved to Newark in 1747, was debating yet another move. The debate was prompted by religious and economic considerations. But there was another issue that weighed heavily on their minds. The trustees of the fledgling college believed there was a close relationship between environment and human conduct. The right environment would nurture a young mind and encourage the growth of a godly spirit; the wrong place could corrupt it.

The village of Princeton (originally "Prince-Town") answered the call in two ways. First, the trustees were among the evangelical Presbyterians—the so-called New Lights—who were establishing Protestant churches throughout the British-American colonies at a fast pace and seeking qualified ministers to tend to the spiritual needs of the growing flock. They needed an institution of their own to train young men to take the word deep into the wilderness. It would be an expensive undertaking, and the trustees required that the chosen community donate land and wooded lots for fuel and building materials to help underwrite the cost. Several communities expressed interest, but it was the citizens of Princeton who came forward. Its selection seems almost preordained: the trustees were eager for a site, according to college president and trustee Aaron Burr Sr., "more sequestered from the various temptations attending a promiscuous converse with the world, that theatre of folly and dissipation." Princeton donated the required land and wood; the absence of urban folly and dissipation was a distinct plus.

Yet it was also an odd site, housing a small collection of buildings halfway between Philadelphia and New York. Hardly more than a change of horses passed through on the well-traveled mud rut that was rather grandly called the "Kings Highway." In retrospect, it seems improbable that one of America's pre-eminent universities would be located in this isolated place. Even more improbable, on the day Nassau Hall opened its doors in 1756, it was said to be the largest building in the colonies—and it stood in an open field. From the perspective of two and a half centuries later, Nassau's siting would be like finding the Empire State Building on the high plains of Wyoming.

Unlike its predecessors, Harvard, William and Mary, and Yale, which were developed within colonial towns, the College of New Jersey put down its roots in country soil. Carpenter-builder Robert Smith, with the assistance of Dr. William Shippen, designed Nassau Hall to be approached by way of a large lawn or green that gradually sloped up to the building, stepping back a considerable distance from the King's Highway with a sweeping vista of fields and wooded stream valleys in the background. In donating this particular four and a half acres to the

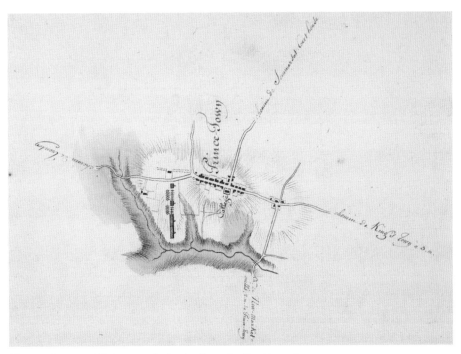

Topographic map of Princetown by Louis–Alexandre Berthier, 1781

college, the FitzRandolph family enabled the new school to build on one of the higher elevations in the area, thus affording commanding views to the north and south. This preoccupation with views and vistas guided the development of the university, continuing to the present day.

The openness of the land also had a profound, yet subtle, impact on the formation of the campus. Occupying the distance between what is today Nassau Street and Nassau Hall, the intervening green is more than a neutral area between town and college; it is the open space, the campus, the collegial center that holds the two elements in balance. Perhaps it is not surprising that the current use of the term *campus*, derived from the Latin word for *field*, had its origin at Princeton around 1770. The adoption of the ancient word by most American institutions of higher learning suggests that the term succinctly embraces a wide range of ideas and principles first articulated at Princeton. The natural setting of wooded stream valleys was also a formative influence on the college's early development. The valleys provided access routes to the town and campus from the south that represented distinctive experiential thresholds for both, while also offering views of fields and woodlands from their higher elevations.

If the vistas direct one's line of sight out into the world, and if the openness of the land provides an emotional centering, the architecture offers the contrary dimension of enclosure. As the mediator between humankind and nature, architecture also reflects complex and shifting attitudes toward privacy, community, nature, ambition, and purpose. For nearly three centuries the physical

Front Campus, view toward Nassau Street, ca. 1874

development of the university has articulated and reflected succeeding waves of enlightenment, religious revival, literary creativity, and scientific rationalism. Princeton's campus reflects many perspectives about the place of humankind in the scheme of things.

The story of Princeton's main campus is not about any one extraordinary building. There are no heroes here. The campus is an admirable ensemble, a whole that is greater than the sum of its parts. Despite changes in architectural fashion and educational curriculum, the university has sustained over the centuries a nearly unwavering commitment to vistas, open space, and enclosures (or outdoor rooms). Importantly, there is an uncompromising investment in proximity and the pedestrian realm: today most campus locations are within a ten-minute walk of the Frist Campus Center.

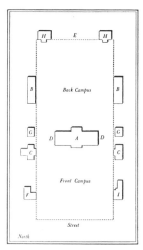

1836 Joseph Henry Plan

An architectural walk around the northern and oldest precinct of the campus is made up of three expanding circles, each beginning at or near Nassau Hall—the magnetic north of the university. The three walks have something of the character of a geological excavation, the oldest layer beginning at Nassau Hall. The historic center, organized in the early nineteenth century by Benjamin Latrobe's paired Geological and Philosophical Halls that flanked Nassau Hall, and Joseph Henry's 1836 master plan, the campus's first, reflected the neoclassical ideals of balance, symmetry, clarity, and simple geometric forms. Not surprisingly, the fabric of the earliest colonial and Georgian buildings is least intact, as the university has grown to the south, east, and west over the years and adopted new forms in response to a changing world. Nevertheless, much remains, in part because Princeton's prevailing spirit is to conserve and to think over long-term horizons, and in part because it is also frugal, more likely to recycle or even move an entire building than tear it down. For instance, Henry House, originally built in 1837 and today standing northeast of Nassau Hall, has occupied four sites on campus and each time it was moved very carefully, as if it were a well-loved piece of furniture.

Nassau Hall (left) and Maclean, or President's House (right), engraving by Henry Dawkins, 1764

1 Nassau Hall

Robert Smith and Dr. William Shippen, 1756; Renovation: Benjamin Latrobe, 1803

NATIONAL HISTORIC LANDMARK · When Nassau Hall opened its doors in 1756 it was widely acclaimed. It was capable of housing 150 students and their teachers, and it was one of the most admired and imitated. War, conflagration, and the work of succeeding generations of architects have pounded its walls. But those walls have held, a testament to the skill of its builders, both those who set the stone and those who planted the seeds of a great university. During the Revolutionary War, Nassau Hall served alternately as barracks, a hospital, and a prison for Continental and British troops. During the Battle of Princeton, in January 1777, George Washington's forces drove the British from the building, which sustained extensive damage within and without. Washington's victory is commemorated in a portrait by Charles Willson Peale, which can be seen today in Nassau Hall's Faculty Room. When the colony of New Jersey declared itself an independent state in 1776, its first legislature met in Nassau Hall and its first governor, William Livingston, was inaugurated there. When the town of Princeton served temporarily as the nation's capitol, the Continental Congress met in Nassau Hall during the summer and fall of 1783. In recognition of the building's role in the birth of the nation, the National Parks Service designated Nassau Hall a National Historic Landmark in 1960.

When Edward Shippen arrived in Newark on January 24, 1753, he was prepared to discuss with his fellow trustees how the College of New Jersey was to be housed in its new Princeton home. The plans he carried called for a structure

190 feet long and 50 feet deep. Although the original documents do not survive, they appear to have been based on a design sketched in Philadelphia by Shippen's brother, Dr. William Shippen, in collaboration with Robert Smith. Born in Dalkeith, near Edinburgh, Scotland, Smith had apprenticed with a builder and may have worked for the great Scottish designer William Adam. Smith gave the trustees a building with a level of craftsmanship that put the new college on the map.

Smith developed Shippen's plans for a rectangular, three-story-plus English basement structure, a central projected pedimented pavilion, hipped roof, and cupola. However, the trustees overrode Smith's preference of brick for the exterior walls, and so it fell to a local mason named William Worth to suggest a less costly alternative—the local sedimentary rock known as Stockton sandstone—which Worth most likely quarried from a site on the south bank of what today is Lake Carnegie. Similar stone is evident in the walls of Stanhope Hall and West College. The local stone has also become a symbol of the powerful idea that had established the College of New Jersey in the first place: like the university, the twenty-six-inch-thick walls of Nassau Hall seem capable of handling everything that anyone can throw at them.

The plan and elevation of Nassau Hall follow the prevailing Georgian architectural style of the mid-eighteenth century. To say "Georgian" means a preference for symmetry: what is on the left side of the front door is repeated on the right, both inside the building and out. The central entrance pavilion on the north (front) side was repeated on the opposite side—in plan—by the original prayer hall. The external

Nassau Hall, north facade

stairs and doorways on the front were repeated on the rear. Window openings are regularly spaced horizontally and vertically on both front and rear sides. Also typical of Georgian architecture, the windows, entrances, and edges of the structure are clearly articulated and proportional to one another. The seeming efficiency of having all functions under one roof made Nassau Hall a model for colleges then being founded up and down the eastern seaboard and beyond, including Brown, Dartmouth, Rutgers, and the University of South Carolina. In fact, Nassau Hall influenced collegiate architecture well into the nineteenth century, as can be seen at nearby Princeton Theological Seminary's Alexander Hall. However, at Nassau Hall functional efficiency also meant Spartan accommodations. As President Burr wrote to a Scottish donor: "We do everything in the plainest and cheapest manner, as far as is consistent with Decency and Convenience, having no superfluous Ornaments."

Princeton historian T. J. Wertenbaker points to the contemporary pattern books that builders and carpenters regularly consulted as the sources for Smith's designs, in particular Batty Langley's *Builder's and Workman's Treasury of Designs* or James Gibbs's *A Book of Architecture*. If we remove the "superfluous ornaments" (President Burr's characterization) from Gibbs's design for King's College, Cambridge, we have a close model for Nassau Hall—the proportions, the hipped roof, the central facade topped by a pediment, the ornamental urns. The central doorway, with the head of Homer dominating the flat arch, clearly was borrowed from Langley's book, while the cupola is a replica of the upper part of the cupola of St. Mary-le-Strand, London, shown in Gibbs's book.

The sources Smith may have consulted are less important than the larger point of what the trustees were telling the world. By turning to current fashion and by building on such a massive scale, they announced that the evangelical wing of the Presbyterian Church and the College of New Jersey were here to stay. Nor were the trustees averse to an extra bit of insurance: they immediately picked up on the suggestion of New Jersey's royal governor Jonathan Belcher (1747–57) to name their first and major building after the late and highly esteemed William III, King of England (1689–1702), Prince of Orange and Nassau.

After repair of the damage sustained during the Revolutionary War, Nassau Hall was gutted by a fire in 1802. The trustees immediately embarked on a fundraising campaign to rebuild. Their efforts were so successful that the college was able to undertake an ambitious building campaign that went beyond renovations of Nassau Hall to include two additional new structures. The architect for this work was Benjamin Latrobe. Born and educated in England, Latrobe moved in 1798 to Philadelphia, where he worked as the first professionally trained architect in the United States. His primary work at Nassau Hall was to reduce fire hazards, replacing wood with brick, stone, and metal in the construction of floors, stairs, and roof. He also introduced Federal-style elements: triangular pediments, a fanlight, and a clock tower. As can be seen in the continuing story of Nassau Hall in Walk Two, some of these functional and aesthetic improvements were short-lived.

Maclean House

2   Maclean House
Robert Smith, 1756; Landscape: Lynden Miller, 2005

NATIONAL HISTORIC LANDMARK · One other legacy of the university's eighteenth-century history remains in Maclean House. For many years Maclean was the official residence of the college president, thus its earlier name, "President's House." Between 1878 and 1966 it served as the home of the dean of the faculty. Today Maclean is the home of the Alumni Association. The house takes its name from John Maclean Jr., vice president and later president of Princeton (1854–68). President Maclean was behind the creation of the Alumni Association in 1826, which played a decisive role in securing Princeton's financial stability. Evidence of Maclean's genius was his ability to convince former U.S. president James Madison (Class of 1771) to become its first president. From this auspicious beginning, the Alumni Association grew in stature to become an influential counterweight in the late nineteenth and early twentieth centuries to the often-reactionary board of trustees that was dominated by Presbyterian ministers.

President Aaron Burr Sr. (1748–57) was the first in a succession of chief executives who would, for over a hundred years, call this modest house on the town's main street home. Over time Maclean House was significantly altered: the roof was raised, dormers inserted, a front porch attached, two bays added on the east and west sides, and the brick painted yellow. Before the addition of the front porch and side bays, the house was basically a simple rectangular block, except for the rear stair tower. Placing the stairs at the rear allowed for a spacious center hall. Unlike the interior of Nassau Hall, where none of the original fabric survives,

Maclean is relatively intact. The finishes, raised paneling, turned balusters in the stair rails, and a fluted arch in the hall confirm that Smith was a gifted carpenter.

The garden behind Maclean House is a gift of the Class of 1936. Although the first occupants would most likely have planted vegetables, this landscape is ornamental and meant to suggest an eighteenth-century garden, as imagined by garden designer Lynden Miller in 2005. On the other side of the house, on the front lawn near Nassau Street, stand two gnarled sycamores. Almost as old as the house itself, the trees are commonly known as the "Stamp Act Sycamores," having allegedly been planted in 1765 to commemorate the repeal of the Stamp Act. In a campus justifiably renowned for its landscape, it comes as a surprise to learn that these two sycamores may have been the only trees intentionally planted on campus before the early nineteenth century.

3   Stanhope Hall

Benjamin Latrobe, 1803–5; Renovation: Hammond Beeby Rupert Ainge, 2007; Landscape: Michael Van Valkenburgh Associates, 2007

Stanhope Hall is one of two original buildings designed by Latrobe after he restored Nassau Hall. Once called Geological Hall, the building was later named for Princeton's seventh president, Samuel Stanhope Smith (1795–1812), who had also served as acting president during the years when President John Witherspoon (1768–94) was an active member of the Continental Congress. Its mate, Philosophical Hall, which stood on the opposite side of the green, to the east, was Stanhope's mirror image in every detail—arched windows, central pavilions, strong pediments, and the rich ochres of the local Stockton sandstone. The practice

Stanhope Hall

of designing paired or matching buildings was a neoclassical trait that would be repeated again in the next thirty years of Princeton's growth. Philosophical Hall contained a kitchen, a dining hall, a room for the "philosophical" apparatus (scientific equipment), recitation rooms for classes in mathematics and natural philosophy, and an observatory. Although in good condition, Philosophical Hall was torn down in the early 1870s to make way for the college's first freestanding library, Chancellor Green Library.

Its surviving twin has a distinguished history. Originally it was home to Princeton's book collection and its debating and literary societies—the American Whig and the Cliosophic—as well as study halls for freshmen and sophomores. Stanhope today houses the Center for African American Studies. To fully appreciate the impact it would have had when built, Stanhope has to be seen as the surviving element of a three-piece ensemble: Latrobe's remodeled Nassau Hall in the middle and Stanhope (Geological) Hall and Philosophical Hall as arms or pavilions. On the west side of the building is one of the largest and oldest American elm trees on campus.

4   West College
Architect unknown, 1836; Addition and renovation: Aymar Embury, 1926; Renovation: KSS, 1996; Landscape: Quennell Rothschild & Partners, 2002

Oval with Points
Henry Moore, 1969–70; bronze

Like Stanhope Hall, West College is also the extant half of a pair. It was originally built as one of two identical dormitories sited opposite each other and flanking what would later become Cannon Green. For some time it was the home of the university store, but West College is currently used for offices, including those of the dean of the college, the dean of undergraduate students, the registrar, undergraduate financial aid, and student employment. Built at a cost of $13,000 in 1836, West College was designed to be 112 feet long and 32 feet wide with eight suites on each floor. Along with East College, its companion that was demolished in 1897, West College was among Princeton's first structures specifically built to house its growing student population. The designs of East and West Colleges followed strict guidelines laid down by the trustees governing their size, building material, and siting, and were deliberately oriented to catch the prevailing westerly breezes.

Between Stanhope and West College stood a dormitory, Reunion Hall, demolished in 1965. Built in 1871, Reunion celebrated the reconciliation of two factions of the Presbyterian Church. Jack Kennedy roomed in Reunion during the first semester of his freshman year, in 1935, until he withdrew for medical reasons. (As student folklore tells it, a physician advised him to take it easy and transfer to Harvard.) Where Reunion Hall stood, there is now an abstract bronze sculpture by Henry Moore. One of the most photographed sculptures on campus, *Oval with Points* has

"Oval with Points"

West College

an amorphous shape that counters the formalism of Princeton's architecture. Moore often found his inspiration in nature, and this work resembles an East African elephant skull kept in his studio. The inner curve is visibly burnished from people sitting on or sliding through it, a use that delighted the artist.

Like Nassau Hall, West College has been reshaped by changing needs and fashions over the years. Perhaps inspired by Reunion Hall, West College and East College underwent Victorian reroofing projects in the 1870s that gave both mansard roofs. Practical as well as stylish, the steep slope of the new roofs transformed the attics into useful living space. Six decades later, architect Aymar Embury (Class of 1900) remodeled and expanded West College on its west side in a Colonial Revival style. Embury also altered and lowered the roof to an approximation of its original shape and height. The 1996 renovation provided contemporary work space for administrative offices accompanied by a paved and planted terrace on the east side that faces Cannon Green.

5   **Whig Hall and Clio Hall**
     Charles Steadman and John Haviland, 1838; Reconstruction: A. Page Brown, 1892; Whig Hall Renovation and addition: Gwathmey Siegel, 1972 and 1997; Renovation: Farewell Mills Gatsch, 2009; Clio Hall Renovation and addition: Hammond Beeby Rupert Ainge, 2005

South and east of West College stand two pristine Greek Revival temples, Whig and Clio Halls. Until the end of the Civil War, the pair defined the southern boundary of the Princeton campus. They would also complete the rhythm established to the

Whig Hall (left) and Clio Hall (right)

north by Latrobe's Geological and Philosophical Halls—and continued by East and West Colleges—as another set of essentially duplicate buildings, only in this case they did not face one another, but turned ninety degrees and looked back to the south elevation of Nassau Hall. This grouping of buildings essentially fulfilled Joseph Henry's 1836 master plan for a front and rear campus, centered on Nassau Hall and flanked by buildings on either side of open green space.

At the time of their completion, Whig and Clio appeared to be the termini of parallel walks that ran from Nassau Street past the east and west sides of Nassau Hall. This is not the view one sees today. The seemingly timeless serenity of Whig and Clio belies what is in fact a complex history. Although the current buildings mimic the design of the original structures, neither is the same size or the same material as the original construction nor do they stand in the same place.

The first decades of the nineteenth century were a period of great student unrest at the college, much of which was directed toward liberalizing the curriculum. Finding little support among the faculty and even less among the trustees, the students took on the challenge themselves. They re-formed the American Whig Society and Cliosophic Society, two rival literary and debating societies that had been established at Princeton in 1769 and 1770, respectively, shortly after the inauguration of John Witherspoon as president of the college. For most of the nineteenth century these societies, and similar ones at other colleges, were the primary resource for student life independent of the formal college structure.

Both organizations not only provided much-needed opportunities for social interaction, but also offered an alternative curriculum. Here, students could acquire the communications skills so important to nineteenth-century politics, commerce, and religion—not to mention the social networking that continued long after gradu-ation. Furthermore, the libraries of both societies were a necessary supplement to the meager resources of the college's library, which would not have its own freestanding building until 1873. In short, Whig and Clio were part fraternity, part athletic club, and part student union. Their attraction was only heightened by the fact that membership was a closely held secret, so secret that the front doors had combination locks that only members could open.

Housed in Stanhope in the early decades of the nineteenth century, both societies eventually required separate freestanding structures. In 1835 the Cliosophic Society formed a building committee, which commissioned the highly regarded carpenter-architect Charles Steadman to buy a design from distinguished Philadelphia architect John Haviland. At the time, this was a common way of doing business. Haviland sent back the specifications for a classical edifice modeled after the Greek temple of Teos. Haviland turned to the temple on the Ilisus for the Ionic capitals that grace the six columns supporting the pediment, which is more classi-cally eclectic than archeologically precise. Steadman's work was so well received that he was asked to provide the Whig Society with a copy located to the east of Clio. Both structures were paid for by their respective societies, not by the college, which no doubt dictated the use of inexpensive building materials—wood, stucco, brick, and a lot of white paint. Due to these materials, the structures were potential fire hazards and in constant need of repair.

What finally prompted their remake may not have been fire but the declining fortunes of both societies that occurred in the later decades of the nineteenth century. Perhaps motivated in part by concern over the rise of the decidedly

Whig Hall, 1972 renovation

upper-class eating clubs, the college administration intervened by commissioning the architect A. Page Brown to house both organizations in more stately edifices. Brown certainly had the credentials to give the job a touch of class, since he had received his training in the New York offices of McKim, Mead and White, one of the leading architectural firms of the day. Both the college and the architect believed that the reputations of Whig and Clio would be invigorated through grander building designs.

Both of the original buildings were torn down in 1890 and replaced by the present structures. Exteriors that had been wood and stucco became slabs of marble two inches thick. Likewise, the original modest wood columns were replaced by solid marble copies, twenty feet high and three feet in diameter. Inside, Brown designed libraries, reading rooms, club rooms, and, on the third floors, spacious senate chambers. Brown also moved Whig and Clio closer to one another, in order to create uninterrupted lines of sight from the north of Nassau Hall south to the fields and woodlands of the Stony Brook valley beyond.

As a result of a 1969 fire that gutted the interior and east wall, Whig under-went a dramatic redesign by the New York firm of Gwathmey Siegel and Associates in 1972, for which the firm received an AIA Honor Award. By removing the solid east wall and deeply carving into the resulting imaginary plane to reveal a glassed-in cross section of the interior spaces, the architect created a more dramatic experi-ence of the building, especially at night when it glows like a lantern. Twenty-five years later the firm designed the semiattached, circular elevator tower on the south side.

In 2005 Hammond Beeby Rupert Ainge renovated Clio Hall to accommodate offices for the dean of the graduate school and the office of admission and to make the building accessible with a rear addition entered from McCosh Walk. The entire second floor hosts the reception room for the office of admission in a gloriously renovated space with wooden Ionic columns and an oval-domed, luminous ceiling.

6   Cannon Green

It is difficult to imagine that well into the nineteenth century organized sports were often actively discouraged as unmanly and frivolous. This opinion was by no means unique to Princeton. And so, at Princeton, Cannon Green became the place where students worked off their energy. Today—apart from Class Day ceremonies during commencement and bonfires when Princeton's football team defeats Harvard and Yale in the same season—Cannon Green is a quiet refuge.

The tree-shaded open green space—bordered by Nassau Hall, East Pyne, Whig and Clio Halls, and West College—takes its name from the large cannon at the center, whose muzzle is deeply buried into the ground. A relic of the battles in and around Princeton during the Revolutionary War, the cannon had been hauled to New Brunswick to defend the city during the War of 1812. It became an object of contention between Princeton and Rutgers over the years that it lay marooned in New Brunswick. In 1835 a posse of Princeton citizens and students led by Winston

Cannon Green and Nassau Hall

Churchill's grandfather, Leonard Jerome (Class of 1839), retrieved the peripatetic cannon, which arrived in its present position in 1840. The largest trees on Cannon Green, some of which are up to five feet in diameter, are white ash. It is likely the trees were planted in 1836 when Joseph Henry laid out the grounds. Although it is no longer the physical center of the campus, Cannon Green remains Princeton's historic and spiritual heart.

7 Henry House

Joseph Henry, 1838; Renovation and addition: Aymar Embury, 1948; Renovation: T. Jeffrey Clarke, 2000

NATIONAL HISTORIC LANDMARK · In a community distinguished by a long history of relocating buildings, rather than tearing them down, Henry House has been the most mobile. Henry House began its history west of Nassau Hall between Stanhope Hall and West College. It was moved in 1871 for the construction of Reunion Hall. When the Chapel was constructed in 1925, Henry House was moved a short distance north to a site that would eventually accommodate Firestone Library. In 1947 Henry House was picked up again for the library construction and transported to its current site northeast of Nassau Hall.

Several renovations have considerably altered the exterior of Henry's quietly elegant Federal design centered by a pilaster-framed entrance that is pierced by a simple fanlight and sidelights. Like Maclean House across the lawn, the brick is painted yellow. Henry House is now part of a four-building complex known as the Andlinger Center for the Humanities.

Henry House

Besides being a capable amateur architect and teacher of the subject, Henry also established Princeton's reputation as a leader in the study of physics. His experiments with the telegraph, which included stringing a wire between his office in Philosophical Hall and his house, predate those of Samuel F. B. Morse. (It was a convenient way for Henry to let his household know he was about to return for lunch.) Henry was lured away from Princeton in 1846 to assume a national position as the first director and secretary of the Smithsonian Institution.

A veritable Renaissance man, Henry, inspired by Latrobe's model of three decades prior, created the first master plan, in 1836, for the future growth of the campus, which represented neoclassical ideals of balance and symmetry. However, in the second half of the nineteenth century a new spirit would profoundly reorient the plan of the campus, and the individual buildings themselves, away from the calculated symmetry of the rational to the equally calculated spontaneity of the romantic.

8   FitzRandolph Gate
McKim, Mead and White, 1905

The university has three works by the eminent twentieth-century architectural firm of McKim, Mead and White, two of which are elaborate and ceremonial gates. The best known, FitzRandolph Gate, is an appropriate place to conclude a tour of the original campus, since it honors the Princeton family that donated the four and a half acres upon which the College of New Jersey built its first permanent structures. The bequest of Augustus Van Wickle, a descendant of the FitzRandolph

FitzRandolph Gate

family, the gates employ an iconography that refers to the intertwining histories of college and nation: the republican eagles that regard one another from the central limestone gateposts represent America; the urns on top of the flanking posts recall the decorative urns on the original central pediment of Nassau Hall. The Class of 1970 further expanded the symbolism of FitzRandolph Gate when it broke the tradition of planting ivy at the base of Nassau Hall and requested instead that the main gate—which since 1905 was closed except on ceremonial occasions—be left open permanently, signifying the university's engagement with the world beyond the campus. The gate remains open to this day.

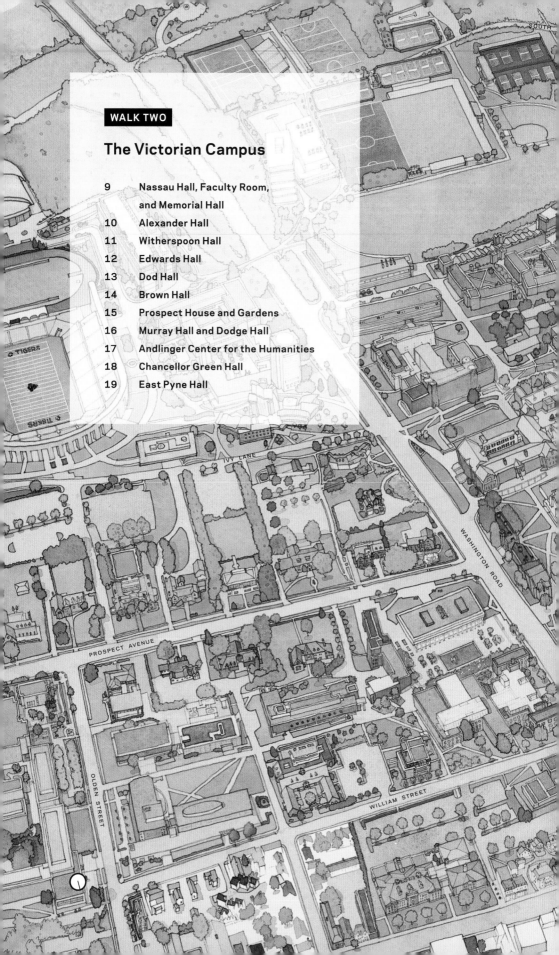

WALK TWO

The Victorian Campus

The Victorian Campus

THE VICTORIAN CAMPUS

Certainly from our current perspective several generations later, the exuberant Victorian legacy is one of the treasures of the Princeton campus. No other period comes close to the intoxication Victorian architects had when handling building materials—granite, marble, limestone, brownstone, and slate in all its colors, tile, brick, terra-cotta, and so forth. If it could be quarried or forged, the Victorians wanted it polished, chiseled, rusticated, carved, and applied as generously as possible.

Unlike the buildings of Princeton's colonial and Georgian periods, which can best be understood as elements of a larger plan, Princeton's Victorian campus reveals a different way of organizing separate elements into a coherent whole. Rather than a rigorously symmetrical, formal pattern, a new organic architecture was set within what Ralph Adams Cram—the university's first supervising architect (1907–29)—later referred to as a "pleasure garden." It is the difference between eighteenth-century Newtonian physics, which seeks unchanging, immutable laws of nature, and Darwinian biology with its emphasis on the evolutionary growth of the species. Great Victorian landscape architects, such as Andrew Downing and Frederick Law Olmsted, were advocates of the oblique angle and the curved walk that constantly revealed surprises. But the genius behind the College of New Jersey's new direction was the gifted Scottish educator James McCosh, who arrived in 1868 and served for twenty years as the college's eleventh president. More than any other individual of his time, McCosh was the decisive force behind the evolution of the Princeton campus.

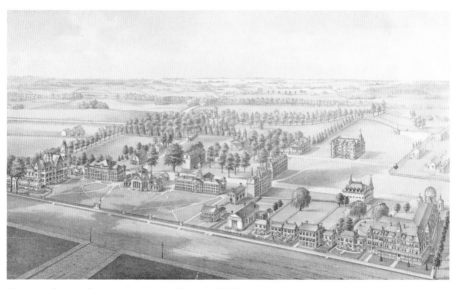

Aerial rendering of campus looking southeast, by Hudnut, 1875

Aerial rendering of campus looking southeast, by Rummell, 1906

Struck by its relative barrenness, McCosh immediately set out to transform the grounds of the college into an English nobleman's park, which he regarded as "the highest model of landscape gardening." It was McCosh who persuaded the trustees to retain the services of a landscape gardener "to furnish a plan for the improvement of the College" and oversaw the planting of several hundred trees. That was an extraordinary change in direction. The Princeton one sees today began with McCosh, who, along with his wife, Isabella, would walk around the campus with cuttings tucked underneath his arm, always in search of more ground to plant. It was no idle boast when McCosh told a visitor, "It's me college. I made it."

During this period increasing enrollment, liberalized curriculum, emerging scientific disciplines, the study of art and archaeology, and athletics drove the need for new buildings. The college erected a procession of buildings from University Place to Washington Road, parallel to and facing Nassau Street, but set back approximately in line with Nassau Hall. While Chancellor Green Library and Pyne Library maintained the alignment, if not the symmetry, of the historic campus, the expansion to the south—from Witherspoon Hall to Brown Hall—followed a diagonal that extended into farmland purchased by the growing college, and buildings were located picturesquely in the parklike landscape. This tension between orthogonal and diagonal, level and sloping, outward and inward has informed campus planning at Princeton ever since.

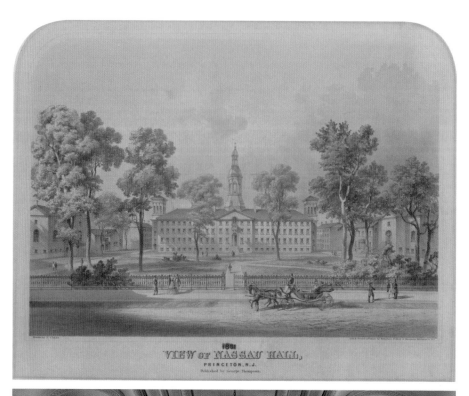

Nassau Hall, College of New Jersey, 1851; Nassau Hall faculty room

Nassau Hall
Renovation and addition: John Notman, 1857

Faculty Room
Renovation: Raleigh C. Gildersleeve, 1906

Memorial Hall
Renovation: Day and Klauder, 1919

Pair of Tigers
Alexander Phimister Proctor, ca. 1910; cast bronze
Gift of the Class of 1879

In Walk One our encounter with Nassau Hall was with its Georgian ancestors. Just as the fire at the beginning of the century was an invitation for Benjamin Latrobe to reshape Nassau Hall in the Federal style, a second disastrous fire in 1855 provided yet another opportunity. The college then turned to architect John Notman, designer of the first Italianate-style building in Philadelphia, the Athenaeum (1845), and many residences, including Lowrie House in Princeton and Prospect House on the Princeton campus. Notman's objectives were threefold: to quickly repair a vital piece of the campus fabric; to upgrade the structure to state-of-the-art fireproof construction; and to give Nassau Hall the beauty appropriate to its prestige, which, for Notman, meant converting it into an Italianate villa.

Notman was a devotee of the Florentine school popular in the 1850s and 1860s. Queen Victoria's Osborne House had set the style, after which square towers, stone balconies, rounded arches of doors and windows, and low roofs with deep, overhanging eaves became fashionable motifs for the affluent in England and America. Notman removed all but one of the existing north and south entrances of the original Nassau Hall and replaced them with square stair towers on the east and west sides. Notman's flanking stone towers rose a full story above the original roof, like massive bookends containing Robert Smith's Georgian structure. These somewhat awkward so-called pepper pots never won many converts and during renovations in 1906—following the recommendation of university trustee Moses Taylor Pyne—the tops of Notman's towers were lowered to align with the existing roof.

The remaining entrance at the front—Nassau Hall's central but modest Georgian doorway and the window above—was enlarged to become the present ceremonial one-and-a-half-story arched Florentine entry. Notman emphasized the symbolic impact of the doorway as the main entrance to the college by placing at the third story a stone balcony with an arched Palladian window that breaks through the cornice into the central pediment. A keen observer can see the outline of a red oak leaf, the state tree, carved in relief in the center of the three stone brackets

supporting the balcony. The vertical thrust provided by the greatly enlarged doorway and the piercing of the cornice is continued by a monumental cupola. The
cupola no doubt achieves Notman's intent to rise above the canopy of trees and
provide an unforgettable point of reference to the heart of the campus.

Notman enlarged the former prayer hall on the first floor by an addition on
the south for use as a library and portrait gallery. To increase the light in an era of
meager artificial illumination, he added a monitor, or clerestory, since removed.
At that point the library had scarcely more than ten thousand books and was open
only an hour or so each week. In 1878 the trustees determined that students would
no longer be housed in Nassau Hall. Gradually, as classrooms, faculty offices, and
laboratories replaced student rooms, interior alterations reflected this change in
program: the old wooden staircases were replaced by winding brownstone steps
in the two new towers; partitions were placed across the east and west hallways;
and the old cross hallways that accommodated the stairs were united with adjacent
rooms to create single chambers.

In 1906 Nassau Hall underwent another major renovation. The task fell to
Raleigh Gildersleeve, whose work appears elsewhere on campus. The former library,
which had been transformed into a museum of natural history (the E. M. Museum) in
1875 by Princeton's first professor of geology and physical geography, Arnold Henry
Guyot (1854–84), became the Faculty Room.

In keeping with his ambition to elevate the university's status and inspired by
a deep Anglophilia shared with the influential trustees, President Woodrow Wilson

Nassau Hall, museum 1875–1909 (Faculty Room), ca. 1886

(1902–10, Class of 1879) conceived a ceremonial room modeled after the British House of Commons. Gildersleeve transformed the space into a council chamber. The large windows on the east and west walls were divided by freestanding columns and the clerestory was removed. A rich cornice was installed around the room, the vaulted ceiling was pierced by lunettes over each window, and the walls were paneled in English oak. The walls are hung with portraits of the university's previous presidents, some of its founders, and a few other important figures, an enduring tradition dating back to the original prayer hall. The Faculty Room continues to host meetings of the faculty and trustees, but also represents Princeton's institutional memory.

Beyond the necessary improvements over time to the heating, cooling, and lighting systems, as well as the welcome addition of plumbing, the building that emerged after Notman's redesign and Gildersleeve's fine-tuning is today's Nassau Hall—with one major additional alteration, Memorial Hall, which was dedicated on Alumni Day, February 21, 1920. The First World War had a sobering impact on the campus and the entire community. As a solemnly grand commemorative statement, the administration and trustees decided to place Memorial Hall at the historic heart of the university—Nassau Hall. The Philadelphia firm of Day and Klauder, which played a central role in Princeton's architectural history, was commissioned in 1919 to redesign the large entrance hall. The dignified and resolutely Beaux-Arts, high, quiet, and spare space makes the room feel like a chapel. The marble panels inset into the bays between the marble pilasters that process around the room bear the names of those alumni who died in American wars, from the Revolutionary War to wars in Southeast Asia. Carved into the wall next to the adjoining Faculty Room is the inscription *Memoria Aeterna Retinet Alma Mater Filios Pro Patria Animas Ponentes* ["Alma Mater keeps in eternal memory her sons who laid down their lives for their country"]. If Notman's redesign of Nassau Hall marked the exuberant beginning of Princeton's Victorian campus, Memorial Hall represents a somber end.

On the low pedestals flanking Nassau Hall's front entrance sit a pair of bronze tigers gazing past FitzRandolph Gate out to Nassau Street. At the same time that orange and black became known as Princeton's colors, the tiger emerged as the university's mascot. In 1911 this pair of tigers replaced the lions that had guarded the entrance to Nassau Hall since 1889. Sculptor Alexander Phimister Proctor traveled with a circus for weeks, sketching and studying the tiger after which the bronze sculptures were modeled.

10   Alexander Hall
William A. Potter, 1894; Renovation: James Grieves, 1984

Walking west from Nassau Hall through the open space that until the 1960s had been occupied by Reunion Hall, one approaches the rusticated brownstone and gray granite walls and turrets of a horseshoe-shaped structure that seems to be somewhere between a church and a nineteenth-century city hall. Alexander Hall,

Alexander Hall, south facade

originally known as Commencement Hall, was built as a fifteen-hundred-seat assembly hall to accommodate large meetings of students and faculty, including the annual commencement. Its size is a measure of Princeton's accelerating growth in the closing years of the nineteenth century and honors three generations of Alexander men who served as Princeton trustees.

In a profession in which achievement and recognition do not often come until middle age, William Appleton Potter was much the wunderkind. A major force in creating the architectural heritage of both the college and the nearby Princeton Theological Seminary, Potter landed his first commission on the Princeton campus, Chancellor Green Library, when he was still in his twenties. He grew up in Philadelphia, the son of Bishop Alonzo Potter and half brother of Edward Tuckerman Potter, also an architect. He learned his art in college rather than on construction sites, which distinguished him from most architects of the first half of the nine-teenth century, who received their training through apprenticeships in the building

trades. Potter's genius did not reside in originality, but in the skill with which he incorporated the ideas of others. For example, the great round Romanesque arches that lead into cavernous door-ways reveal that he was inspired by the work of the great nineteenth-century American architect Henry Hobson Richardson. Other Richardsonian features are the steep gabled roof,

Alexander Hall facing Nassau Street, ca. 1894

Alexander Hall, Richardson Auditorium

tall dormers, heavy and rough stone walls, the horizontal emphasis, and the zigzag detail under the eaves.

Alexander Hall faces Nassau Street, an important defining characteristic of Princeton's Victorian campus. The new academic and classroom facilities that were built during McCosh's tenure and the years immediately following lined up along Nassau Street. Succeeding changes to the university's master plan, along with the disappearance of key buildings, have obscured this arrangement. Yet old photographs reveal the complementary relationship with the buildings of the town on the north side of Nassau Street: Alexander Hall, Maclean House, Nassau Hall, Chancellor Green Library, Dickinson Hall (destroyed by fire, 1920), and the John C. Green School of Science (destroyed by fire, 1928), all joining with the old University Hall (demolished, 1916) on the northwest corner of the campus and the First (now Nassau) Presbyterian Church, to look out into the community. The neoclassical First Presbyterian Church continues to stand between Alexander Hall and Nassau Street on a site not owned by the university. Dormitories and other student facilities were sited to the south, deep into the campus behind this public streetscape.

As the university later turned inward and away from Nassau Street, the south side of Alexander Hall assumed a new importance in the overall campus plan. Today the massive southern elevation, with its great Tiffany quatrefoil window, helps define the northern edge of a loosely organized quadrangle that has become colloquially known as Alexander Beach. Particularly noteworthy is the exuberant exterior bas-relief sculpture, said to have been designed by J. A. Bolger and executed by J. Massey Rhind, which embraces the sides of the great window and supports it from below. The sculpture depicts the arts and sciences paying tribute to Learning, the central seated figure, who holds a large book between his left hand and knee. On his left stand figures representing Oratory, Theology, Law, History, Philosophy, and Ethics; to his right stand Architecture, Sculpture, Painting, Poetry, Music, and Belles Lettres. The horned figure in the large upper left panel represents Moses and on the upper right side sits Christ, thus illustrating the words of Princeton's official seal, "*Vet Nov Testamentum*" ("the Old and New Testaments").

Renovations of Alexander Hall have made it friendlier to its users. In 1928 glass walls were inserted between the arches of the rusticated brownstone ambulatory to create a sheltered lobby space for the assembly hall. In 1984 the assembly hall was renovated as a concert hall and renamed Richardson Auditorium in memory of a Princeton alumnus. The new hall—with reduced seating capacity, larger stage, and improved acoustics—is used for concerts by the Department of Music, student and community groups, and touring professionals. Jacob A. Holzer's splendid mosaics behind the stage on the south wall, which illustrate scenes from Homer's *Iliad* and *Odyssey*, were carefully preserved. The 1984 renovation also included the construction of an underground addition to the basement to provide public restrooms, as well as rehearsal and reception spaces. In 2006 accessible restrooms were added on the ambulatory level.

Over the years the reputation of Alexander Hall has had precipitous ups and downs. On a tour of Princeton, Frank Lloyd Wright was said to have stated that Alexander Hall was the only interesting work of architecture on campus. No doubt Wright was being characteristically perverse, but he did have a point: the dexterity Potter showed in manipulating forms and the sheer delight he took in his palette of textures and colors, down to the malachite crosshatches and semicircles in the leaded-glass windows, are a treasure. Arguably the high-water mark of Princeton's Victorian phase, Alexander Hall was also one of the last facilities built in a style other than the soon-to-be-mandated Collegiate Gothic. Under pressure from the trustees, Potter himself would adopt the ascendant Gothic style for his later Princeton building, Pyne Library.

11   Witherspoon Hall
Potter and Robertson, 1877; Renovation: Goody Clancy, 2003;
Landscape: Quennell Rothschild & Partners, 2003

Named in honor of Princeton's sixth president, John Witherspoon (1768–94)—the only sitting college president and clergyman to have signed the Declaration of Independence—Witherspoon Hall is part of Rockefeller College, one of the university's six residential colleges. Prior to the Civil War, Princeton was the college of choice for many Southern students. After the war support from the former Confederate states declined, and so President McCosh turned his sights to the emerging northern industrial class. Witherspoon was built to attract this new class with the prospect of a good education in luxurious accommodations. One of the earliest occupants of the grand dormitory was Woodrow Wilson, Class of 1879.

The dormitory is sited on an elevation overlooking the former train station, making it the first building on campus that acknowledged the significance of the railroad as an entrance to the community and campus. Five stories high and distinguished by a great tower (removed in the 1940s) on the west side facing the tracks, Witherspoon was the first building to be seen as the train approached the campus. In effect, it was both a gateway and an advertisement for an increasingly confident College of New Jersey.

Built to house 140 students in eighty rooms, Witherspoon was the first of six dormitories constructed during President McCosh's tenure to accommodate increasing college enrollment. This modern dormitory's amenities are many: indoor plumbing, dumbwaiters, wood paneling, fireplaces, stained-glass windows, and special corridors for servants. No expense was spared to create what was acclaimed in the architectural press as the most beautiful dormitory of its time. The facade of the building is particularly exotic. The ground floor is constructed of dark blocks of Newark brownstone. The floors above are of blue-gray Pennsylvania marble set off by bands of the darker Newark brownstone. Each band of windows is of a different shape.

Victorian architects regarded the roof as the crown of a building, and Potter and Robertson employed various design elements to reflect that ideal: gables and dormers break the roofline; large, asymmetrical towers rise from the west end; the southwest corner sports a turret with a conical cap; and the ridge line is decorated with stone ornaments called crockets.

Witherspoon Hall

To dwell on the exuberance of the exterior design risks overlooking its practical attributes. The interior plan is far more residential than the massiveness of Witherspoon's footprint might suggest. Intimacy is achieved by breaking down the interior into four distinct buildings, with dividing walls, stair halls, and separate entryways. The architect designed Witherspoon Hall to be well ventilated through high ceilings and an elevated siting. The manipulation of the building's form also opened up the interior to natural light.

12 Edwards Hall
Edward D. Lindsey, 1880; Renovation: Fulmer and Wolfe Architects, 1985

An increase of wealthy students from the North required a highly visible gesture to show that there was a place at Princeton for those of modest means. This was the genesis of "the poor man's dormitory," appropriately named after the great evangelist, theologian, and third president of the college, Jonathan Edwards (1758). Until the 1960s students paid different rates for dorm rooms, a sliding scale set according to amenities.

Edwards Hall bespeaks a parsimonious hand. Witherspoon Hall was designed by an architect; Edwards was designed by Curator of Buildings and Grounds and Professor of Architecture and Applied Arts Edward D. Lindsey (1876-80). While Witherspoon had suites, Edwards was made up entirely of single rooms. The cost of building Edwards was a third that of Witherspoon, and not simply because the latter was one story higher. The materials used to construct Edwards were more

Edwards Hall

Dod Hall

common—Trenton brownstone was laid randomly and trimmed with a lighter sand-stone. There is no grand porch at the front of the building, which faces east, but rather a pair of modest arched entrances at the base of Edwards's two square cren-ellated towers. Not surprisingly the building soon acquired a reputation for being dark and dirty.

An extensive renovation in 1985 by the firm of Fulmer and Wolfe superseded the earlier reputation. The roof was raised to create a fifth floor, the towers were capped with pyramidal roofs, and the gloomy exterior fire escapes were removed by incorporating fire safety within the interior. With these improvements in place, the dormitory's single rooms—preferred by today's undergraduates—became a virtue rather than an expediency. For its skillful efforts, the restoration architect earned an Excellence in Architecture Award from the AIA's New Jersey chapter. Edwards is now one of the dormitories of Mathey College.

13   Dod Hall

John Lyman Faxon, 1890; Renovation: Newman Architects, 2005;
Landscape: Princeton University Office of Physical Planning, 1998

This upperclass dormitory has created challenges for generations of Princeton's architects and master planners: the location infringes on the sight line leading south from Nassau Hall through the terrace between Whig and Clio Halls to the playing fields. Ralph Adams Cram's proposal—in the context of his 1909 master plan—to move the building westward and reduce its height was not implemented. Variously described as Italianate or Romanesque Revival, Dod tends to be regarded more highly by students who value the light and airy rooms than by architectural critics. When Dod opened, rents for the one- and two-bedroom suites were between the costs of Witherspoon and Edwards. The primary exterior stone is granite from Bull's

Dod Hall entry detail

Brown Hall

Island near Stockton. The lighter window trim and stringcourses are limestone, while the darker course below the roofline is brownstone. Like Edwards, Dod opens to the east through three entryways. The central door is flanked by turrets with conical caps and framed by a Romanesque arch supported by column shafts of Georgia Creole marble. The interior cast-iron staircases were an important development in the technology of fire safety at the time. The dormitory is named after Albert B. Dod, a highly regarded professor of architectural history and mathematics (1830–45).

14   Brown Hall

John Lyman Faxon, 1892; Renovation: CUH2A, 1970; Atkin Olshin Schade Architects, 2010; Landscape: Michael Van Valkenburgh Associates, 2010

Brown is the fourth in the series of dormitories (beginning with Witherspoon and continuing with Edwards and Dod) that defines a gentle downward sloping diagonal, running from northwest to southeast. In some ways Brown Hall is the most restrained of the parade of Victorian dormitories initiated by President McCosh.

Architect John Lyman Faxon's skill is evident in lightening the overall mass of the building, not only by the change in color and materials, but also because the masonry elements themselves are smaller above than they are below. The flat-jack window arches of the lower two stories, for example, suggest the compression that comes with weight, which is appropriate for the base; the smaller, rounded arches of the windows along the upper two stories introduce an equally appropriate sense of lightness as well as a vertical note in an otherwise horizontal composition. Along this theme, the first two floors are built of rusticated blocks of warm gray Gloucester granite laid in Florentine ashlar style, whereas the top two floors are of orange Roman brick trimmed with terra-cotta and brick quoins. If one looks up to the cornice, small terra-cotta lion heads are visible at regular intervals (at the time of construction the tiger had not yet displaced the lion as the school's official mascot). The corners of the building are further articulated by pairing the windows at the ends of each row, breaking up what might otherwise be a monotonous march of windows across the facade.

In an era of gas lighting, natural daylight was a high priority for building interiors. Faxon achieved this in two ways: the windows of Brown Hall are large and generous, and the interior court serves as a light well. By using a more reflective golden yellow brick for the upper stories of the courtyard, Faxon enhanced the effect of natural light. The interior court also provided needed ventilation in the days prior to air-conditioning.

Faxon's four-story Florentine palace was one of the last buildings erected before the advent of Princeton's Collegiate Gothic–style era in 1896. At the time Brown Hall enjoyed fine views: the rolling countryside stretched to Stony Brook and the main line of the Pennsylvania Railroad to the south and the floral oasis of Prospect Gardens to the east. In 2010 the university created a new exterior portal through the south facade, which provides a pathway and north–south views through the building, as well as a required means of egress from internal corridors.

Prospect House

Prospect House
John Notman, 1852; Addition: Princeton University Office of Physical Planning, assisted by Warren Platner, 1969; Interior renovation: Venturi, Rauch and Scott Brown, 1988

Prospect Gardens
James and Isabella McCosh, 1878–88; Ellen A. Wilson, 1902–10; Beatrix Jones Farrand, 1912–43; Princeton University Office of Physical Planning, 1997–2000; Lynden Miller, 2005–13

Sherrerd Green
Michael Van Valkenburgh Associates, 2013

Moses
Tony Smith, 1967–68, fabricated 1969; painted mild steel

Venetian Wellheads
Limestone, Bequest of Dan Fellows Platt, Class of 1895

Titan
Michele Oka Doner, 2004; bronze
Gift of Michele Oka Doner in honor of the seventieth birthday of Micky Wolfson Jr., Class of 1963

Centaur
Dimitri Hadzi, 1954–71; cast bronze
Gift of Brian P. Leeb, Class of 1918

NATIONAL HISTORIC LANDMARK · Prospect House was the residence of the school's presidents from James McCosh in 1878 to Robert Goheen in 1968. The main section of Prospect Gardens south of the Italianate house comprises a semi-circle that contains a series of terraces that step down the sloping site. Prospect Gardens highlights yet again how President McCosh transformed the lives of Princeton students, the faculty, the campus, and the land itself. President and Mrs. McCosh had a love for gardens and shaded walks. Under their influence, the grounds of the Princeton campus—which prior to the Civil War had been as austere as the architecture—blossomed into a parklike environment. Princeton hired the school's first landscape architect, Donald Grant Mitchell (1870-75), who, together with his patrons, set the campus on an enlightened course that persists to this day.

Prospect House had been donated to the college in 1878 by Alexander and Robert Stuart, wealthy Scottish-American merchants and Presbyterian-minded

Prospect House Gardens vista, 1908

philanthropists, also benefactors of the Princeton Theological Seminary. The house was built for Thomas F. Potter, the son of a wealthy Charleston merchant, and designed by John Notman, who specialized in institutional buildings, churches, and villas, and was responsible for the 1857 renovation of Nassau Hall in the Italianate style. Notman's skill was such that he could accommodate whatever fashionable revival style his clients called for. But he is best remembered for his Italianate designs. The poetry of Shelley, Byron, and the Brownings, along with the musical compositions of Mendelssohn and Brahms, suggests the depth of the widespread nineteenth-century passion for the Italian Renaissance, a passion that culminated in the art of the pre-Raphaelites and the influential architectural writings of the great Victorian essayist and critic John Ruskin. The Italianate was a style especially attractive to newly rich industrialists and tradesmen in Philadelphia—as well as in New York, New Orleans, Cleveland, Chicago, and Detroit—who were moving out of the city to the nearby countryside. Having one's own Tuscan villa instantly communicated the message of "to the manor born." The Italianate was also a style that comfortably straddled the great divide separating the restrained neoclassic, as exemplified at Princeton by Whig and Clio Halls, from the exuberance of the Romanesque, as seen in Alexander Hall. As such, it is the aesthetic link that connects the first and second halves of the nineteenth century.

Apart from the prominent off-center tower, the spacious interior may be the most noteworthy aspect of the house. Not only do the rooms welcome light and air, they relate to the natural circulation of inhabitants, rather than follow an abstract geometry in the manner of, for example, the symmetrical rectangles of a formal Georgian plan. In other words, far from being arbitrary, the external form is determined by what goes on inside. This was a major change in residential design that continues to resonate up to the present day.

The central part of the north elevation is the most formal, appropriately so since it is here, through the porte cochere, that visitors enter the house. Notman composed this elevation with advancing and receding planes—characteristic of the Italianate style—featuring three rounded arches of the porte cochere, three balustraded balconies, and groupings of three window openings. The most relaxed side of Prospect is at the back, where the dining room, verandah, and conservatory were originally located. Indeed, the interior plan seems to draw the visitor past the formal public rooms at the front to the delightful private spaces at the rear with their views of the garden and the vistas beyond.

Prospect House is set in a five-acre park consisting of both formal and informal landscapes that have evolved over time. Sherrerd Green—the front (north)

Prospect House Gardens

lawn—is manicured and punctuated by an ancient tulip poplar tree and a large-scale sculpture titled *Moses*, by Tony Smith. Known for their distinctive black finish, Smith's sculptures explore the geometric relationships between form and space. *Moses* received its title from the visual affinity the artist found with depictions of the biblical figure of Moses, including works by Michelangelo and Rembrandt. The east and west sides of the park gradually slope to the south amid informal plantings of ground cover, shrubs, and trees. Campus walkways meander among the wide variety of plantings, which include a dawn redwood, a rare species when planted in 1948. Two Venetian wellheads are found among the plantings. For centuries Venice relied on wells for part of its water supply; now, they serve as markers of history, spanning the different artistic eras during which they were created. After the modernization of water management they became popular with collectors and could be purchased from art dealers.

The south side of the park is ringed with densely planted hemlock trees that form a backdrop to the formal gardens. When residing in the house, President Wilson erected an iron picket fence around the property to prevent short-cutting through the grounds. The boundaries remain, but the fence is gone except on the southern perimeter. Paths through the park are clearly defined by stone gateposts: the original ones at McCosh Walk, and more recent ones designed by Machado and Silvetti at the east and west entries to the gardens. Tucked away in a grove of trees is the sculpture *Titan*, by Michele Oka Doner. Oka Doner's primary interests revolve around the natural world, particularly ancient and fossil forms. *Titan* suggests these primordial relationships through its fossil- or shell-like surface, evoking cycles of life and death. The hollow, spongelike figure evokes both growth and decay. Coming from a body of work that marks the artist's return to an interest in the life-size human form, this sculpture was hand patinated by the artist and intended for placement in a natural outdoor setting.

The gardens are the inner sanctum of the park. The semicircular plan with two radiating paths is centered on a fountain and ringed with trees. Over the years garden designers, including Beatrix Farrand and Lynden Miller, and university architects, landscape architects, and grounds staff have maintained and improved the gardens. Nine seasonal planting beds define the edges of the three pie-shaped segments of the garden. Low shrubs form a backdrop to the planting beds and an edge to the interior lawn areas. Tall, slender arborvitae trees frame a central axis, and trimmed holly trees punctuate the corners of each bed.

The fountain sculpture was added in 1971. Dimitri Hadzi's pipe-playing centaur reflects the artist's modernist approach, which bridges abstraction and figuration. It also calls upon his lifelong interest in mythology. In myth, the artist noted, centaurs are physical but also intellectual beings; the heroes Achilles and Hercules were both students of centaurs. The fountain was commissioned by President Robert F. Goheen (1957–72), a classicist, when Prospect House was still home to the university's president.

Traversing the garden is a broad bluestone walk that provides entry to the garden's gravel pathways. This east–west promenade, known as Garden Walk,

Dodge Hall

separates the formal gardens to the south from a stepped embankment rising north, toward the house. At the upper level a rose garden with perennials is bordered by a clipped yew hedge. At midlevel a lawn terrace with benches overlooks the formal gardens.

After President Goheen moved off campus to the Walter Lowrie House, also designed by Notman, Prospect House was converted and remodeled into a dining and social center for faculty and staff. Warren Platner consulted on the design of a modern two-story, cast-in-place, concrete and glass dining wing at the southeast corner. Platner recommended frameless glass walls to capitalize on the garden view. While uncompromisingly modern, the addition is still an appropriate companion, enhancing rather than upstaging the historic structure. The Victorian interior finishes and furnishings have been restored to an approximation of the interior McCosh might have seen when he moved in.

16   Murray Hall and Dodge Hall

Murray Hall
J. Morgan Slade, 1879; Renovation: Francis F. A. Comstock, 1933

Dodge Hall
Parish and Schroeder, 1900

Two Planes Vertical Horizontal II
George Rickey, 1970; stainless steel

North and slightly west of Prospect is the pair of structures called Murray-Dodge, linked by a cloister. During the course of its long history Princeton has witnessed episodes of religious revival. In the 1870s one such surge washed over campus, the focus of which was the Philadelphia Society, the oldest collegiate religious organization in the country. As the revival gained steam, it soon became obvious that the society needed space in which to meet and pray. Murray Hall was the result, paid for not by the college but by students and alumni. Murray lines up on the east–west axis defined by Whig and Clio Halls. The grouping indicates a deliberate effort to identify a precinct or zone behind Nassau Hall on the other side of Cannon Green for student extracurricular activity. The gleaming temples of Whig and Clio could not have been more different from the large, rusticated brownstone blocks of first Murray and then Dodge Hall. But there is a higher, perhaps unintended logic to the arrangement: the cool, white classical shapes of Whig and Clio served the rational exercise of the intellect; the darker, vaguely ecclesiastical detailing of Murray Hall spoke to the irrational yearnings of the soul.

The easternmost of the two structures, Murray Hall, was built using Trenton brownstone in a Victorian Gothic style, which characteristically emphasizes the masonry. It is organized as two distinct volumes connected by a vestibule, which serves as a hinge between the two parts. The room to the south, illuminated by a clerestory, was designed to be a large auditorium-cum–prayer hall that seated four hundred. After the interior was destroyed by fire in 1933, it was rebuilt to house the two-hundred-seat Theatre Intime, where plays produced by students are staged. The room to the north is a high-ceilinged octagonal reading room.

Having outgrown Murray Hall by the end of the nineteenth century, the Philadelphia Society commissioned architectural firm Parish and Schroeder to design a two-story building immediately to the west. Dodge rose up in the ascendant Collegiate Gothic style. Parish and Schroeder followed several strategies to make the two distinct buildings seem to be one piece. The firm connected the buildings with a fifty-two-foot-long covered walkway, or cloister, pierced by a procession of pointed-arch windows, used the same brownstone as was used in Murray, and redesigned the Murray roof. To give the resulting ensemble a focus as well as a presence on campus, the architects designed a fifty-one-foot-high tower pierced by oriel windows for the northeast corner of Dodge Hall.

A century later the Murray-Dodge complex continues to minister to the social and extracurricular needs of students. Today Dodge is the headquarters of the university's student religious organizations and houses the offices of the dean of the chapel. At the south and tucked between the two buildings is another of Princeton's delightful garden "rooms." In the center is a polished marble tablet given by the Class of 1969 on the occasion of their twenty-fifth reunion. The inscription, quoting lyrics from Joni Mitchell's song "Woodstock," celebrates the spiritual revival of the counterculture of the late 1960s and early 1970s. To the north, situated at the highest point of campus, George Rickey's sculpture *Two Planes Vertical Horizontal II* holds the distinction of being the only kinetic outdoor work in the Campus Art collection. The two squares can turn 360 degrees on a horizontal axis, and the whole assembly can rotate fully around its vertical axis with the help of a strong breeze.

17   Andlinger Center for the Humanities

Scheide Caldwell House
Schwartz/Silver Architects, 2004; Landscape: Quennell Rothschild & Partners, 2004

Remembrance
Toshiko Takaezu, 2000; cast bronze
Princeton University

President Shirley M. Tilghman's (2001–13) initiative to promote cross-disciplinary research and teaching within the humanities, and between the humanities and other divisions of the university, is exemplified by the Andlinger Center for the Humanities. Supported by a lead gift from Gerhard Andlinger (Class of 1952), the center's facilities include three renovated buildings—Chancellor Green Hall, East

Pyne Hall, and Joseph Henry House—as well as the new Scheide Caldwell House. Schwartz/Silver Architects of Boston designed the Scheide Caldwell House in 2004 to relate to the residential scale of the Henry House and to create a three-sided courtyard framed on the east and west by the houses and on the south by Chancellor Green. Music scholar and bibliophile William H. Scheide (Class of 1936), whose personal library is housed within Firestone Library, provided funds for the new building in honor of his aunt Gertrude Scheide Caldwell. Schwartz/Silver designed the building's exterior in a contemporary version of neoclassical architecture, using white-painted wood clapboard and black-painted shutters flanking tall,

Andlinger Center for the Humanities: Scheide Caldwell House (left), Chancellor Green (center), and Henry House (right); 9/11 Memorial Garden and "Remembrance"

mullioned windows. The interior features a two-story open atrium providing daylight and facilitating communication among the building's mix of programs in cultural studies.

The courtyard features a raised lawn, plantings, and paved walks at the perimeter. On the south side of the courtyard, an east–west walkway connects Nassau Hall's front lawn to Firestone Plaza, providing access to the shaded terrace of Henry House and a cafe in the newly accessible lower level of Chancellor Green. Quennell Rothschild and Partners designed the landscaped path, which features river birch trees and flowering shrubs. On the west side of Chancellor Green is the 9/11 Memorial Garden and *Remembrance*. A bronze bell hanging between two wooden posts, *Remembrance* guards the alcove of the memorial garden, where a circle of bronze stars commemorates the thirteen Princeton alumni who died in the attacks of September 11, 2001. Serene and silent, the bell has potential for both resonance and reverberation, and the surrounding plant life exemplifies renewal.

18 Chancellor Green Hall

William A. Potter, 1873; Renovation: Schwartz/Silver Architects, 2004; Landscape: Quennell Rothschild and Partners, 2004

The construction of Chancellor Green Library represented one of the first major projects built during President McCosh's tenure. This vitally needed facility was made possible by a new funding strategy. Until McCosh became Princeton's president, it had been common practice to name a facility after a revered figure (Stanhope and Nassau Halls), its function (Philosophical Hall), or its site (East

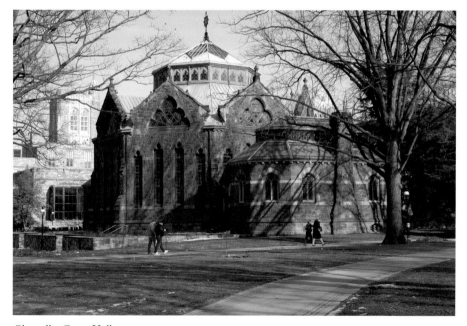

Chancellor Green Hall

Chancellor Green rotunda, ca. 1875

Chancellor Green rotunda

and West Colleges). It was McCosh who began the lucrative practice of offering to name new facilities after significant donors. In this instance an exceptionally generous trustee, John C. Green, underwrote the library to honor his younger brother, Henry Woodhull Green, the chancellor of New Jersey's equity courts.

The building of the library also represented the first major breach in the early nineteenth-century neoclassical quadrangle developed by Latrobe and Joseph Henry. The change in course necessitated tearing down an older structure: Latrobe's Philosophical Hall. It was razed, not because there was no other land available, but because McCosh wanted Princeton's first free-standing library to occupy a highly visible and symbolically strategic site between Nassau Hall and the then-existing college chapel. Even more significant, the library faced out toward Nassau Street, rather than inward toward the campus. The shift in the campus's orientation is key to an appreciation of McCosh's strategies for reviving the college and, in the process, reinventing it. The decision to orient the library's two entrances toward Nassau Street was motivated by the same spirit that prominently sited Witherspoon dormitory to overlook the train station. Princeton's new buildings were externally directed to the world beyond the campus. As McCosh said in his farewell address, "I viewed edifices as a means to an end."

McCosh's commitment to the future was evident in his efforts to design and build state-of-the-art facilities. The library was the centerpiece of this commitment, signaling a revived college intent on achieving world-class status among institutions of higher learning. The college sought advice from the faculty and prominent architects on every detail, from building materials and shelving to reading rooms to light and ventilation. It took a surprising risk in its selection of a designer, turning to the twenty-nine-year-old unproven architect William A. Potter for his first major commission.

Potter played with geometric shapes, creating a series of three octagons along an east–west axis. The central octagon is the dominant structure, known as the rotunda, where the librarian supervised the books and the students from a raised, circular desk. Potter designed decorative wooden bookcases on the main level and balcony, which line the perimeter of the octagon and radiate toward the

*Chancellor Green Hall, north entry
column capital*

center. Each side of the main building is capped by a pediment and pierced by stained-glass lancet windows. At the center of the roof is a stunning stained-glass octagonal skylight. Unlike with Pyne Library (later called East Pyne Hall), which Potter designed two decades later, the interior of Chancellor Green remains structurally intact, including the gilded ironwork of the perimeter balcony. The balcony is supported by slender columns topped by capitals of luxurious gilded flowers. The university renovated and restored the rotunda in the early twenty-first century, starting with the skylights and clerestory windows. With the opening of Pyne Library in 1897, Chancellor Green became primarily a reading room. A succession of other uses followed. In 2004 Schwartz/Silver—the architect for the concurrent renovation of East Pyne Hall—replaced the main level flooring with a two-tone wood parquet pattern that recalls the original library floor, installed a glass-enclosed elevator to the mezzanine, and custom-designed study carrels for the mezzanine alcoves. Princeton-based architect and emeritus professor Michael Graves selected furniture and fabrics for the space. As a result, the Chancellor Green rotunda—despite its primary function as a quiet study space for the Andlinger Center—is one of the most sought-after venues for receptions and other events on campus.

The outside of the building is Victorian Gothic, with brownstone towers, faceted facades, steep roofs set off by varicolored slate, and pointed and foliated arches over doors and window openings. No opportunity for iconographic ornament was overlooked. For example, the polished marble pillars that support the two north entry porticos are topped by limestone capitals, which are carved to resemble stacks of books with their authors' names chiseled into their "spines."

The Victorian ensemble is a carefully choreographed and innovative response to scholars' needs. An abundance of daylighting was essential. This suggests that the complex geometry of the library was not arbitrary, but in fact an imaginative strategy to flood every corner of the interior with light to accommodate scholarly pursuits. To minimize glare, Potter used stained glass in the transoms and skylight. Chancellor Green was so admired that Princeton awarded Potter an honorary master of arts degree, as well as commissions for several other major buildings on campus, including Pyne Library and Alexander Hall.

William A. Potter, 1897; Renovation and addition: Schwartz/Silver
Architects, 2004; Landscape: Quennell Rothschild & Partners, 2004

Picnic Table

Scott Burton, 1978–79; cast concrete
Museum purchase, with a grant from the National Endowment for the Arts
and a matching gift from the Mildred Andrews Fund

East Pyne Hall began its tenure on campus in 1897 as university's main library, first called the Stacks Building and then Pyne Library. It is an impressive Tudor Gothic design connected to the equally impressive Victorian design of Chancellor Green by a "hyphen." After Firestone Library opened in 1948, the interior of East Pyne was extensively remodeled. It now houses the classrooms and offices of the university's foreign language and literature departments.

In style, East Pyne is a transitional building. It attempts to bridge the gulf between the fanciful Victorian of the McCosh era and the emerging passion for Collegiate Gothic ushered in by Princeton's Sesquicentennial in 1896. In his design Potter resisted the trustee's mandate to create a Gothic design based on Oxford-Cambridge precedents—a mandate made forcefully by trustee Moses Taylor Pyne and abetted by Professor Andrew Fleming West—but relented when he risked losing the commission. Potter's resulting Gothic design retained some of the Victorian flourishes of his earlier designs for Chancellor Green and Alexander Hall, but was on the main evolutionary path toward the Collegiate Gothic style. That path was blazed by the firm Cope and Stewardson in its design for the contemporaneous Blair Hall and was later validated by Ralph Adams Cram, who presided over the Collegiate Gothic era of the campus's development. Pyne Library was Potter's last work for Princeton. Soon after he was appointed supervising architect of the United States Treasury, the highest office held by an architect in the federal government.

Once the decision had been made to incorporate the existing Chancellor Green Library as the main reading room of the new library complex, Potter chose the same brownstone cladding for Pyne Library for the sake of harmony. However, the decision to preserve Chancellor Green resulted in another distinctly unharmonious consequence. With Chancellor Green to the north, Nassau Hall to the west, and the relatively new Dickinson Hall to the east (destroyed by fire in 1920), the new library could only be sited to the south of Chancellor Green. This required razing the school's first freestanding chapel—designed by John Notman and completed in 1847—along with the well-loved East College dormitory. The destruction of these two buildings, East College in particular, provoked a great outcry from the alumni, who called it the "Crime of Ninety-Six." A further consequence was to alter the neoclassical symmetry of the Cannon Green quadrangle, although Potter aligned the west wall of Pyne along the foundation of East College.

Potter's main challenge was how to design a structure that by definition was a large warehouse for books. As a major repository for paper-based collections, it had to be fireproof. It also had to be well illuminated inside and, in an era before air-conditioning, the library had to be well ventilated. Potter addressed the need for light and fresh air by opening up the center of the structure and maximizing the use of glass in the walls of the resulting interior courtyard, which also provided indirect natural light for the library. Advances in construction technology allowed the floors in the stack areas to be paved in thick, translucent glass, thus admitting even more light.

The most distinctive feature of the building is a large tower that rises over the western arch. A shorter, crenellated tower marks the eastern arch. The archways and court allow through passage—first to carriages and now to pedestrians—and mark the trace of an east–west road that at one time extended from Washington Road to University Place. As he had at Alexander Hall, Potter turned to the sculptor J. Massey Rhind to decorate the solid planes of the exterior walls. Two of Princeton's eminent presidents, both of whom were Scottish Presbyterian ministers, occupy monumental niches on opposite sides of the west archway: John Witherspoon stands at the left with his hands folded, looking out benignly at the college he steered through the Revolutionary War when the campus was literally a battlefield; at the right stands President James McCosh, holding a large tome befitting his role as a teaching president who modernized and expanded the college's academic program. Above the statue of McCosh, niches are occupied by sculptures of James Madison (Class of 1771) and lawyer Oliver Ellsworth (Class of 1776). Additional empty niches on the exterior and within the courtyard suggest that Pyne Library was intended to become a type of Princeton Valhalla over time. Beneath a sundial placed flush against the south side of the west tower is an inscription: Pereunt et Imputantur ("They Pass Away and Are Charged to Our Account").

East Pyne Hall

Since the new library complex would be able to house as many as 1,250,000 books, the trustees calculated it would take at least two centuries before all the shelves were filled. But by 1947, just fifty years later, the stacks were overflowing and the larger Firestone Library was being built to accommodate the growing collections and provide reader space for the spike in post–Second World War student enrollment.

In 2004 the university renovated the building again to meet the needs of the new Andlinger Center for the Humanities. Schwartz/Silver Architects created entrances to the building on the north and south sides of Thompson Court, on axis with Chancellor Green. Below the courtyard additional basement space was excavated to accommodate a seventy-seat auditorium and a language resource center. The lower level connects via a "hyphen" to the Chancellor Green cafe. On the upper floors the architects reorganized and renovated space for language departments and created common spaces on the perimeter to bring daylight into the corridors and promote easier circulation.

The sculpture *Picnic Table*, by Scott Burton, is located south of the building on a lawn visible from Chapel Drive. Burton championed functional art, creating works that he described as "sculpture in love with furniture." Calling to mind the simplified geometric forms of minimalism, Burton's table, an inverted cone balancing on a wide circular base, offers students and passersby a place to socialize or study.

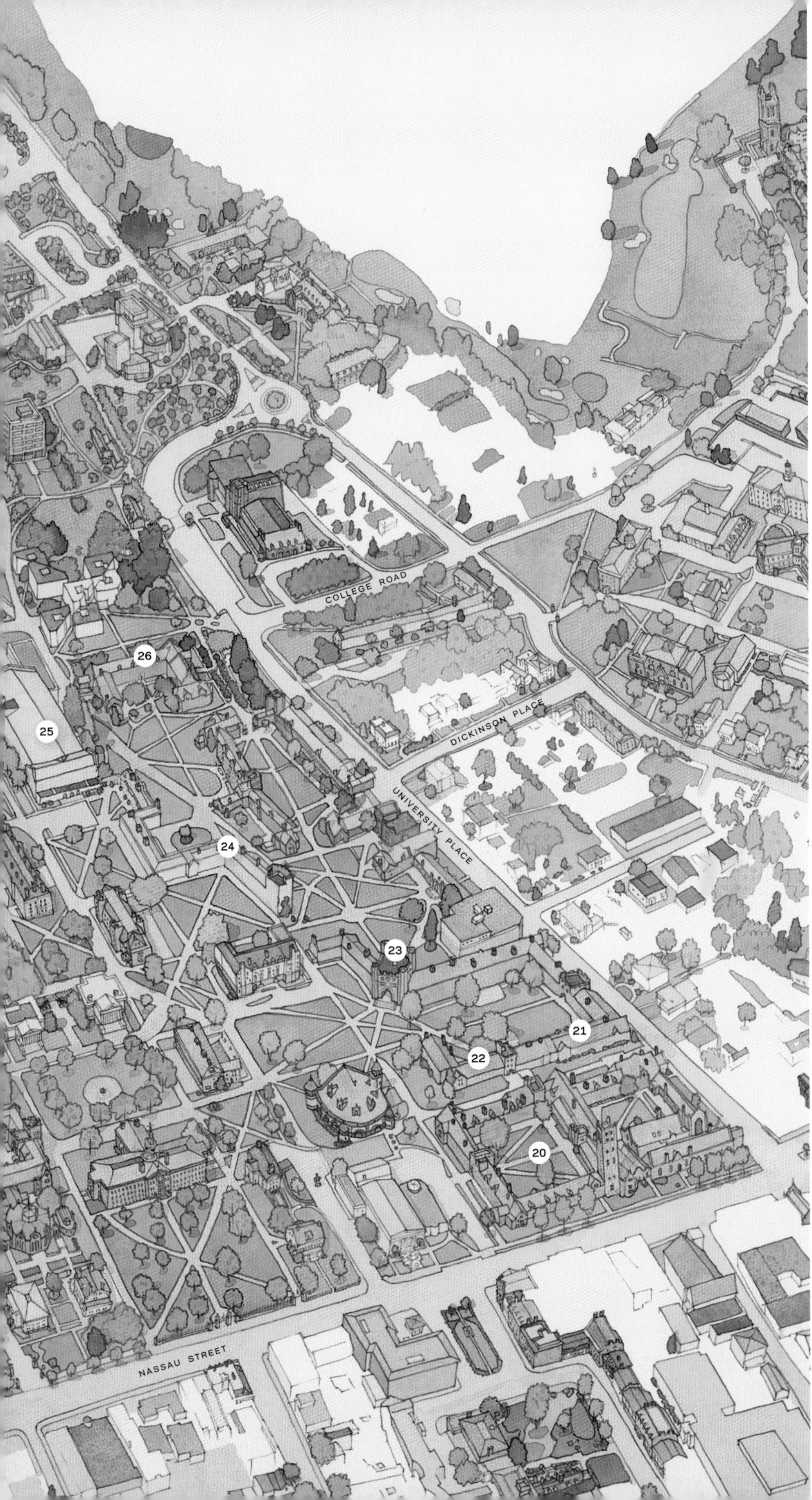

COLLEGE ROAD

DICKINSON PLACE

UNIVERSITY PLACE

NASSAU STREET

26

25

24

23

22

21

20

Collegiate Gothic Era

FROM COLLEGE TO UNIVERSITY

Approaching the eve of the twentieth century the College of New Jersey was well into the process of reinventing itself. Having weathered a low period in the years leading up to the Civil War, the college had righted itself during the dynamic tenure of President McCosh (1868–88), who had dramatically transformed the institution and its impact on the world, just as President John Witherspoon had done in the eighteenth century. In the last two decades of the nineteenth century, the college, along with its peer institutions, introduced graduate and professional studies into the curriculum and began conferring master's and doctoral degrees. While *college* remained the term for the parts of these institutions devoted to undergraduate studies, the expanded institutions renamed themselves *universities*. By 1896 Princeton University was alive with new confidence. With powerful northern industrialists and financiers as patrons, a new and much-enlarged physical plant, and a faculty increasingly distinguished by excellence in teaching and research, Princeton was poised to take its place on the world stage. The newly named Princeton University held a three-day celebration in October 1896 to mark its Sesquicentennial.

Princeton adopted a style of building meant to identify it as the new standard bearer of a glorious tradition stretching back to medieval Paris and Oxford. The irony is astounding: to achieve the credibility of a great modern university, Princeton reached back into history and dressed itself in Gothic stones.

Collegiate Gothic was mandated by the trustees in 1896. Three men drove this decision: Moses Taylor Pyne, Andrew Fleming West, and Woodrow Wilson. All had visited England and were impressed by the character of Oxford and Cambridge Universities—the secluded quadrangles, the separation from the

Aerial rendering of campus looking southeast, 1920

world of action, the sense of higher purpose and community, the apparent spirituality, the dignity of learning, the commitment to educate leaders, and the sheer beauty (down to the purple chains of wisteria that hung from the walls of ancient stone tracery). All three were eager to re-create what they had seen.

In America the closest source of inspiration was Philadelphia. In the late 1880s and through the 1890s, both the University of Pennsylvania—which had moved to a new site in West Philadelphia in 1873—and Bryn Mawr College—which had been founded in 1880—commissioned the young Philadelphia firm of Cope and Stewardson to design a series of Gothic Revival buildings. Both schools needed instant credentials for marketing purposes, which meant the image of a distinguished history, a distinction made persuasive by deliberately siting buildings in an irregular way as if the campus had arisen over time.

When Pyne, the rich and influential chairman of the Trustee Committee on Grounds and Buildings (1886–98), saw that the design vocabulary of Cambridge and Oxford could be spoken so eloquently on his native mid-Atlantic shores, he put his influence (and money) to work. The trustees directed Princeton's preferred Victorian architect, William Potter, to design the new library funded by Pyne's mother as a Tudor Gothic structure. Potter resisted but eventually relented. And it was clear to Pyne that Cope and Stewardson would not require similar coaxing. With the construction of Blair Hall the same year as Pyne Library (1897), Cope and Stewardson became the new preferred architectural firm, to be followed soon after by Day and Klauder and, most importantly, Ralph Adams Cram.

Blair Hall was the first true embrace of Princeton's long, fifty-year commitment to Collegiate Gothic. Professor and later university president Woodrow Wilson (1902–10) embraced Collegiate Gothic as the coming of age for the university and also an affirmation of Princeton's sacred mission to teach the values and culture of the English-speaking peoples.

The trustees' decision to mandate Collegiate Gothic as the official style was significant in several ways. First, the decision committed Princeton to a departure from previous eclectic styles in favor of a single new style. To coordinate such a sweeping undertaking, the university created the post of supervising architect, one of the first American universities to do so, and selected Ralph Adams Cram for the position in 1907. Cram's firm had recently won the commission to plan and design new buildings at the U.S. Military Academy at West Point, New York. Cram immediately began a comprehensive plan for future development of the campus, which was first published in 1909 as *A Plan for the Architectural and Topographical Development of Princeton University*, referred to herein as the 1909 master plan.

Second, the university was broadcasting a new message. While President McCosh had set out in the late nineteenth century to construct a contemporary institution of higher learning, designed in eclectic styles popular at the time, Collegiate Gothic architecture, as Wilson put it, would turn imaginations back

"A Plan for the Architectural and Topographical Development of Princeton University," by Ralph Adams Cram, Revised 1911

a thousand years "to the earliest traditions of learning." Collegiate Gothic architects like Cram did not consider their work antiquarian. Instead they were simply picking up a tradition that had been interrupted by the Renaissance.

Third, and perhaps most significantly, the university turned inward, away from Nassau Street. In part this was an inevitable consequence of expansion on newly acquired land to the south. But it was also an expression of a belief that young men needed to sleep, eat, and study away from the distractions of the world. The erection of the FitzRandolph Gate between Nassau Street and Nassau Hall in 1905 was the visible expression of the boundaries of the campus community. Indeed, it was in this period that gates went up around colleges and universities across America. At Princeton, FitzRandolph Gate would remain shut (except on special occasions) for nearly seven decades.

Cram's plan established a formative framework for campus development, inaugurating the era when the campus achieved its iconic cloistered greens and Collegiate Gothic walls. Cram would have preferred to replace the picturesque arrangement of buildings from McCosh's era with a more orderly arrangement of courtyards and quadrangles that reinforced the sense of the campus as a community, rather than a series of individual structures. (Cram referred to the campus's previous development as "handicapped by the defiant individualism of a light-hearted past" and McCosh's contributions as the "go as you please" method of designing and placing buildings.) However, pragmatism persuaded him to accept the landscape and buildings from McCosh's time and to plan the next generation, in the third ring of development centered on Nassau Hall, as ensembles of buildings and courtyards that housed dormitories to the west and academic buildings to the east, primarily in the available space around the perimeter of the campus. The central area of campus maintained McCosh's mode of buildings in a park. Cram located buildings along paths of travel, using landscape and pathways rather than geometry to define sites. This approach confirmed Princeton's characteristic focus on pathways and vistas—even Cram's courtyards were typically three-sided or featured views out to the spaces beyond.

The need to accommodate a growing student body prompted expansion of the campus (and relocation of the train station) to the south, and the construction of an ensemble of dormitories on the former site of the railroad tracks that to this day are among Princeton's most delightful and endearing.

Aerial view of Blair and Witherspoon Halls (background), Foulke and Lockhart Halls (foreground), date unknown

Blair Walk "haystacks"

This was also a formative period for the campus landscape, due to the hiring of Beatrix Farrand in 1912 as consulting landscape gardener, a position comparable to the one created in architecture for Cram. A study of the architecture on Princeton's historic campus cannot be lifted out of the context of the landscape that was designed to receive and complement it. Any appreciation of this organic art must focus on Farrand. Her work and the rules she established for Princeton's landscape design are as defining an element of the Princeton style as Collegiate Gothic. Farrand's association with Princeton began with the Graduate College in 1912 and lasted thirty-one years. She was the only woman among the founders of the American Society of Landscape Architects. A memorial bench and a small garden dedicated to her memory at the northwest corner of Cram's splendid University Chapel offer an insight into the nature of their creative relationship and her unique contribution: Cram and his colleagues sought to lift the spirit; Farrand gave that spirit roots in the nurturing ground.

For an art as ephemeral as landscape architecture, it is a tribute to Farrand's genius and Princeton's enlightened stewardship that so much of her work survives and flourishes. On the historic campus, a few of her masterworks include the recently restored Blair Walk paved with bluestone and lined with an allée of yews pruned in a "haystack" profile; the great cream-colored blossoms of the specimen *Magnolia grandiflora* on the southwest corner of Pyne Hall; the cascading waves of winter-blooming yellow jasmine on the facade of 1901 Hall; the graceful fragrant chains of white and purple wisteria on the east side of Foulke and Henry (woody loops of wisteria vines were a signature of Farrand); the bluestone walks that connect the archways of Holder Court; the espaliered *Magnolia kobus* on the south wall of McCosh Hall and the espaliered cornelian cherry on the east wall of Laughlin; the entire precinct around the Chapel; and the informal walks that lead to Lake Carnegie through the woodlands. Even after Farrand's relationship with Princeton ended, succeeding landscape architects and gardeners followed the design and planting principles she laid down.

Her first principle was simple: "A campus is a place for trees and grass, nothing more." Within this basic premise, she developed a practical approach to the landscape that encompassed a holistic picture of vistas and pathways, as well as plants. Some critics initially considered her plantings around the Graduate College as too sparse. But she understood, unlike many suburban gardeners, that a landscape design evolves with time. Her pragmatic approach vetoed designs and materials that were high maintenance. Summer-blooming plants were rejected for the sensible reason that no one would be on campus to see them. For this reason, plantings had to maintain their interest in the winter months when classes were in session, which meant attractive shapes, berries, and the occasional evergreen. Plant materials were selected to complement rather than overwhelm the architecture; this included the use of espaliered trees and clipped vines to heighten a particular element, such as a bay or the turn of a strategic corner. Plants native to the area were preferred. Above all, Farrand believed that nature was to the spirit what books were to the mind: "We all know education is by no means a mere matter of books, and that aesthetic environment contributes as much to mental growth as facts assimilated from a printed page."

Holder Hall courtyard

20   Holder Hall, Hamilton Hall, and Madison Hall
Day and Klauder, 1910–17; Renovation: Venturi, Rauch and Scott Brown, 1981; Renovation: Einhorn Yaffee Prescott, 2008; Landscape: Quennell Rothschild & Partners, 2005; Michael Van Valkenburgh Associates, 2007, 2009

The Bride
Reg Butler, 1956–61; cast bronze, aslip technique

Walk Three begins to the west of Nassau Hall at the Gothic arch that leads into Holder Court and the ensemble of dormitories and dining halls known as Holder, Hamilton, and Madison Halls. Commenting on this Collegiate Gothic ensemble, with its picturesque quadrangles and shaded cloisters, Cram said, "In this great group of collegiate buildings at Princeton—Holder Hall and the University Dining Halls— Messrs. Day and Klauder reach the highest point thus far in their authoritative interpretation of Gothic as a living style."

Day and Klauder fit the U-shaped plan of Holder Hall between Nassau Street on the north, the First (now Nassau) Presbyterian Church on the east, and Cram's Campbell Hall on the south. The open part of the U-shaped University Hall, built in 1876 at the corner of Nassau Street and University Place as a hotel and acquired in 1884 by the university for use as a dormitory and dining hall. Holder Tower anchors the northwest corner of this composition. Hamilton Hall, the next piece of the ensemble, was added as a southwest extension of Holder. Hamilton Hall is named for John Hamilton, the acting governor of the province of New Jersey, who granted the first charter to the College of New Jersey in 1746. Demolition of University Hall in 1916 provided the site for Commons, the final piece of the ensemble. Commons (now Madison Hall) contained five separate dining halls where all freshmen and sophomores were served their meals. A north–south cloister closed the U of Holder Hall, provided access to the dining halls, and created today's Holder Court. The configuration of Commons, together with Hamilton, created another smaller courtyard, Hamilton Court. Some might quarrel with the inward-looking design, but that was precisely what the university asked the architects to do.

The importance of this remarkable ensemble—based on Day and Klauder's study of the fourteenth-century New College at Oxford—cannot be overstated. For one, the 140-foot-tall Holder Memorial Tower, modeled after Canterbury Cathedral, fixed in the minds of students and visitors alike an indelible image of Princeton as an old and venerable campus steeped in tradition. On a more practical level, the complex addressed two of the most pressing issues faced by the growing university—where to house and feed the increasing number of students. President Wilson believed that if students had no other social options apart from the Prospect Avenue eating clubs, and if there were no place to sleep at the end of the day apart from off-campus housing, it would be next to impossible to achieve the bonds of an ideal community of scholars. How else could an attitude of "service to the nation," Wilson's great phrase, be nurtured among the undergraduates? This is the context for understanding what drove the great burst of dormitory construction in the first decades of the twentieth century, as well as various attempts to provide an attractive alternative to the eating clubs.

Whereas Cram's praise for Day and Klauder addressed more scholarly matters in its "authoritative interpretation" of the Gothic style, succeeding

Madison Hall Commons, ca. 1930–50

Hamilton Hall courtyard

generations have focused on the beauty of the work, including the skill that handled the limestone tracery of the cloister on the west side of Holder Court. The arch at the center of the cloister leads to Hamilton Court. The contrast between the two courts—Holder to the east and Hamilton to the west—epitomizes the architect's shrewd understanding of how to manipulate one's emotional response. Holder Court invites crowds and communal undertakings. It is a spacious parade ground into which residents of the various buildings that ring the court enter. On the other side of the arch, Hamilton Court is intimate, landscaped, romantic, and quiet. Entrance to the court from the east is gained by stepping down a flight of stairs; from the west, by climbing a narrow flight of stairs from University Place. This is a restorative place, enhanced by classic Farrand plantings: a magnolia tree in a bed of roses hugs the north wall, balanced by a spreading willow oak near the south wall. A sculpture, *The Bride*, also enhances the court. The artist Reg Butler worked on *The Bride* over a span of five years, in a tree-filled garden similar to the Gothic courtyard in which the sculpture resides today. Butler's casting technique allowed him to capture minute details, resulting in the sculpture's treelike textured surface.

The great arch on the east side of Holder Court has special significance: as the foundation for Holder Hall was being dug, workmen discovered the remains of a burial ground belonging to the FitzRandolphs, the family that had donated the original four and a half acres for the Princeton campus. President Wilson had the contents of each grave placed in a separate box and reinterred under the arch. A commemorative plaque on the south wall has inscriptions by Wilson and Andrew Fleming West, the first dean of Princeton's new Graduate School; West's poetic Latin inscription reads, *In Agro Jacet Nostro Immo Suo* ("In Our Ground He Sleeps, Nay, Rather, in His Own").

In 1981 Philadelphia architectural firm Venturi, Rauch and Scott Brown renovated the entire complex to accommodate two of the university's newly formed residential colleges, Mathey and Rockefeller. The firm transformed the five separate dining halls of Commons into dining facilities and common rooms that now serve the two colleges. Holder Hall and Tower serve as residences of Rockefeller College, which also includes Madison, Witherspoon, Campbell, and Buyers Halls. In 2007 the university worked with Michael Van Valkenburgh Associates (MVVA) to restore the Holder courtyard with new paving, lawn, and flowering trees. The long and narrow space between Campbell-Joline and Holder-Hamilton, a former roadway, was converted to a pedestrian walkway in the 1970s. In 2009 the university enhanced the space with a landscape design by MVVA that includes new pavements and plantings of crape myrtle and redbud trees.

21   Joline Hall
Charles Z. Klauder, 1932

As far back as President Wilson's tenure at Princeton, there was a commitment to complete the university's westernmost quadrangle by joining Campbell Hall (1909) to the east and Blair Hall (1897) to the south. This was not possible until Halsted Observatory was torn down in 1930. Halsted's replacement, the FitzRandolph Observatory, was built in 1932 in the far southeastern part of campus. Joline feels very different from its surroundings, perhaps because of the long, narrow site, a diminishing enthusiasm for Gothic architecture, or the worsening financial straits affecting the entire country due to the Great Depression. There is little of the imagination or invention that animates Holder and Hamilton Halls. Instead, Joline is much more sober, even streamlined. Whatever the constraints that shaped it, Joline was the last new dormitory Princeton would construct for over fifteen years. Today Joline Hall is one of the residential dormitories of Mathey College.

22   Campbell Hall
Cram, Goodhue, and Ferguson, 1909

Ralph Adams Cram designed Campbell Hall shortly after his appointment as supervising architect to the university. He designed the building—an undergraduate dormitory now part of Rockefeller College—to embody his vision of a Collegiate Gothic campus. Cope and Stewardson had set a high bar with their designs for Blair Hall, Little Hall, and University Gymnasium some ten years earlier, but Cram's primary interest as a planner was the relationship of one building to another, particularly as the buildings defined courtyards, pathways, and vistas.

Cram's 1909 master plan indicated a three-sided dormitory quadrangle bordered on the south and west by Blair Hall. The site Cram designated for the L-shaped Campbell Hall defines the northeast corner of this quadrangle. Cram's plan for Campbell required demolition of Bonner-Marquand Gymnasium, built in

Campbell Hall

1869. Construction of the Brokaw Memorial (1896) and the University Gymnasium (1903)—both on the site of today's Dillon Gymnasium—rendered the older gym expendable.

Cram's Collegiate Gothic template included schist as the primary facing material; carved limestone trim around windows and doors, and for arches, stringcourses, and quoins; wood doors; metal-framed, mullioned casement windows; brick chimneys; copper gutters and downspouts; and pitched slate roofs with dormers. He terminated gable ends and projecting bays with parapets of schist and limestone trim. He placed entryways to the rooms on the courtyard sides of the building and an archway on the north side that aligns with one that Day and Klauder subsequently designed for Holder Hall (see p. 88). This alignment, sensitive to context, is characteristic of the best planning and design evident on the Princeton campus over the years.

23   Blair Hall and Buyers Hall
Cope and Stewardson, 1898 and 1907; Renovation: Einhorn Yaffee Prescott, 2000; Landscape: Quennell Rothschild and Partners, 2002

For all the echoes of Oxford and Cambridge, Blair Hall owes more to Main Line Philadelphia than to the Tudor gate towers of England's oldest universities. The design of Blair Hall, down to the distinctive crenellated tower with its four corner turrets, is derived from an earlier Cope and Stewardson building, Rockefeller Hall, at Bryn Mawr College. The dramatic impact of Blair is due to its elevated siting on the hill that overlooks the former location of the train station. The university asked Cope and Stewardson to address three challenges: provide space for the growing student population; screen the campus from the noise and smoke of the nearby train line (known as the PJ&B—Princeton Junction and Back—or "Dinky"); and give Princeton

Blair Arch

a new ceremonial entrance that acknowledged the mode of arrival at campus for most students and visitors in the closing years of the nineteenth century. The architects delivered on all three counts—and more. Cope and Stewardson's achievement seemed to be visual proof of the wisdom of the trustees' decision to adopt Collegiate Gothic as the official style.

Blair provided much-needed dormitory space, and the imposing stone walls closed the campus off from the outside world of belching steam locomotives. Approached from below by a steep flight of stone stairs, Blair Hall has an imposing, fortress-like air, distinguished by the arch at the foot of the central clock tower. The function of the building as a line of demarcation or screen is underscored by the orientation of all entryways north, toward the campus, to the expansive green lawn loosely defined by Witherspoon, West College, Alexander, Campbell, and Joline Halls. The western end of this space, a three-sided court defined by Blair, Joline, and Campbell, has stone walls draped in wisteria. Its central east–west path passes by the state's largest London plane tree and continues west through an arch to University Place beyond. Quennell Rothschild and Partners renovated the courtyard landscaping in 2002.

Blair's function as a screen and as the university's main gateway was considerably diminished by the relocation of the train station to the south in 1917. Nevertheless, Blair Hall retains much of its majesty, as anyone who walks the long landscaped path from the current train station to the foot of the stairs discovers. A distant presence that grows larger with each step, Blair remains a symbol of the Princeton campus, capturing the genius of the place. In 2000, following an extensive renovation, the university renamed the portion of Blair Hall south and east of the arch and stairs Buyers Hall. Buyers serves as a dormitory for Rockefeller College and Blair serves Mathey College.

Train station (foreground), Blair and Witherspoon Halls (background), ca. 1900–1916

Little Hall (left) and Dillon Gymnasium (right)

24 Little Hall

Cope and Stewardson, 1899 (north section) and 1902 (south addition);
Renovation: Venturi, Rauch and Scott Brown, 1983; Renovation:
KieranTimberlake, 2001; Landscape: Quennell Rothschild and Partners, 2003

In its second project for the university, Cope and Stewardson extended the Gothic
western wall that had started with Blair Hall. Little Hall follows the property line
of the campus as it existed before the train station and tracks were moved south.
This explains the dormitory's curious zigzag shape, or what undergraduate F. Scott
Fitzgerald—who enrolled with the Class of 1917 but did not graduate due to poor
health and the First World War—called the "black Gothic snake of Little." While
descriptive of the shape, the words "Gothic snake" do not prepare one for the many
delights of this dormitory. Whereas Blair is formidable as the former grand ceremonial entrance to campus, Little has a charm that is due to its modest role on the
campus. The graceful bays, the Flemish gables, the Tudor chimney stacks, the pedimented doors, and the broad gesture of the oriel window in the four-story crenellated tower are the decorative grace notes of Little Hall's delightful composition.

25 Dillon Gymnasium
Aymar Embury, 1947

Dillon Gymnasium is sited immediately south of Little Hall along Elm Drive. With
Firestone Library, it has the distinction of being among the last structures on campus built in the Collegiate Gothic style. Dillon Gymnasium was the third of a series
of ever-larger athletic facilities that began with Bonner-Marquand in 1869. Next
came Cope and Stewardson's University Gymnasium (1903), which was the largest

Dillon Gymnasium

gym in the country when it opened but was destroyed by fire in 1944. Dillon, similar in many of its exterior details to University Gym, rose three years later out of the ashes.

A college gym can inspire an almost spiritual affection in those who have spent time within its walls, as either players or spectators. Cope and Stewardson's gymnasium accomplished this. When University Gym was destroyed, trophies and all, Princeton slated the new gymnasium to be built in the same spot and to re-create the look of its predecessor. Firestone Library was intended to be Princeton's showcase bicentennial project, but it was Dillon Gymnasium that took that honor.

For all its similarities, from the use of local stone (Wissahickon schist) and limestone (salvaged from the older building) to the great crenellated entry tower, the architect Aymar Embury's design respects rather than mimics the original building. Princeton's growth over the years and the influx of returning Second World War veterans necessitated a larger facility. Dillon's main interior space is more than double the size of the original gym. Embury (Class of 1900) dressed Dillon with carved gargoyles; it was the last building on campus that animated its walls with a full program of these wonderful stone creatures. Compared to Firestone Library, where the few grotesques are applied halfheartedly to the surface, the cartoonlike athletes carved in stone on Dillon still show some playfulness that never fails to delight.

Dillon Gymnasium

26 Pyne Hall Ensemble

Landscape
Beatrix Jones Farrand, ca. 1922–28

Pyne Hall
Day and Klauder, 1922

Foulke Hall and Henry Hall
Zantzinger, Borie, and Medary, 1924

Laughlin Hall and 1901 Hall
Day and Klauder, 1926

Lockhart Hall
Day and Klauder, 1928

As Cram had envisioned in his 1909 master plan, land occupied by the train tracks, station, and coal yard of the railroad spur that extended from Princeton Junction to the base of Blair Hall could be better utilized for undergraduate dormitories. The realization of Cram's vision was enabled in 1917 when the railroad relocated the station one-quarter mile south, removed the tracks, and relocated the yards. The demand for more dormitories—largely based on enrollment of veterans of the First World War—was quickly met over a period of six years (1922–28) by the construction of Pyne, Foulke, Henry, Laughlin, 1901, and Lockhart Halls. Pyne Hall anchors the southern end of a range of Collegiate Gothic dormitories that begins with Holder Hall on the north.

Day and Klauder aligned Pyne, 1901, and Laughlin parallel with the existing west walls of the ensemble of Blair, Buyers, Little, and Dillon Gymnasium. The architectural firm of Zantzinger, Borie, and Medary aligned Foulke and Henry Halls with the east side of University Place. These predominantly north–south alignments create one large quadrangle and two linear courtyards. The large quadrangle defined by Blair, Buyers, Little, Laughlin, Foulke, and Lockhart is a crossroads of the western extent of McCosh Walk and the northern extent of Blair Walk. McCosh continues westward up a flight of stairs and through an archway in Lockhart to University Place. The linear courtyard between Laughlin and 1901 Halls and Foulke and Henry Halls is carefully composed, although by two different firms. Blair Walk traverses this space, and an archway between Foulke and Henry leads to University Place. The linear courtyard between Laughlin and 1901 and the Little-Dillon buildings is more amorphous due to the presence of a service drive and cul-de-sac. However, the space is enlivened by a pathway leading from the arch and stair between Little and Dillon, entryways to Laughlin and 1901, and careful attention to landscaping and paving. It contains a mile marker post, a remnant of the railroad

Henry Hall tower and Blair Walk; Pyne Hall courtyard with Chinese magnolia tree

spur. Laughlin and 1901 feature entryways on both sides, a rarity on campus determined by their siting between two courtyards.

The small courtyard created by the U-shaped plan of Pyne Hall provides a sheltered open space for Pyne residents, but is also part of the larger composition of buildings, spaces, and pathways. Day and Klauder elevated the courtyard to provide some separation from the linear courtyards, but also placed an archway in the south wing that suggests future expansion to the south, although Cram's

Henry Hall with Beatrix Farrand landscape, 1931

master plan did not anticipate this expansion. Fifty years later, I. M. Pei and Partners recognized Day and Klauder's intent by framing a view from the Spelman Halls complex centered on the Pyne arch. Day and Klauder also placed archways in the east wing—with a flight of stairs leading to the gymnasium—and in the west wing leading to Blair Walk. The Pyne courtyard features two large saucer magnolia trees that provide shade in the warm months and a profusion of pink petals in the spring.

Finding the funds to build Pyne Hall—and the other dormitories in this grouping that soon followed—presented the university with a challenge. However, in April 1921 one of Princeton's greatest benefactors, Moses Taylor Pyne, died, and Princeton's alumni contributed funds for a major project that would honor his memory. In his position as chairman of the Grounds and Buildings Committee, Pyne had persuaded the trustees to adopt Collegiate Gothic as the school's official style and had funded a number of the school's significant initiatives. It was preordained that his fellow Princetonians would generously underwrite the campus's major residential expansion in his name. Funding opportunities were offered by the configuration of separate entryways, rather than long double-loaded corridors that are featured in Princeton's Collegiate Gothic dormitories. These individual entries are today designated as gifts of the Classes of 1902, 1906, 1908, 1912, 1920, 1921, 1922, and 1923. Nearly fifty years after it was dedicated, Pyne became the first dormitory to house undergraduate women.

The architects of these six dormitories designed in varying expressions of the Princeton Collegiate Gothic style. They used argillite stone as the primary exterior wall material, which contrasts in color with the schist stone used for the adjacent

Blair, Buyers, Little, and Dillon Gymnasium buildings. Beatrix Farrand enhanced the buildings, courtyards, and pathways with plantings, including Chinese magnolias in the Pyne courtyard; espaliered wisteria in the Foulke, Henry, and Laughlin archways; and Japanese yews flanking Blair Walk.

27   Cuyler Hall Ensemble

Landscape
Beatrix Jones Farrand, ca. 1913–30

Patton Hall and Wright Hall
Benjamin Wistar Morris, 1906; Renovation: Goody Clancy, 1999

Cuyler Hall
Day and Klauder, 1913

Walker Hall and 1903 Hall
Charles Z. Klauder, 1930

This grouping of undergraduate dormitories provides one of the most delightful environments on the Princeton campus for its inhabitants and visitors. While the ensemble is composed of individual buildings constructed over twenty-six years, they define spaces and frame views in informal yet calculated ways. They share the Collegiate Gothic style as expressed by two different architectural firms, Day and Klauder and Benjamin Wistar Morris, using two different types of exterior stone. They take advantage of the sloping topography and relationship with existing buildings to the north to transform the simple function of housing students into a complex spatial experience.

Morris designed Patton Hall as a linear building roughly following the diagonal alignment established from Witherspoon Hall to Brown Hall. To the west, across the road now known as Elm Drive, stood University Gymnasium. Morris chose schist for the walls, though he used larger blocks and a rough split-face surface to distinguish the appearance of Patton's walls from the earlier Collegiate Gothic dormitories like Blair and Little. Window frames, sash, and mullions are wood, not metal as in the earlier dormitories. During the 1999 renovation, which added a story and corridor to the east side of the building, the architects Goody Clancy created an archway in the tower portion of the building. The archway allowed a pathway from the now-developed western part of the campus to join the pathway system created by later buildings in the Cuyler ensemble that lead to Frist Campus Center. At the time of the renovation the university named the northern section of the building Wright Hall.

In 1913, continuing President Wilson's policy to house all undergraduates on campus, an additional dormitory was built just north of Patton Hall. Cuyler Hall, named for Wilson's classmate Cornelius Cuyler, shares a wall with Patton, but the

Cuyler Hall; Patton and Wright Halls (left), Cuyler Hall (right)

buildings are different in two ways: while Patton is linear, Cuyler is L shaped, forming a two-sided courtyard; and while Patton's walls are schist, Cuyler's are argillite. Day and Klauder chose argillite because of the increasing scarcity and cost of schist. Quarries in the Princeton area initially supplied argillite, but later quarries in Pennsylvania along the Delaware River supplied it, marketed as "Princeton stone." While schist is gray in color with specks of sparkling mica, argillite—a clay-bearing material—has varying shades of ochre, brown, and purple.

Considered by almost every commentator as the most handsome of Princeton's residential halls, Cuyler Hall is Collegiate Gothic at its most inventive. There is a richness of detail and materials, from the overscaled stone chimneys

1903 Hall, ca. 1930–50

and thick slabs of slate on the roof, to the extravagant ceiling of the Pitney archway (installed in 1921), which honors the long relationship between the Pitney family and Princeton. If a spider could spin stone webs, the ceiling inside Pitney archway would be the result with rosettes, leaves, coats of arms, and shields caught like so many flies. Cuyler was one of Princeton's smallest dormitories at the time of its construction, which lends to its reputation as a privileged place. Designed and constructed at the same time that the great steel plates of the Titanic were being riveted together, Cuyler looks back to an era of handcraftsmanship and proposes an idyllic alternative to the industrialization of the late nineteenth and early twentieth centuries.

After a pause of seventeen years—during which time dormitory development shifted to the western side of campus in the Pyne Hall environs—the university commissioned Charles Z. Klauder to design two additional dormitories adjacent to Patton and Cuyler Halls. Klauder used an L-shaped plan for Walker Hall and a U-shaped plan for 1903 Hall. Incorporating exterior stairs, terraces, archways over existing paths, and courtyards defined by walls of the existing and new buildings, Klauder melded the four buildings into an ensemble. There are three north–south paths that traverse the ensemble. One from the Cuyler courtyard leads through Pitney arch and continues down a staircase along the eastern flank of Wright-Patton Hall. Another descends a set of stairs and is defined by the eastern wall of Cuyler Hall and the open courtyard of 1903 Hall. The third traverses the sloping open courtyard of Walker Hall and continues through an archway at the inside corner of the L-shaped building. This sublime environment is compromised only by practical necessities: a trash enclosure and a parking lot. These north–south pathways intersect several east–west pathways that connect Elm Drive on the west and Prospect Gardens and Frist Campus Center on the east.

1879 Hall

28 1879 Hall and Marx Hall

1879 Hall
Benjamin Wistar Morris, 1904

Marx Hall
Kallmann McKinnell and Wood, 1993

The former residential hall 1879 Hall, built early in the twentieth century, is evidence of the direction in which the campus might have grown had the trustees not been able to secure large parcels of land to the south shortly thereafter. No other dormitory was built this far east afterward. A handsome exercise in brick Tudor Gothic, 1879 Hall was hugely popular with Princeton's upperclassmen for the very reason that it was the closest student residence to the Prospect Avenue eating clubs. Just how handsome it appeared to students can be gathered from a contemporary hand-

Woodrow Wilson's office, 1879 Hall

book: "The suites consist of a study, in which is set an open fireplace, and two single bedrooms, separated from the study by a passage opening from the stair hall." The building's use for residential life ended in 1960, when the university converted it to teaching spaces and offices for the Departments of Religion and Philosophy. The conversion is a reminder of the continuing authority of Cram's 1909 master plan, which

Marx Hall

identified this precinct as an academic rather than a residential zone.

When Wilson was president of Princeton (1902–10), he had an office in the tower over the vaulted archway, a privilege no doubt earned by his membership in the class that had donated funds for construction of the dormitory. This room has its own special entrance, an impressive limestone and brick open stone stairway along the inside of the northeast corner of the arch. In designing the passageway through the center of 1879 Hall, Morris was not simply interested in traffic control; he seized the opportunity to engage in visual choreography. Like a telescope, the arch is placed so that it focuses the eye, leading the line of sight forward and out to a vista down Prospect Avenue or, if approached from the east, to a view of the great outdoor room of 1879 Green. The progression from light to shadow back to light is a source of theater, a script that is reversed at night, but with the same effect; there is a dramatic sense of entering and departing.

Collegiate Gothic archways are like decorated rooms: a lamp sways slightly in the breeze; the ribs of the triple-groined vaults give texture; the limestone ornaments that pin the intersecting ribs of each groin are carved with oak leaves or the heads of snarling tigers. Students often gather here to sing to capture the spirit of the place.

Marx Hall (left) and McCosh Hall (right)

In 1993, as the Departments of Religion and Philosophy grew and technology and media required new types of teaching spaces, the university constructed an addition to 1879 Hall, Marx Hall. The site plan and exterior design reflect a contextual sensitivity characteristic of postmodern design. The architects extended the linear alignment of 1879 Hall to the north, narrowing the gap between McCosh Hall and 1879 Hall. While some in the community criticized the university for "walling off" the campus, the reduced open space better defines the meeting of McCosh Walk and Washington Road. Over time the university further improved this transitional space and connecting walkways with new landscaping, paving, lighting, and signage (see Walk Seven). The architects Kallmann McKinnell and Wood artfully adopted the Tudor Gothic proportions, fenestration, and brickwork of 1879 Hall while introducing modern materials and details. In lieu of limestone trim around window openings, they used steel painted a putty color resembling limestone. They articulated the trim by fabricating arrises (sharp edges) in welded steel rather than carved stone. To assert the modernity of the addition, the architects split the gable-roof masonry to reveal air louvers, which serve a similar function to the chimneys of the 1904 building.

29 McCosh Hall and Dickinson Hall

McCosh Hall
Raleigh C. Gildersleeve, 1907

Dickinson Hall
Charles Z. Klauder, 1930

Impressive in size even today, McCosh Hall was built to accommodate a big idea—President Wilson's revolutionary preceptorial system of instruction. The university chose Collegiate Gothic for what was Princeton's largest classroom and office complex at the time and selected German-trained Raleigh C. Gildersleeve of New York, out of seven competing architects, to design the building. The L-shaped building is four hundred feet long on the leg that runs parallel to McCosh Walk and one hundred feet on the northern extension that fronts Washington Road. Gildersleeve's academic background may have been less an argument for his selection than the fact that he was the clear favorite of Moses Pyne. He had designed two dormitories for the influential trustee on the north side of Nassau Street, which featured retail outlets on the ground floor. In addition, he had remodeled Pyne's great estate on the west side of town, Drumthwacket, which today serves as the official residence of New Jersey's governor.

However, Pyne's powerful support and a winning competition entry did not make it easy for Gildersleeve. President Wilson and the trustees involved themselves intimately in the design process, requiring Gildersleeve to modify his concept in a number of ways: the gargoyles favored by the architect were deleted from the pronounced buttresses, which at the time were a new design element on campus, and the window lintels on the first floor were altered from curved to straight. But the broad outlines of Gildersleeve's proposal remained, including the choice of limestone as exterior cladding with a brick backing as an extra measure of fire protection.

The interior features four lecture halls of varying size paneled entirely in oak. As a testament to their versatility, they are the longest continually used teaching spaces on campus. There have been many renovations over the years, the most recent in 2013 when McCosh 50—the largest of the lecture halls—was equipped with cameras, monitors, and speakers that enable on- and off-campus e-learning. In addition to the lecture halls, there are numerous faculty offices, precept rooms, and nine separate entrances from campus to minimize crowding when classes change. Although McCosh Hall has always been impressive in size, especially when first built, every inch of new space was needed to house President Wilson's ambitious educational program, which required a great increase in the size of the faculty.

Dickinson Hall replaced another classroom building of the same name. The original Dickinson—designed by George B. Post and built in 1870 on the site of the current Firestone Plaza—burned down in 1920. Currently Dickinson Hall houses the Department of History. The building fills the Washington Road frontage between McCosh Hall and the University Chapel. While the exterior of all three buildings is constructed of limestone, Klauder's design for Dickinson Hall is far more restrained than its illustrious neighbors.

30   McCosh-Dickinson-Chapel Courtyard
Landscape: Princeton University Office of Physical Planning, 1996

Mather Sundial
After Charles Turnbull; based on 1579–83 design; executed ca. 1907; carved limestone (Portland stone) with gun metal for gnomons (sundial points) Princeton University, gift of Sir William Mather, presented in 1907

The three-sided court formed by the connected facades of McCosh Hall, Dickinson Hall, and the Chapel is somewhat elongated and tapers slightly toward its western open end. When viewed from there, the false perspective subtly modifies the perception of space to create a sense of an intimate courtyard with Mather Sundial as focal point.

The lawn, pavements, and plantings were renewed by the university in 1996, a project that helped spark a resurgence of interest in the campus landscape. Over time the court's perimeter pathway had become an asphalt roadway with muddy edges more

Mather Sundial and McCosh Hall

suitable to trucks than people. It was removed and redesigned into a pedestrian-scaled walk that could also handle wheeled traffic. Paved in concrete unit pavers, the walk uses low beveled curbs of bluestone and granite bollards to protect the central green. The green itself is crisscrossed by curbless bluestone walks for pedestrians only. The circulation hierarchy proved successful and the approach was subsequently adopted for courtyard landscaping at Holder, Blair/Joline, Whitman, and other pedestrian realms where occasional vehicle access is a requirement. Today's tranquil courtyard was once the site of the bitter battle between President Wilson and Dean West over the site for the proposed Graduate College (see Walk Ten). Later, a dispute between Cram and Klauder over the design of Rothschild Arch, which spans between Dickinson and the Chapel, led to Cram's resignation as supervising architect.

The Mather Sundial was given to the university in 1907 by Sir William Mather, a member of the British Parliament. Carved in England from stone quarried on the Isle of Portland, it is a copy of one erected in 1579 by Charles Turnbull in Corpus Christi College, Oxford. Mather gave the sundial to Princeton as a symbol of the connections between the United States and England and their institutions of higher learning.

The sundial takes the form of a cylindrical shaft, surmounted by a square stone and carved with four coats of arms. The column is topped with an astronomical model known as an armillary sphere and surmounted by a pelican. The pelican, the symbol of Corpus Christi College, was a medieval symbol for Christ's sacrifice, for it was believed that the pelican pierced her skin to feed her chicks with her own

McCosh–Dickinson–Chapel courtyard

blood. The inscriptions on the highest base include selections of poetry and information about the donation of the sundial, although most of this has worn away. For much of the past century, sitting on the steps at the base of the sundial was a privilege reserved for members of the senior class. Now all students are welcome to sit on the steps and on warm days the sundial is often the site of outdoor class discussions.

31   University Chapel
Cram and Ferguson, 1928

James McCosh
Augustus Saint-Gaudens; bronze relief, recast
Princeton University, presented in 1929 by the Class of 1879 on its fiftieth reunion

Abraham and Isaac: In Memory of May 4, 1970, Kent State University
George Segal, 1978–79; cast bronze
The John B. Putnam Jr. Memorial Collection, Princeton University, partial gift of the Mildred Andrews Fund

The university's first space dedicated to prayer and worship was located in what today is Nassau Hall's Faculty Room, although the room itself was then not as large. The first freestanding chapel, designed by John Notman, was built in 1847 on the site where East Pyne Hall now stands. A modest building, its construction nevertheless provoked great controversy when the surprised trustees discovered it followed what they considered to be a popish cruciform design. It was replaced in 1881 by Marquand Chapel, which was designed in high Victorian splendor by Richard Morris Hunt but was destroyed by fire in 1920 during a house party weekend. The loss of Marquand Chapel and the patriotic afterglow of the First World War no doubt provided the climate necessary for a great gesture.

The $2.5 million Chapel that replaced Marquand is a work of extraordinary beauty. It was created out of the sense of mission that drove two men: Ralph Adams Cram and President John Grier Hibben (1912–32). For Cram, who was a high-church Episcopalian, the architecture of a university intended to create "culture and character." For Hibben, the architecture of the new Chapel would be a symbol of "the continuity of the religious tradition of Princeton, which had its origin in the faith and hope of the early founders." The complementary purposes of both men begot a building of beauty and holiness that, apart from being one of the world's largest college chapels, exemplifies the Collegiate Gothic style that transformed the campus.

The choice of a site on the east side of campus was in part dictated by the location of the destroyed Marquand Chapel. There was another compelling reason

University Chapel

University Chapel interior

for the site: the university's undergraduate center of gravity was moving eastward. In developing its design, Cram and Ferguson took a hybrid approach, turning to a number of sources for inspiration, most notably the chapel at King's College, Cambridge. The building of the Chapel represented an amalgam of traditional and modern construction techniques. Although the roof framing is fireproofed steel supporting concrete slabs, the walls and columns are monolithic load-bearing masonry (Pennsylvania sandstone and Indiana limestone).

One first encounters the architect—literally—at the west entrance. In 1991 a ninety-six-year-old stonemason named Clifford MacKinnon revealed he had carved his own head, along with that of his boss, Cram, as one of a pair of crockets or "grotesques" on either side of the Chapel's entry portal. Cram to the right is easily identifiable by his glasses. The tympanum—the triangular space immediately above the double set of doors of the west entrance—depicts the "majesty of Jesus Christ" as described by St. John in the Book of Revelations. The inscription of the scroll in Christ's lap is translated, "Who is worthy to open the book?" The figures holding books on either side of the seated Christ are the symbols of the four Evangelists: the lion (St. Mark), angel (St. Matthew), eagle (St. John), and ox (St. Luke). Beneath this scene are carved words from the University Shield—an open Bible with the inscription "*Vet Nov Testamentum*" ("the Old and New Testaments") and the university's motto, *Dei sub numine viget* ("Under God's power she flourishes").

On the south facade, built into the angle between the transept and the nave, is the Bright Pulpit, which bears a quotation from John Bright, the nineteenth-century English politician and advocate of religious freedom: "An instructed democracy is the surest foundation of government, and education and freedom are the only sources of true greatness and happiness among any people."

The interior of the Chapel is divided into four parts that suggest the outline of a cross, with a total length of 270 feet. The elevation is composed of three sections, or stories, beginning with the arcade at the base, then the triforium at the middle level, and the clerestory at the top. The first room entered is a low-ceilinged hall called the narthex. From here one proceeds to the nave, named after President Hibben, which is the largest area of the Chapel. The sensation one experiences after moving from the low-ceilinged narthex into the great expanse of the nave demonstrates the power of architecture to choreograph an emotional response. From the pavement to the crown of the vault, the distance is seventy-six feet.

The pews, made from army surplus wood first intended for Civil War gun carriages, seat nearly two thousand people for religious services, as well as theater, dance, and musical performances. Known for its outstanding baroque quality, the Chapel organ has 125 stops and ten thousand pipes. At the rear in the triforium on the north wall of the nave is an antiphonal organ. In the west gallery below the window is a fanfare trumpet for ceremonial occasions.

Proceeding down the center aisle, one comes to the widest section of the nave, where the perpendicular or long arm of the cross intersects the short or horizontal arm. Attached on either end of the crossing are two transepts: Marquand to the left (north) and Braman on the right (south). The bronze cross is the work of Stephen Zorochin, a campus security guard. A relief of James McCosh is located in the north transept. Created by Augustus Saint-Gaudens, the renowned sculptor of the Beaux-Arts style, the original was severely damaged in the 1920 fire that destroyed the original Marquand Chapel. This relief, a copy, was made from a cast made from the original.

At the very end of the nave is the chancel, reached by a low set of steps. To the left of the stairs is a mid-sixteenth-century pulpit from France; to the right is the lectern. The eagle standing over the snake represents Christ's victory over evil. The chancel—paneled in oak carved in England from Sherwood Forest trees—required a hundred

"Abraham and Isaac: In Memory of May 4, 1970, Kent State University"

woodcarvers who worked on this project for over a year. The oak statues on the ends of the choir and clergy stalls represent musicians, scholars, and teachers of the church. In the center of the chancel wall is the Great East Window ("The Love of Christ"). The chancel is flanked by six bays of windows, the first two representing Psalms of David, and the remaining four depicting cycles from four great Christian epics—Dante's *Divine Comedy*, Sir Thomas Malory's *The Death of Arthur*, John Milton's *Paradise Lost*, and John Bunyan's *Pilgrim's Progress*.

The intricate stained-glass windows throughout the Chapel memorialize figures from Princeton's history and depict scenes from the Bible, literature, history, and philosophy. Of these, the most important are the four Great Windows at the building's four extremes, each depicting a central Christian theme: north, Endurance; east, Love; south, Truth; west, Life. At the center of each window is the figure of Christ depicted, respectively, as martyr, lover (the central scene is the Last Supper), teacher, and savior (the scene is the Second Coming). It also depicts John Witherspoon, the sixth president of the college, in the Great South Window ("Christ the Teacher"). He stands in the right lancet, beside the medieval scholar Alcuin, and above the seven liberal arts—arithmetic, geometry, astronomy, rhetoric, dialectic, grammar, and music—that constituted the curriculum at the time the great cathedrals were built. In the wall below is a verse from the Gospel of St. John: "Ye shall know the truth, and the truth shall make you free." William Selden (Class of 1934) tells the stories of the richly leaded stained-glass windows that pierce the massive Chapel and make the walls appear *light*—in both senses of the word—in his book *Chapels of Princeton University*.

Outside, the grounds in the immediate vicinity of the Chapel reveal their own special pleasures. Against the north transept is a small formal garden designed by landscape architect Howard Russell Butler (Class of 1876). The garden of evergreens and white azaleas is a suitably modest and reflective memorial to Hibben, the driving force behind the construction of the Chapel. On the lower plaza between the Chapel and Firestone Library is a sculpture depicting a contemporary version of Abraham and Isaac in an allegory for the May 4, 1970, tragedy at Kent State University. A poignant visualization of humankind's struggle between ideology and paternal love, it mirrors the conflict that led to the death of four students at the hands of the Ohio National Guard. Though Abraham looks poised to strike his son, the artist emphasized that Genesis 22 ends without tragedy, as Isaac is spared. A happier memory is discovered in a gracefully curved bench next to the Chapel at the northwest corner. It memorializes Beatrix Farrand, whose living monument is the natural beauty that distinguishes the Princeton campus. The inscription reads, "Her love of beauty and order is everywhere visible in what she planted for our delight."

The Chapel has served as the site of individual and collective celebration, thanksgiving, grief, and debate for both the university and the community.

32 Firestone Library
O'Connor and Kilham, 1948; Addition: O'Connor and Kilham, 1961; Addition: Kilham, Beder, and Chu, 1971; Addition: Koetter Kim and Associates, 1988; Renovation: Shepley Bulfinch with Frederick Fisher and Partners, 2011–18 (estimated completion)

White Sun
Isamu Noguchi, 1966; Seravezza marble

Atmosphere and the Environment X
Louise Nevelson, 1969–70; Corten steel

The heart of a great university is its library, and Princeton's library is second to none in the country. Firestone Library—with its current collection of more than eight million volumes on-site and in satellite repositories—represents a studied attempt to resolve a fundamental paradox: books need to be protected, but unless they are accessible they have no value.

For colonial Americans, a gift of books was valued as much as a gift of money, perhaps even more so. The wisdom contained within a book is beyond time and the vicissitudes of human circumstance—but the books themselves are not. Initially housed in Nassau Hall, precious volumes repeatedly fell victim to the catastrophic fires that reduced the structure to its massive exterior walls. Fire was not the only threat; there was also policy. Because they were precious, books were kept under lock and key except one hour a week when students were allowed limited access.

There was also an issue of space. Unlike the considerably younger Princeton Theological Seminary, which had built a freestanding facility as early as 1843, the college, even after the Civil War, was forced to store its books in whatever space was available. The lack of a separate library facility and the meager size of the collection appalled newly appointed President McCosh when he arrived from Scotland in 1868. The library at that point consisted of no more than fourteen thousand volumes. The two student debating societies, Whig and Clio, alleviated the problem somewhat by offering their own libraries. But a library for "members only" could never replace the need for a college facility that served the needs of the entire student body as well as the faculty.

McCosh's commitment to growth and access soon bore fruit. He transformed the formerly anemic accessions policy into a rapidly rising tide of new books, and liberalized the school's lending policy and the hours during which books could be accessed. Students met his initiatives with an explosion of use. First Chancellor Green Library and then Pyne Library—both of which had been intended for the use of many generations—were overwhelmed. By the end of the 1920s it was clear to the trustees that a larger facility had to be built. Charles Z. Klauder produced sketches in the early 1930s that depict a Collegiate Gothic structure with a

Firestone Library with "John Witherspoon" in foreground

monumental, if not theatrical, Gothic interior. Klauder's conception focused on vertical storage of books that, had it been built, would have yielded a structure along the lines of the soaring Cathedral of Learning he had designed for the University of Pittsburgh.

In 1944 President Harold Dodds (1933–57) convened a distinguished task force of college librarians, library consultants, and young architects, including Robert B. O'Connor (MFA 1920) and Walter H. Kilham, whose firm had been founded in New York the year before. Called the Cooperative Committee on Library Building Plans, this task force not only was charged to develop a plan to meet the needs of faculty and students, but also was given carte blanche to create a revolutionary prototype for what a modern library should be. It was to be a "laboratory-workshop library," consisting of open stacks and reading areas within the stacks. This arrangement contrasts with closed stack libraries where patrons request books at a main circulation desk and read them in a large reading room. To protect books from ultraviolet rays, the stacks would be located underground in a loft structure with a horizontal organization. Firestone Library was the architects' response to this new program. By employing what was then a fairly revolutionary use of a flexible modular system of organization, the architects and their consultants imaginatively tackled the twin challenges of storage and access. In the process they were able to create the world's largest collegiate open stack library.

The grade of the site, sloping down toward Nassau Street, allowed for a large facility that would not overshadow the nearby Chapel. One enters from the south into what appears to be the ground floor of a relatively modest building, but is in fact the fourth level of a seven-story structure. The three floors above and the entrance tower are constructed of structural steel clad in rustic buff limestone, Wissahickon schist, and Mount Airy granite to complement the nearby Chapel and McCosh Hall. The three floors below grade are constructed of reinforced concrete.

Understanding that a modern library must always be a work in progress—clearly demonstrated by the rapid obsolescence of Princeton's earlier facilities—the architects designed a deliberate porosity into Firestone's envelope. The entrance, which faces and defers to the Chapel, has an appropriately formal facade that conveys an air of permanence. The other elevations, however, were clearly intended to accommodate lateral additions as the pace of acquisition inevitably grew. In 1961 O'Connor and Kilham designed an octagonal addition on the southeast corner to house the John Foster Dulles Library of Diplomatic History. In 1971 the firm was called back again to add to the stack areas by expanding the two lowest below-grade floors at the northwest corner. Seventeen years later the firm of Koetter Kim and Associates was commissioned to add approximately fifty thousand square feet of stacks, office space, and major reading rooms. The architect accomplished this by expanding the two lowest floors at the northeast corner.

Whereas the original architects deliberately minimized natural daylight in the stack areas to protect the books from ultraviolet rays, Koetter Kim welcomed the outside in. Having access to new technologies and materials, the architects

Firestone Library, third-floor reading room

designed a carefully organized system of roof penetrations that wash the space with light and allow those inside to have refreshing views out. The three large skylighted reading rooms also orient the user in what might otherwise seem like a directionless maze. The largest of these rooms runs along what had been the north outer wall of the existing building with an eastern view toward Washington Road. The exposed stone wall of the existing building and the use of arched trusses to support the glass skylight that covers the entire space yields a space conducive to scholarly research.

If the inside of the addition employs a wide variety of design strategies to enliven the below-grade space, understatement is the prevailing note outside. As the slope of the site falls away toward Nassau Street, the addition slowly emerges out of the ground, ultimately forming a low wall at its northern edge, penetrated by windows that offer views into the stacks and carrels. The twenty-foot-wide setback area between the length of the wall and Nassau Street serves as an urban park. Passersby are invited to relax and watch the street scene outside beneath the two parallel rows of zelkova elms. The textures and colors of the elements that appear above grade are chosen to complement the main building, which rises at some distance in the background. The roof terrace, which is visible from the main building, supports a modest green space comprising a formal pattern of lawn areas and pathways. At the northeast corner, a semicircular stair tower capped by a sloping glass roof brings daylight into the building and anchors this edge of the central campus.

On the lawn between the west side of the library and Nassau Street stands Louise Nevelson's sculpture *Atmosphere and Environment X*. Princeton has the distinction of having Nevelson's first monumental outdoor sculpture in Corten steel.

Atmosphere and Environment X relies on light and shadow to give depth to the surface's geometry, which appears lacy and weightless or bold and structured, dependent on the play of natural light.

Like most research libraries in the twenty-first century, Firestone is adapting to digital resources and user preferences. A comprehensive, phased renovation of the building—guided by a university steering committee and the design team of Shepley Bulfinch and Frederick Fisher and Partners—is scheduled for completion in 2018. There will be increased emphasis on the quality and variety of reader spaces, while maintaining a balance with the collections. Compact shelving is used on the lowest level, where floor loads permit, to shelve more books in less space while preserving Firestone's open stack policy. Reader tables are interspersed within traditional open shelving, restoring the concept of the "browsing alcoves" articulated by planners of the 1948 building. The online catalog replaced the card catalog cabinets that were once a feature of the main floor, and wireless internet and mobile devices offer a twenty-first-century version of browsing. Readers are given priority at the perimeter of above-grade levels, where daylight is abundant. Open carrels, lounge seating, reader tables, and group study rooms replace the original, private, enclosed study carrels (nicknamed "phone booths").

In the main floor lobby the architects replaced the wooden security barrier with a low glass partition and the parquet floor with wide oak planks, but kept the plaque marking the contributions of the Classes of 1922 through 1929 and Isamu Noguchi's sculpture *White Sun*. Noguchi created *White Sun* while developing *The Garden (Pyramid, Sun, and Cube)* at Yale University. Princeton's is one of several study versions; others include a black granite sun now in Seattle. Drawing on both Eastern and Western cultural traditions, Noguchi's sculptures appear to possess the quality of effortlessness, a virtue Japanese artists once valued above perfection.

Public areas on the main floor include the renovated lobby and a new glass-enclosed, museum-quality gallery for exhibitions of rare books and special collections, as well as the Cotsen Children's Library. Charter Trustee Lloyd E. Cotsen (Class of 1950) donated his collection of rare children's books, artwork, and educational toys—some dating from the fifteenth century—to the library and provided funds for the renovation of a two-story space (originally a study hall) accessible from the main lobby. In 1997 Henry Smith-Miller (Class of 1964) designed a glass-enclosed "wall of books" in the space to store these rare materials, which are visible to visitors but only accessible to scholars. Schoolchildren and families also enjoy James Bradberry's "Bookscape," a storybook come to life with topiary animals, reading nooks, a wishing well, and a tree house.

West of the main lobby beyond the security barrier is the Trustee Reading Room, a study space heavily used by undergraduate students. The room features a mezzanine, a luminous ceiling with pendant fixtures, and windows on three sides. Glass panels—designed by Venturi, Scott Brown and Associates—etched with the names of all Princeton presidents and trustees are superimposed on north-facing windows. On the third floor the former faculty lounge was converted into a read-ers' space where a tapestry by John Nava hangs. The two-story room features a mezzanine and full-height windows embellished with Gothic tracery that overlook Firestone Plaza.

33   Firestone Plaza
Zion and Breen Associates, 1977; Redesign: Quennell Rothschild and Partners, 2003–4

John Witherspoon
Alexander Stoddart, 2001; cast bronze
Princeton University

Song of the Vowels
Jacques Lipchitz, 1969; cast bronze

Firestone Plaza has an irregular perimeter defined by East Pyne Hall, the Chapel, and Firestone Library, but a strong axial orientation. In the nineteenth century William Street extended across campus from Washington Road to University Place (then Railroad Avenue). College Avenue, to the east of the original FitzRandolph property, ran north–south from Nassau Street to Prospect House. Vestiges of both roads remain as pedestrian walkways through Firestone Plaza: one is in the location of the former William Street and the other, Chancellor Way, is the former College Avenue.

Firestone Plaza

The plaza, an artful blend of bluestone paving, granite benches, planting beds, and trees, provides access to the main arched entry portico of Firestone Library and to the west portal of the Chapel. The plaza also hosts events, such as a farmers' market and social gatherings. Robert Zion, consulting landscape architect (1974–82), first designed the plaza in 1977. The current plaza's plantings, pavements, and benches are the work of consulting landscape architects Quennell Rothschild & Partners (2000–2005).

Two sculptures—*John Witherspoon* and *Song of the Vowels*—grace the plaza. Witherspoon is memorialized in a twenty-first-century bronze figure, which has a twin in his native Scotland. Sculptor Alexander Stoddart, also a Scotsman, included everyday objects to symbolize his subject's character: a Bible, lectern, and eagle represent, respectively, Witherspoon's contributions as renowned preacher, beloved teacher and president, and champion of American independence. In *Song of the Vowels*, Jacques Lipchitz fused the harp with the harpist to form a powerful hybrid. Inspired by symphony concerts in Paris, the work embodies the cubist principles of structure and form for which the sculptor was well known. Seventh of an edition of seven, Princeton's version is unique in that it adds a square base to the pedestal, an element not found in earlier casts.

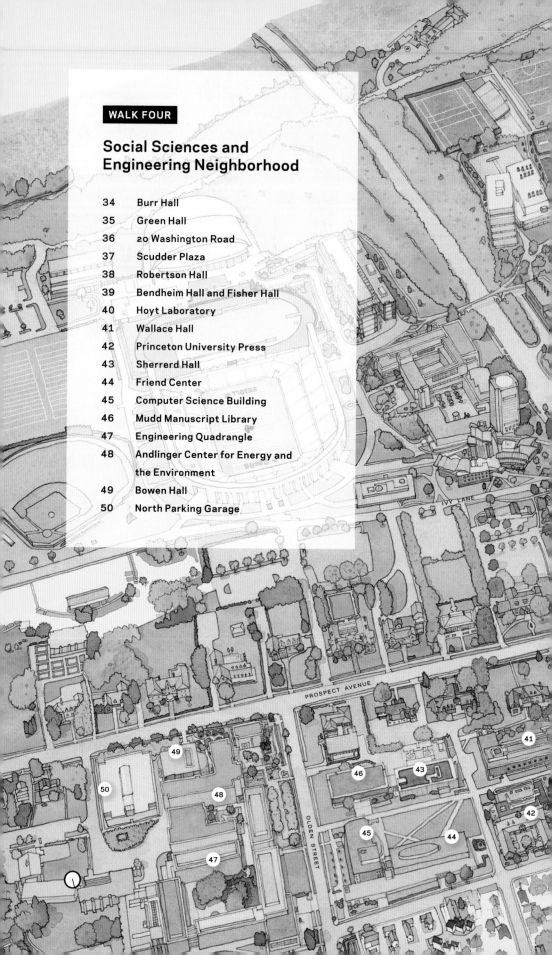

WALK FOUR

Social Sciences and Engineering Neighborhood

SOUTH DRIVE

ELM DRIVE

WASHINGTON ROAD

WILLIAM STREET

NASSAU STREET

38

37

39

36

40

35

34

Social Sciences and Engineering Neighborhood

CREATING A NEIGHBORHOOD

As the university expanded in the late nineteenth century beyond the close-knit confines of the historic campus around Nassau Hall, land eastward across Washington Road became prime space for the emerging scientific disciplines of chemistry and biology. Today the campus that lies east of Washington Road and north of Prospect Avenue is framed on each end by two of Princeton's three storied professional schools—the School of Engineering and Applied Science and the Woodrow Wilson School of Public and International Affairs—and is connected by a pedestrian spine, Shapiro Walk, along the east–west axis (see Landscape Walks).

The university's public and international affairs program, founded in 1930, became the Woodrow Wilson School in 1948 and moved into its new head-quarters in 1965. Around the same time, major laboratories for mechanical and aerospace engineering—located on the Princeton Forrestal campus since the 1950s—moved to the new Engineering Quadrangle and consolidated with other engineering departments in the mid-1960s. The site of the Engineering Quadrangle had been university athletic fields since the early twentieth century. Largely as a result of the post–Second World War buildup in international affairs, engineering, and applied sciences, this area of campus came to be defined as a neighborhood of buildings for innovation, home to many of the country's leading thinkers and researchers in these fields.

The early and mid-twentieth-century buildings along today's Shapiro Walk were developed over 125 years with no consistent plan or design and no particular focus or organizing principle. Burr Hall was the first academic building to be sited east of Washington Road—at the intersection of Nassau Street—and signaled the institution's need to expand beyond its original boundaries. It was built as a chemical laboratory in 1891 to relieve overcrowding in the John C. Green Hall of Science (previously located on the site of Firestone Library). Two additional science buildings constructed in the late 1920s, Frick Laboratory for chemistry and Green Hall for mechanical and electrical engineering, represented the leading edge of what Supervising Architect Ralph Adams Cram clearly intended for the emerging campus east of Washington Road. But this never happened. Frick and Green were built in the final days of the Roaring Twenties. After the devastating 1929 stock market crash and ensuing national Depression, construction at Princeton—like all American campuses—ground to a halt. Before new building resumed, Collegiate Gothic had largely gone out of fashion. As the neighborhood developed, the design of individual buildings reflected the prevailing architectural idiom of their time: Collegiate Gothic (Frick and Green Halls), various forms of modern architecture (from Robertson Hall to Friend Center), postmodern architecture (Computer

Aerial view of campus east of Washington Road looking southeast, date unknown

Science Building and Bowen Hall), and contemporary design (Wallace and Sherrerd Halls).

In the larger context the neighborhood is bordered by Nassau Street to the north, Murray Place to the east, and Prospect Avenue to the south. Between William Street and Nassau Street lie private retail and residential properties and the visual arts studios of the Lewis Center for the Arts at 185 Nassau Street. The single-family private residences to the east along Murray Place are buffered from the Engineering Quadrangle by building setbacks and dense plantings. Current and former private eating clubs, several of which were repurposed for university use, line the section of Prospect Avenue from Washington Road to Murray Place, known as "the Street" (see Walk Five). South of Prospect Avenue are athletic fields and science buildings. As cross-disciplinary research and teaching between engineering and the natural sciences continue to grow, there are opportunities to link those buildings to this neighborhood through north–south connections, such as the walkway next to Cannon Club linking Prospect Avenue and Ivy Lane, and Roper Lane between Cottage and Cap and Gown clubs.

Burr Hall

34   Burr Hall
Richard Morris Hunt, 1891; Addition and renovation: Allan Greenberg Architect with KSS *Architects, 2005*

Burr Hall, located at the southeast corner of Nassau Street and Washington Road, was initially designed as a chemistry laboratory. It is the only surviving example on campus of the work of Richard Morris Hunt, the architect of Marquand Chapel (destroyed by fire in 1920). Perhaps best known for New York's Metropolitan Museum of Art and the Biltmore estate in Asheville, North Carolina, Hunt's architectural style oscillated between Beaux-Arts pomp and an almost classical, restrained use of masonry and massing reminiscent of the

Burr Hall addition

American architectural genius H. H. Richardson. For Burr Hall, Hunt chose a Renaissance Revival vocabulary. The top floors are of Haverstraw brick laid in red mortar. The ground floor, which flares out slightly like a skirt, is of Trenton sandstone, as are the belt courses and window trimmings. Mock battlements add visual interest to the straightforward flat roof.

The Department of Chemical Engineering moved to the new Engineering Quadrangle in 1962, leaving Burr Hall to be renovated for the social sciences. The Department of Anthropology was the first beneficiary of this renovation, joined later by a collection of regional and international studies programs. To accommodate these expanding programs, an addition was constructed in 2005. Designed by the classically trained architect Allan Greenberg, the addition fits seamlessly and snugly into the inverted southeast corner of the building. A narrow but welcoming passageway between Burr and Green Halls connects Washington Road to a new entrance, marked by a glass canopy. Greenberg continued the rusticated base and horizontally banded brick of Hunt's design, but added a chamfered corner with turret atop Hunt's battlements. Behind this facade is a multistory circulation and gathering space defined on two sides by the former exterior masonry walls.

35   Green Hall
Charles Z. Klauder, 1929; Addition: Voorhees, Walker, Foley, and Smith, 1950; Renovation: Francis W. Roudebush, 1963; Renovation: Nalls Architecture, 2003

Green Hall and the former Frick Laboratory next door are among the few Collegiate Gothic buildings east of Washington Road. Green Hall memorializes the important contributions of John Cleve Green, founder of the university's Engineering School and the donor behind Chancellor Green Library. In the mid-nineteenth century, Green stepped up to the challenge facing Princeton to help meet the nation's growing need for graduates trained in the theoretical and applied sciences. Historically, America's liberal arts colleges had held to a classical curriculum, but by the close of the Civil War the emergence of public land grant colleges offering technical training in mechanical and agricultural arts was evidence of the demand for college graduates in the applied sciences. The Lawrence Scientific School at Harvard and Sheffield Scientific School at Yale were founded in 1847. Princeton followed suit in 1874 with the founding of the John C. Green School of Science. The Green fortune endowed chairs, subsidized faculty salaries, and funded the laboratories and classrooms for the new school. Green financed McCosh's vision of distinguished achievement in chemistry, physics, electrical engineering, and civil engineering.

Princeton's first science laboratory, the original Green Hall, was built in 1874 and designed by William Potter, architect of Chancellor Green Library. It stood on the west side of Washington Road where Firestone Library is now located. In 1877 the building doubled in size, but by the 1920s, engineering advances during the previous decade left it inadequate. In 1928 fire destroyed the building.

Charles Z. Klauder's design for the new Green Hall faithfully followed Cram's 1909 master plan, in which he had proposed a building to replace a civil engineering laboratory constructed in 1904. The structure would front the east side of Washington Road and extend from Burr Hall to William Street. Klauder's design, similar to that of the original Frick Laboratory, is a restrained version of Collegiate Gothic. Both use the same argillite and limestone trim for exterior walls as the

Green Hall

earlier twentieth-century Collegiate Gothic buildings on the historic campus, but combined with advances in structural practice, including concrete structural frames to support the floor and roof loads. The exterior, and particularly the interior, reflected the research laboratory function, rather than a domestically scaled and detailed dormitory.

In 1962 the occupants of Green Hall moved to the newly constructed Engineering Quadrangle, and the building was renovated for the Departments of Psychology and Sociology. Eno Hall—the first building constructed for the Department of Psychology (1924)—was also designed by Charles Z. Klauder. Evolutionary cycles in curriculum and infrastructure brought further changes after fifty years: in 2013 the psychology department and the Princeton Neuroscience Institute moved to new buildings in the Natural Sciences Neighborhood, again presenting the opportunity to renew the venerable Green Hall.

36   20 Washington Road (formerly Frick Chemistry Laboratory)
Charles Z. Klauder, 1928; Landscape: Beatrix Jones Farrand, 1928; Addition: O'Connor and Kilham, 1963; Addition: Payette Associates, 1984; Renovation and Addition: KPMB *Architects, scheduled completion 2016; Landscape: Michael Van Valkenburgh Associates, scheduled completion 2016*

In the late 1920s Pittsburgh steelmaker Henry Clay Frick offered to endow a law school at Princeton. President Hibben had a different agenda and persuaded Frick to instead endow the chemistry department, one of the last in a succession of science and dormitory buildings commissioned during Hibben's twenty-year tenure

(1912–32). With Hibben's patronage and Cram's guidance on planning and architectural matters, Klauder designed fifteen major Collegiate Gothic buildings on the Princeton campus, including Frick Chemistry Laboratory and Green Hall. (Frank Miles Day, Charles Z. Klauder's partner, died in 1918, but the firm retained the name of Day and Klauder until 1927.)

Beatrix Farrand created a nestling habitat at Frick, where the gnarled wisteria vines seemed to grow out of the stone. The Collegiate Gothic facade masks what was, at the time it was built, a thoroughly modern interior that featured two of the most extensively used lecture halls on campus. While the exterior of the 1928 building and the 1963 addition are expressions of Collegiate Gothic design, the Washington Road frontage and shallow elevated terrace depart from the early Princeton tradition of a building generously set back from the street and surrounded by landscaping. Modest three-story towers on the north and south ends of the two-story western facade and a double-arched entrance are rendered in the mandated Collegiate Gothic style. However, there is no steeply pitched roof dressed with gables and gargoyles. The concrete frame structure was intended to be fire-resistant and to accommodate open-plan laboratories with large windows on light courts.

In the 1960s the university expanded the building to the east to accommodate new technologies and a growing student population. A 1968 fire and a $1.5 million grant from the Kresge Foundation brought internal modifications and upgrading. But by the turn of the twenty-first century requirements for chemistry research and teaching had rendered the building obsolete. Once the university decided in the early 2000s to proceed with the construction of a new chemistry

20 *Washington Road, south facade rendering*

20 *Washington Road west facade, photomontage*

building, the opportunity arose to repurpose the original building. When the building reopens (scheduled for 2016) the Department of Economics will move from Fisher Hall, the Woodrow Wilson School will relocate several of its centers, and the Princeton Institute for Regional Studies and other international initiatives will move from Burr Hall into renovated offices, classrooms, conference rooms, and social spaces.

Goals for the renovation include integrating the building into a more campus-like setting with strategies such as landscaping former service areas and light courts, and removal of the loading dock, exterior fire escapes, and a bridge connection to Hoyt Laboratory. Entries will be opened on each facade and a bridge to Scudder Plaza will be installed to facilitate interactions with academic departments in adjacent buildings and other parts of campus. Two large atria within—one at the Washington Road entry, one at the Scudder Plaza entry—will provide communal spaces shared by the various disciplines housed in the building. An addition, built on the second-floor roof, will link the two projecting three-story wings on the Washington Road side and will provide classrooms as well as a second exit for the wings. On the east side an eight-foot-wide section of the building added in 1984 will be removed, exposing the stone facade of the 1963 addition, which will be renovated with new windows. The architectural treatment will refresh the historic character of the original Collegiate Gothic building, while providing contemporary additions to accommodate the programs and enhance collaboration.

A transformation of this magnitude demonstrates Princeton's commitment to preserve its heritage and provide for future generations of scholars and students.

37   Scudder Plaza

Yamasaki and Associates, 1965; Renovation: Quennell Rothschild and Partners, 2002

Fountain of Freedom

James FitzGerald, 1966; cast bronze
Princeton University

Scudder Plaza represents the nexus of the social sciences at Princeton and a significant public space shared by campus and community. As an architectural composition, Scudder Plaza is like no other quad on campus. Here stand four episodes of twentieth-century architecture: the Collegiate Gothic former Frick Laboratory on the north; an austere Cold War brick-box-cum-cylinder in Corwin Hall; postmodern Bendheim and Fisher Halls on the east; and a flamboyant recollection of the Parthenon in Robertson Hall on the south. Scudder Plaza's ample benches, play of water, and tulip magnolias mediate this stylistic dialogue.

The eminent modern architect Minoru Yamasaki designed the plaza in tandem with his design for Robertson Hall, the Woodrow Wilson School's main building. The centerpiece of the plaza is a shallow reflecting pool and sculptural fountain. The spires and crevices of the *Fountain of Freedom* mimic natural patterns of wind and water erosion, metaphorically representing the aspirations and frustrations of Woodrow Wilson. At six tons and twenty-three feet high, the fountain is one of the largest cast bronze sculptures in the United States.

The plaza's composition, unlike the informality of the Victorian-era campus and the picturesque quality of the Collegiate Gothic campus, is grand and

Scudder Plaza and Robertson Hall (right)

monumental. Quennell Rothschild and Partners' 2002 renovation softened the plaza by recladding it in warm-brown Canadian granite and adding areas for seating at both ends of the pool, shaded by honey locust trees. While the plaza is level, the land around it slopes from Washington Road to the south and east. Stairs at the northeast corner lead to Shapiro Walk and the engineering and other social sciences buildings, and stairs at the southeast corner along Bendheim and Fisher Halls lead to Prospect Avenue. A landscaped berm sloping to Shapiro Walk will replace a retaining wall that created a precipitous separation between the plaza and former Frick Laboratory. The magnolia trees that will line the edge of the berm are replacements for the beloved originals that were removed when the retaining wall was demolished.

38   Robertson Hall
Yamasaki and Associates, 1965; Addition: Ford Farewell Mills and Gatsch, 2002

The World
Harry Bertoia, 1964; bronze
Princeton University

Peyton Hall
Yamasaki and Associates, 1966

Robertson Hall is the main building of the Woodrow Wilson School of Public and International Affairs. The school—founded in 1930 as an interdisciplinary program for undergraduates—was named for Wilson when the graduate professional program was added in 1948. Wilson had articulated his concept of "Princeton in the Nation's Service" in speeches made at the Sesquicentennial celebration in 1896 and later as president of the university in 1902. During President Shapiro's tenure he expanded Wilson's phrase to read, "Princeton in the Nation's Service and in the Service of All Nations." A medallion inscribed with this phrase is located at the intersection of several pathways on the lawn north of Nassau Hall.

As the number of faculty, students, and programs grew, the school moved from spaces in Dickinson and Clio Halls to the former Arbor Inn club—known today as 5 Ivy Lane—and then in 1952 to a purpose-built facility, Woodrow Wilson Hall. Designed by Voorhees, Walker, Foley, and Smith, the building was located at the northeast corner of Washington Road and Prospect Avenue. In the early 1960s the school received a gift to further expand the faculty and to fund construction of a new building. To raise the profile and prestige of the school, President Goheen hired Yamasaki to design the new building as a dramatic architectural statement. Harvard President Nathan M. Pusey, Yale President Alfred Whitney Griswold, and Penn President Gaylord P. Harnwell had each hired renowned modern architects—Le Corbusier, Richard Neutra, Walter Gropius, Josep Lluís Sert, Louis Kahn, Romaldo

Giurgola, Eero Saarinen, Gordon Bunshaft (Skidmore, Owings & Merrill), Phillip Johnson, and Paul Rudolph—to design signature modern buildings. Goheen's strategy mirrored that of his colleagues at Harvard, Yale, and Penn.

Yamasaki's design required moving the existing Woodrow Wilson Hall, which had been renamed Corwin Hall, three hundred feet to the east and demolishing the Observatory of Instruction (1877). To serve Goheen's goal of stimulating students of government to lofty aspirations, Yamasaki designed a building that is at once classically inspired and modernist, with international cultural references and more monumental spirit than typically functional university buildings. Robertson Hall follows the form of a Greek temple: a colonnade surrounding a cella (sanctuary), sitting on a plinth (raised platform), and surmounted by an entablature (architrave, frieze, and cornice). In this case the recessed three-story volume containing offices, classrooms, an auditorium, an atrium lobby, and other public space represents the cella. In the atrium lobby, Harry Bertoia created the globe-shaped sculpture out of densely arranged tubes, each with a branch-like ending, welded to a central core. The artist is most famous for his modern furniture and sound sculptures, but this work, from his *bush* series, reflects his deep love of nature. The cantilevered fourth floor with narrow windows and containing offices represents the entablature.

Below the first-floor plinth, a lower level contains seminar rooms, bowl classrooms, and informal public space. Corridors at the east end of the lower level connect Robertson to Bendheim and Fisher Halls; Corwin Hall, home of the Department of Politics, is connected to Bendheim Hall on the first floors of both buildings. In 2002 seminar rooms and another bowl classroom, as well as a direct stair and ramp connection to Washington Road, were added to the lower level.

The construction and detailing of Robertson Hall are characteristic of modernist design in the mid-twentieth century. Yamasaki embraced the industrial technique of prefabrication, both for ease of construction and precision of manufacture. The fifty-eight load-bearing perimeter columns are formed of precast concrete surfaced with quartz chips. The exterior walls are non-load-bearing travertine veneer and a metal-and-glass curtain wall. Yamasaki's details are minimalist, using slender members, small joints, and concealed fasteners. The white exterior is the color favored by both classical Greek and modern architects. His design achieved Goheen's objective to create an icon for the school and has both admirers and

detractors. In one sense it is Princeton's first postmodern building, at once both traditional and modern.

Yamasaki's success with Robertson Hall led to his commission to design Peyton Hall for the Department of Astrophysical Sciences, completed in 1966. Located on Ivy Lane east of Lewis Library, the building houses an observatory, replacing the one demolished for

Peyton Hall

construction of Robertson. Although the main floor plan is similar to Robertson—a central floor-through lobby with an auditorium on one side and teaching space (originally a library) on the other—the exterior of "Princeton stone" (argillite) above a one-story band of precast concrete window frames is modest by comparison.

39   Bendheim Hall and Fisher Hall
Venturi, Scott Brown and Associates, 1990

Bendheim and Fisher Halls—together with Wallace Hall, and the older Corwin and Robertson Halls to which they are connected, and, in the future, 20 Washington Road—constitute a large complex that serves the social sciences. The architecture of Bendheim-Fisher announces yet another aesthetic in this stylistically diverse neighborhood, an aesthetic that, like Victorian architecture, celebrates color, texture, and light. To see Bendheim and Fisher Halls set at an obtuse angle next to the modernism of Corwin Hall is to appreciate what Robert Venturi's polemic *Complexity and Contradiction in Architecture* (perhaps the single most trenchant critique of the moral language of orthodox modern architecture) had set out to overturn. Both structures are essentially rectangles. Both are brick and glass with limestone trim. But Corwin appears to be the dull shell out of which a far livelier Bendheim and Fisher have hatched. Venturi, Scott Brown and Associates manipulates the geometry of the envelope by rounding the edges, and achieves warmth inside by opening the spaces to sunlight and choosing rich wood finishes. Window mullions are wide, closely spaced, and painted medium gray to relate to the leaded-pane casement windows of Collegiate Gothic buildings.

Venturi (Class of 1947, MFA 1950) and his design partner, Denise Scott Brown, are two names that surface repeatedly in Princeton University's design history after 1980. They gave the campus a visual identity in the 1980s and 1990s that served as a model for a generation of architects working at Princeton and other universities.

40   Hoyt Laboratory
Davis Brody and Associates, 1979; Renovation: HDR, 2013

The university built Hoyt Laboratory as a new structure for biochemistry in the late 1970s, rather than further expand Frick Laboratory. Today, as the boundary between the natural sciences and engineering becomes increasingly porous, the biochemical research conducted here is under the aegis of the School of Engineering and Applied Science. The crisp and clean polish of Hoyt takes its cue from the advanced research into the then-emerging discipline of biochemistry. Compare this to Klauder's design for the Frick Laboratory: a Gothic mask that veiled the innovative research inside. Whereas Klauder invoked a late medieval academic tradition, Davis Brody and Associates used the sleek, modern style to communicate the university's commitment to innovation. The architects use windows decoratively

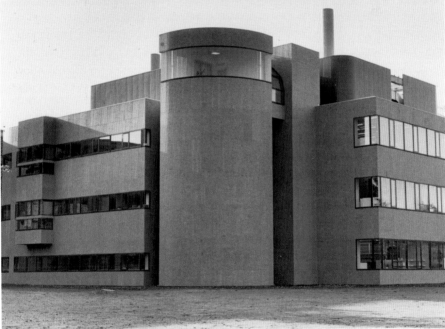

Robertson Hall (left) and Fisher Hall (right); Hoyt Laboratory, date unknown

as well as functionally, which distinguishes this building from the architecture
of the 1950s and 1960s, in which windows were little more than utilitarian openings
for ventilation and light.

When Davis Brody designed Hoyt the firm located the main entry to the
building on William Street. As the Social Sciences and Engineering Neighborhood

developed, the main east-west pedestrian circulation shifted to Shapiro Walk. Once Hoyt is detached from 20 Washington Road (the former Frick Laboratory) during renovation of the latter, the existing walkway from William Street to Shapiro Walk—and the green space between the south side of Hoyt and east side of 20 Washington Road—will feel like more of a campus green. An existing side entrance to Hoyt along this walkway will become more prominent.

41   Wallace Hall

Bohlin Cywinski Jackson, 2000; Landscape: Michael Vergason, 2000; Landscape: Michael Van Valkenburgh Associates, 2009

Wallace Hall is one of several buildings that define the edges of Shapiro Walk. Architects Bohlin Cywinski Jackson planned Wallace Hall with attention to the site conditions on all four sides. The facade facing Shapiro Walk is composed of horizontal bands reinforcing the linearity of the pedestrian path. The main entrance at the northwest corner is emphasized by a two-story freestanding column and overhanging roof. This entrance is positioned to welcome pedestrians descending the steps from Scudder Plaza and is also oriented toward a secondary, narrower passage between Wallace and Corwin Halls that leads to Prospect Avenue. On the south the ground plane is cut back and sloped to a landscaped terrace that provides daylight to the lower level. On the east the building turns the corner with a short extension that defines Charlton Street—an improved service drive—and shelters the south-facing terrace.

Wallace Hall

The building's horizontal banding is reinforced by a glass wall recessed behind freestanding columns at the first floor, a projecting plane of brick at the second floor, a flush glazed wall at the top floor, and cantilevered metal sunscreens at the roofline. There are also cantilevered metal roof canopies over the main entrance and tower. These horizontal elements are juxtaposed against a solid brick tower with a vertical strip window and tall freestanding columns.

Occupants of the building include the Woodrow Wilson School and the Department of Sociology. Central to both the school and the department are the research collections. A grand stair leads from the main entrance to the lower level, where occupants enjoy an outdoor terrace planted with flowering cherry trees. Set within a two-story volume, with one level below grade and one level above grade, and visible from Shapiro Walk through a glass wall, the stair descends along an interior foundation wall clad in stacked courses of black granite.

42 Princeton University Press
Ernest Flagg, 1911; Addition: KSS Architects, 2001

While administratively separate from Princeton University, the Princeton University Press is embedded in the physical campus. The building's main entrance is through a courtyard of the original building on William Street. A staff entrance is located in the addition on the Shapiro Walk side. The Collegiate Gothic style of the original building relates to the early twentieth-century dormitories on the historic campus, and the addition relates to the late twentieth-century modern design of Wallace Hall

Princeton University Press

and Friend Center on Shapiro Walk. When constructed in 1911 the press was the only institutional building on William Street east of Washington Road.

At the turn of the twentieth century the need to publish the research of university professors became a cornerstone of the transformation of American colleges into universities. Charles Scribner (Class of 1875), trustee of the university and renowned book publisher, responded to this need by providing the land, the building, and an endowment for the press. His largess came with an architect—his brother-in-law Ernest Flagg, who had designed Scribner's New York offices and store—and the Collegiate Gothic style of architecture. Initially the press printed the *Alumni Weekly* and later grew into one of the world's most prestigious publishers of scholarly books.

Flagg, although trained at the École des Beaux-Arts, obliged his benefactor by designing a building in the Collegiate Gothic style with argillite stone walls, limestone trim, and a steeply pitched slate roof. Entered through a monumental arched gateway, the domestically scaled courtyard features a central ornamental tree, bluestone pavers, and perimeter planting beds. The courtyard leads to an entrance hall in the center of the U-shaped plan that initially housed the printing presses. In the 1960s the press moved the printing plant off-site and repurposed the hall for exhibitions and receptions.

The press outgrew the original building and in 2001 constructed an addition on the south side. By this time the university had developed the campus between Washington Road and Olden Street, affording the press frontage on Shapiro Walk. KSS Architects responded to this opportunity by placing a conference room with tall windows on the southwest corner of the addition and an entrance plaza near the southeast corner opposite an entrance to Wallace Hall.

Sherrerd Hall

43 Sherrerd Hall
Frederick Fisher and Partners, 2008; Landscape: Quennell Rothschild and Partners, 2006; Landscape: Michael Van Valkenburgh Associates, 2008

Untitled (ORFE/SEAS)
Jim Isermann, 2008; chrome-plated aluminum, steel, acrylic, LED illumination, miscellaneous hardware
Princeton University

Sherrerd Hall houses Operations Research and Financial Engineering (ORFE), a department of the School of Engineering and Applied Science, and the Center for Information Technology Policy. ORFE has close programmatic ties with the social sciences, the Department of Economics, the Bendheim Center for Finance, and policy centers in the Woodrow Wilson School. Together these departments and centers offer undergraduates a course of study that prepares them for business and management professional schools. The expansion of social sciences to the east and engineering to the west along Shapiro Walk allows the disciplines to converge on the site of Sherrerd Hall. The building fills a void between Mudd Library and Wallace Hall, further defining the south edge of Shapiro Walk and screening an electric substation. It also shapes a green bordered by Princeton University Press and Charlton Street on the west, Friend Center on the north, and Computer Science on the east. The convergence of site and program demonstrates the integration of campus and academic planning.

The architect, Frederick Fisher and Partners, brought to the project its expertise in using glass as a primary material and in collaborating with visual artists. The three-story, forty-five-thousand-square-foot building is comparable in size to

both its neighbors, but where Mudd Library is a solid brick mass and Wallace Hall is a composition of multiple materials, Sherrerd's exterior is virtually all glass. The glazing technology, known as "four-sided silicone," minimizes expression of metal mullions on the outside of the building by adhering glass panels to frames behind the glass. The proportions of the glass panels—emphatically horizontal with multiple divisions for each floor level—are visually related to the proportions of the Friend Center glazing across the green. Fisher designed various patterns of vertical and diagonal line segments formed by ceramic frits fused to

Sherrerd Hall glass curtain wall

the glass surfaces. These patterns vary the amount of light and heat energy transmitted through the glass. At spandrel areas—above, below, and at the floor structure for example—where opacity is required, Fisher designed a "shadow box" consisting of a solid panel set back three inches from the outer glass. During the day the shadow box gives depth to the glass wall and at night emphasizes the banding of floor levels. The visual effect of the glass varies, depending on the weather outside and the activities inside. The fritted glass and green roof (water-absorbing, shallow-soil plantings over a waterproof membrane) combine to reduce heat gain and conserve energy.

The entrance to Sherrerd Hall from Shapiro Walk is articulated by a project-ing bay that provides views of Shapiro Walk from the interior and brings natural light to the three-story open stair and common space immediately inside the building. Suspended in the stairwell is a thirty-foot-high sculpture by Jim Isermann. A shimmering lattice of light and mirrors, *Untitled (ORFE/SEAS)* is composed of a modular system of precisely angled panels, one-third of which light up with LEDs. The transparency and reflection of the work symbolize and facilitate the interac-tions that occur in a building of learning. The site-specific work is intended to be viewed over time, a quality that makes it ideal for this frequently utilized staircase. Fisher designed filigreed wood panels to clad walls and to screen lounges within the common space. Wood finishes are also used in faculty offices, conference rooms, and classrooms to "domesticate" the otherwise high-tech quality of the building.

44   Friend Center
Pei Cobb Freed and Partners, 2001; Landscape: Michael Vergason, 2001

Wende
Friedel Dzubas, 1977; acrylic on canvas
Gift of James A. Leach, Class of 1964

Olden House
J. Robert Hillier, 2014

The decision to expand the School of Engineering and Applied Science on the west side of Olden Street was in part a strategy to optimize development opportunities that had been constrained by zoning. The Friend Center site at the southwest corner of William and Olden Streets was zoned for academic but non-research-laboratory uses. In order to free space in the existing Engineering Quadrangle for needed laboratory space, the engineering library and convocation room were moved across Olden Street into the new Friend Center.

The Computer Science department (1989) was the first move in this strategy and the construction of Sherrerd Hall for ORFE (2008) is the most recent, with Friend Center (2001) in the interim. Together these buildings define a green that embraces Shapiro Walk. Pathways lead from Shapiro Walk to a recessed entrance at Friend Center. Another entrance facing Olden Street links via a crosswalk to the raised entrance plaza of the Engineering Quadrangle and makes an internal connection with the Computer Science Building. The north side of the building, facing private residences across William Street, is set back with a landscaped buffer and steps back with a one-story precast concrete base aligned with and fronting the street. On the northwest corner of William and Olden Streets is a three-story, eighteen-unit building designed by J. Robert Hillier to house visiting faculty members. Completed in 2014, Olden House harmonizes with the existing private residences and reinforces the William Street streetscape.

The ground floor of Friend Center contains entrance lobbies, classrooms, a convocation room, and a wide corridor that opens into a four-story glass-enclosed atrium. The atrium provides access to the library and a monumental stair leading to the lower-level auditorium. The walls of the main corridor serve as an exhibition space, most notably the annual Art of Science display of digital images submitted by scientists and curated by artists. The public space is elegantly detailed in a minimalist aesthetic: polished terrazzo floors, smooth plaster-coated walls, frameless glass side rails at stairs and ramps, and polished stainless-steel fittings. A pastel-green full-height atrium wall and a colorful painting complement the predominantly white color palette. The largest canvas painting on campus, *Wende* typifies the monumental scale of Friedel Dzubas's late work. In this painting Dzubas bridges the expressionism of his youth as a noted figure of the New York School and the Color Field style of his maturity.

The library on the upper two floors of the building is enclosed by a glass-and-metal curtain wall. Interior operable wood blinds shade the library space and screen the William Street residences from evening illumination. The Friend Center

Friend Center

engineering library, like the later Lewis Library, represents the trends of information-age libraries, which typically are fitted with fewer book stacks, more group and individual study space, and high-speed wireless internet access, allowing less-formal seating and study arrangements.

45   Computer Science Building
Kliment Halsband Architects, 1989

Home to Princeton's Department of Computer Science, the fifty-seven-thousand-square-foot building includes classrooms and a lecture hall on the ground floor and basement level. Student, faculty, and administrative offices; seminar rooms; and research laboratories are housed in the upper three stories. Sited on the northern edge of Shapiro Walk near Olden Street, the Computer Science Building provides a focus for this important pedestrian way and defines, in the words of its architect, "a language for the development of subsequent buildings that will form a new quadrangle." This quadrangle—bordered by Princeton University Press, Friend Center, Sherrerd Hall, and Computer Science—now has the experience of a campus courtyard.

Kliment and Halsband designed the primary south and west elevations in anticipation of the subsequent buildings and new quadrangle. The firm faceted the south facade, facing Shapiro Walk, into three bays, the center of which is clad top to bottom in limestone. The center bay features an arched opening supported by round columns that lead to an arcade and recessed entries at the ground level. The flanking bays are clad in alternating limestone headers and brick stretchers that

Computer Science Building

Computer Science building detail

enliven the facade. These bays feature a ground-level colonnade composed of flat limestone lintels supported by limestone piers. The west elevation that faces the quadrangle continues the colonnade at the ground level, but infills the openings with metal-framed glass panels. There is another building entry at the north end of the colonnade. The walls of the upper stories gradually revert to a more conventional brick pattern. If the limestone trim framing the entrance bays takes its cues from Princeton tradition, so too do the frames and mullions of the aluminum windows, which are painted gray to resemble leaded panes. The main stairway links the principal entrance on Shapiro Walk with the reception room and tea room on the second floor, the facility's chief social spaces. The tea room has a balcony that looks out to the courtyard formed by Friend Center and Sherrerd Hall. According to the architect, the recessed brick headers visible at the upper left of the west entrance form a conjectural proposition from computer theory in binary code. More subtle than a Gothic gargoyle, this gesture represents a witty return to ornament and symbolism.

46   Mudd Manuscript Library
Hugh Stubbins and Associates, 1976

Rhumba
Richard Erdman, African granite
Princeton University, gift of Charles Erdman III, Class of 1946,
presented in 1991

Mudd Manuscript Library, located on the west side of Olden Street and south side of Shapiro Walk, is home to part of the University Library's Department of Rare Books and Special Collections. It houses the Princeton University Archives and the Twentieth Century Public Policy Papers, including the papers of James A.

Mudd Library

Baker (Class of 1952), Adlai Stevenson (Class of 1922), and Supreme Court Justice John Marshall Harlan (Class of 1922), as well as the records of the American Civil Liberties Union. The building was named for its benefactor, Seeley G. Mudd, a renowned medical educator and philanthropist who funded libraries and science buildings at thirty-three American colleges and universities.

Given the relative isolation of the site at the time Mudd Library was built, the thirty-one-thousand-square-foot building neither deferred nor related to other structures. The building program's strict limitation on direct sunlight on the paper-based artifacts influenced the building's siting and massing. The impact of sun radiation was reduced by the orientation of the building to the north and the over-hang created by the vault, which allows for a generous expanse of glass around the perimeter of the main floor. Windows are located in public and staff areas only. The stacks are entirely enclosed and access is strictly controlled. Sophisticated climate control and fire protection systems further protect the irreplaceable documents. Mudd was the first building at Princeton designed to comply with the university's energy conservation program initiated in response to the Arab oil embargo of the 1970s.

The irregular color and shape of the handcrafted bricks contrast with the smooth manufactured bricks of the Engineering Quadrangle across the way. Outside the building set in the low plantings along Shapiro Walk is the sculpture *Rhumba*. The sculptor Richard Erdman works with stone and bronze, creating abstract sculptures known for their buoyant motion. Here the artist employs rectangular slabs of granite that convey the twisting and turning movements of the dance for which it is titled.

47 Engineering Quadrangle
Voorhees, Walker, Smith, Smith, and Haines, 1962; Renovation: Pei Cobb Freed and Partners, 2000; Landscape: Clarke and Rapuano, 1962

Von Neumann Hall
Charles K. Agle, 1960

Energy Research Laboratory
Sert, Jackson, and Associates, 1979

J-Wing (addition to D-Wing, Duffield Hall)
The Hillier Group, 1993

Upstart II
Clement Meadmore, 1970; Corten steel

Stone Riddle
Masayuki Nagare, 1967; black granite

The Engineering Quadrangle was conceived in the late 1950s in the midst of the university's long-range planning exercise under the leadership of the Board of Trustees and Consulting Architect Douglas Orr (1954–66). For its design they chose an estimable friend of the institution: architect Stephen Francis Voorhees (Class of 1900), principal of Voorhees, Walker, Smith, Smith, and Haines; university trustee; and the university's former supervising architect (1930–49). Orr's model of the campus, first shown publicly in 1959, included Voorhees's fully developed design for a new engineering complex, known as the E-Quad. Construction started in 1960.

Federal research funding and engineering enrollment had increased rapidly in the 1950s, overwhelming Green Hall and other engineering facilities on campus. The James Forrestal Campus—several miles north of the main campus on Route 1—absorbed much of this growth, particularly for research in jet propulsion and atomic energy. However, consolidation of engineering research and teaching activities on the main campus became a priority for the 1960s capital campaign. The 275,000-square-foot program for the complex included four departments (Electrical, Mechanical and Aerospace, Chemical, and Civil Engineering), a library, and administration, and required a large site. Orr's plan identified a site east of Olden Street on land occupied by university athletic fields and related uses. At the time the nearest university buildings, aside from Osborn Clubhouse on the site, were Frick Laboratory to the west and Palmer Stadium to the south.

Separation from the historic campus, combined with the introduction of modern architecture at peer institutions, encouraged Voorhees to chart a new course for the design of campus buildings. Voorhees managed the large scale of

Engineering Quadrangle entry plaza

the complex by positioning six four-story wings—one for each department and two others for the library and administration—around an enclosed courtyard. Von Neumann Hall, an additional freestanding building named for the eminent mathematician and computer pioneer, was constructed concurrently, east of the E-Quad.

The original 1962 series of interconnected buildings (each named for a distinguished engineering faculty member) wrap around a central court. Five of the wings are clad in pastel-orange vertical brick panels alternating with panels composed of stacked metal-framed windows and aluminum spandrels. Both brick panels and window-spandrel panels are the same width, providing vertical relief to the long, linear buildings. The sixth wing, featuring the former library and the main entrance to the complex from Olden and William Streets, is clad in limestone. A sculpture by Clement Meadmore is installed on the plaza outside the main entrance. Meadmore's minimalist *Upstart II* reduces forms to their barest elements for a maximum expression. The work is constructed of only two components and its visual effect is of one soaring projection. The sculpture's steel surface has been left to weather and has formed a rich brown patina.

As departments grew and new fields of research emerged, additions and new buildings were constructed and existing buildings were renovated to accommodate them. While Voorhees's design for the original E-Quad buildings is decidedly utilitarian—an aesthetic characteristic of many research laboratories of the postwar period—subsequent additions and renovations are more adventurous. In 1979 Sert, Jackson, and Associates designed the Energy Research Laboratory with a connection to the Von Neumann Laboratory. In 1993 the Hillier Group designed the J-Wing

Engineering Quadrangle, J-Wing Addition

for the Department of Mechanical and Aerospace Engineering, linked to the D-Wing and the Energy Research Laboratory. Alan Chimacoff, designer for the Hillier Group, composed the exterior four-story elevations with a lower section clad in oversized ironspot brick, separated from an upper section—clad in brick related in color and pattern to the original buildings—by a horizontal band of limestone. Prominent chevron-shaped window bays framed with strong vertical fins and horizontal "eyebrows" pierce the limestone band, uniting the lower and upper sections. Inside Chimacoff separated the addition from the older structure to create a three-story atrium reaching to the clear glass tent of a skylight. The J-Wing addition introduces diffused daylight, different textures and colors, and movement, as bridges span the atrium between the old structure and the new. Just under the skylight, large cables are strung from girders to distribute the roof load. The effect is both decorative and structural. Whereas the structural and mechanical systems in the Voorhees-designed wings are concealed beneath dropped ceilings and other finishes, in the J-Wing Chimacoff reveals these systems. Exposed wires, ducts, cables, air returns, and exhausts as decorative elements are today something of a cliché, yet appropriate in a building that celebrates the practical applied sciences.

Throughout the original wings, spaces were vacated by newly created departments—Computer Science and ORFE—and moved to new buildings across Olden Street. Pei Cobb Freed renovated some of these vacated spaces in an aesthetic resembling its design for Friend Center. On the main floor the former library was turned into a cafe, lounge, and study space, and on the lower level electrical engineering labs were modernized.

Engineering Quadrangle courtyard

Courtyard design has many precedents at Princeton and other colleges and universities. While Princeton planners prefer three-sided courtyards to preserve vistas, the E-Quad courtyard, designed by landscape architects Clarke and Rapuano, is enclosed on four sides to be self-contained. The firm's plan is a metaphor for islands and water, in the manner of Japanese temple gardens, where the islands are raised planting beds and the water is represented by raked, crushed marble. In the 1960s the gravel was raked daily to achieve the desired effect, but its use as a walking surface made this impractical. A sculpture by Masayuki Nagare is set among the plantings. Nagare is known as "Samurai Artist" for his discipline and emulation of traditional Japanese aesthetics. In *Stone Riddle* the contrast between the smooth planes of the horizontal stone and the rough chisel of the base reflects his interest in the principle of yin-yang equilibrium. Nagare termed this contrast *warehada*, "broken texture," seeing it as a way to expose the essence of each surface.

Aerial view of the Engineering Quadrangle with rendering of the Andlinger Center for Energy and the Environment (lower left)

At the court's center is a large, free-form island of lawn, hemlocks, cherry, and pines with a fountain pool at one end. Two smaller islands feature groves of multistemmed birch trees. The stone and gravel paving meanders through the islands, broadening in places to make spaces for sculpture and seating. The lush plantings and curving forms deliberately contrast with the repetitive vertical planes of the surrounding buildings. While the landscaping and sculpture provide pleasant views from the facing offices and labs, access to the space, even for the buildings' occupants, is limited. The new Andlinger Center for Energy and the Environment will improve access to the existing courtyard, while integrating open and inviting green spaces into the new building's program and design.

48 Andlinger Center for Energy and the Environment

Tod Williams Billie Tsien Architects with Ballinger Architects, scheduled completion 2015; Landscape: Michael Van Valkenburgh Associates

Untitled, Bowl for Andlinger Center for Energy and the Environment, Princeton University

Ursula von Rydingsvard, 2013–15; copper

Part of the School of Engineering and Applied Science, the Andlinger Center for Energy and the Environment (ACEE) conducts research and teaching in the areas of sustainable energy development, energy conservation, and environmental protection and remediation related to energy. The ACEE collaborates with other disciplines, including natural sciences, human behavior, public policy, and economics. The university is constructing a 129,000-square-foot complex for the ACEE that will enhance the visual character and campus spaces of the engineering complex east of Olden Street. The multilevel composition of interconnected buildings, gardens, and pathways will be nestled into the southwest corner of the site, requiring demolition of the 1892 Osborn Clubhouse. Tod Williams Billie Tsien's earlier building for Princeton, Feinberg Hall, likewise fit into a tightly constrained site.

Williams (Class of 1965, MArch 1967) and Tsien's design for the Andlinger Center retains the twenty-foot-high brick wall and gateway along the Olden Street and Prospect Avenue sidewalks. In 1911 McKim, Mead and White designed the orna-

mental iron gateway—named in honor of track-and-field athlete Ferris Thompson (Class of 1888)—on the Prospect Avenue frontage. As the ceremonial entrance to the former athletic fields, it beckons students, faculty, and visitors to "enter a garden" and experience a series of landscape spaces integrated with state-of-the-art engineering laboratory facilities.

Ferris Thompson Gateway

Andlinger Center for Energy and the Environment, garden rendering

Within the garden wall—and inserted between the North Garage to the east, Bowen Hall to the south, A-Wing (Hayes Hall) to the north, and E-Wing (Maclean Hall) to the west—the buildings will step down into sunken gardens. There will be three gardens below the campus level: one adjacent to imaging labs and clean rooms; one adjacent to graduate student offices and teaching labs; and one adjacent to the lecture hall and classrooms. The latter will be accessible to the public from the street level via cascading stairs. The gardens and green roofs on the buildings are designed to emulate the integration of buildings and grounds on the historic campus. A street-level pathway will provide welcome access to the existing, somewhat isolated, E-Quad courtyard.

With the exception of two tower elements, the height of the entire complex will be significantly lower than Bowen Hall and the original E-Quad wings. The exterior planar brick walls with large recessed glazed openings will feature Williams and Tsien's characteristic careful and innovative use of materials. The handmade irregular brick used on the facade will describe a contemporary building while resonating with craft traditions that characterize the historic campus.

The Andlinger Center parti consists of interconnected low-rise buildings of varying heights, below-grade levels open to sunken courtyards, abundant land-scaping of courtyards and open spaces, and multiple pathways through the complex connected with existing campus pathways. In its planning, it resembles the new

Butler College dormitories and the Lewis Center for the Arts. While not mandated by a master plan, these site strategies derive from similar campus planning objectives to reduce the impact of new large buildings, reinterpret the traditional relationship of buildings and landscape for contemporary projects, and reinforce pedestrian movement and vistas.

49   Bowen Hall
The Hillier Group, 1993

Bowen Hall is named for the seventeenth president of the university, William G. Bowen (1972–88). As befits a building housing the Princeton Institute for the Science and Technology of Materials (PRISM)—and in contrast to the E-Quad's limited palette—Bowen Hall is an exhibitionistic mix of colors, materials, and asymmetrical forms. The north facade is bracketed by two glass-enclosed stairwells. On the west side the roof of the two-story bay functions as an outdoor terrace. The south entrance opens into a foyer with a set of stairs to an elevated atrium wrapped by the upper floors. The entire space is illuminated by natural light that floods in through a skylight. To the north of the atrium is a sculptural set of spiral stairs, which will provide a connection between Bowen Hall and the Andlinger Center for Energy and the Environment.

The exterior is clad in square ironspot brick. Major variations on the primary rectilinear form, such as the expansive two-story semicircular bay on the west side, are faced with slabs of green granite. Sheltering the main entrance to the building

Bowen Hall

is a simple steel canopy supported by a single polished-steel column, which looks electrified when the sun strikes it. Above the canopy is a panel of acid-etched glazed tile in a fractal pattern familiar to materials scientists. The diagonal grid of the panel contrasts with the prevailing horizontal bands of windows on this elevation. The entrance is set off slightly to the left, flanked by a pair of columns of contrasting shape, texture, and material.

50 North Parking Garage
Machado and Silvetti Associates, 1991

Machado and Silvetti's AIA Honor Award–winning parking garage was the first parking structure built on the university campus. Typically, few architectural demands are made of buildings that house mundane services, such as warehouses and parking garages. The architect was challenged to define a building type destined to be more prevalent on campus in the future, as academic buildings replace existing surface parking lots. Machado and Silvetti not only defined but also elevated a utilitarian facility seldom associated with beauty into a delightful design.

The design of the parking structure relates to the existing McKim, Mead and White brick wall in height, texture, and material. Between the brick wall and the parking structure is a lawn. On the southern side, facing the lawn, Machado and Silvetti clad the building in a green galvanized-steel screen covered with ivy. Flanking the ivy wall, five-story copper panels identify the pedestrian entrances to the garage. In the middle of the south face, a two-story opening provides additional

North Parking Garage

light and transparency to enhance security and safety. The building is constructed of a sand-polished, galvanized-steel frame with poured-in-place concrete slabs. To complement and affirm the garden character of the surroundings, a bronze lattice screen wraps the three floors of the structure above the two-story brick wall. Along the north side the screen pulls free from the wall, creating a high arcade that shelters an east-west path paved with the bluestone common to Princeton's campus walks. The shifting play of light and shadow alters the building's presence throughout the day. The screen and the articulation of the design—the flared cornice, the flying buttress–like supports, the arcade and canopy along the north wall—impart an energy seldom associated with a parking garage.

WALK FIVE

Campus Life, Prospect Avenue, and Varsity Athletics

FACULTY ROAD

SOUTH DRIVE

ELM DRIVE

WASHINGTON ROAD

58

58

58

59

51

52

54

Campus Life, Prospect Avenue, and Varsity Athletics

THE WHOLE STUDENT

"In college, as much learning occurs outside the classroom as within the classroom" is an adage that applies to undergraduate colleges where students live, dine, socialize, and participate in a variety of creative, athletic, religious, and service activities on campus. At Princeton these cocurricular campus life activities, together with teaching and research, are central to the university's mission, but it was not always so.

During the first three decades of the nineteenth century, there were six student rebellions at the College of New Jersey, including the Great Rebellion of 1807, after which the administration suspended three-fourths of the student population. Students rebelled against the lack of cocurricular opportunities and amenities that characterize today's university. In a more constructive response, students created off-campus living and dining arrangements, literary and debating societies, athletic teams, theatrical and musical clubs, and other organizations. The college gradually formalized some of these organizations and added others. Today there are over three hundred student organizations under the aegis of the dean of undergraduate students and more than fifty graduate student organizations.

Until the mid-nineteenth century organized sports were actively discouraged by the college's administration. But the College of New Jersey played Rutgers College in the first American intercollegiate football game in 1869, and in the same year built Bonner-Marquand Gymnasium to replace a primitive

Aerial View of University-owned farmland south of the historic campus, 1940

1859 gym partially paid for by the students themselves. Today the university has thirty-eight intercollegiate varsity teams, sponsors club and intramural sports, and provides facilities for fitness and other recreational activities.

In the early twentieth century the university acquired large tracts south of the historic campus that had been farms through most of the nineteenth century. The transformation of Stony Brook and surrounding wetlands into Lake Carnegie in 1906 provided a natural boundary to the southern edge of university lands. In the first decades of the twentieth century development of the land between the historic campus and Lake Carnegie began with construction of Guyot and Palmer Halls for natural sciences, Palmer Stadium and Baker Rink for athletics, and the private eating clubs on Prospect Avenue.

This walk, starting at Frist Campus Center, proceeding along Prospect Avenue, and continuing farther south through athletic facilities, gives a sense of the variety of experiences available to today's undergraduate students at Princeton. Other examples may be found throughout this book, particularly in the features on Whig and Clio Halls (see Walk One), Murray and Dodge Halls (see Walk Three), and McCarter Theatre (see Walk Seven).

Frist Campus Center from 1879 Green

51 Frist Campus Center (formerly Palmer Hall)
Henry Janeway Hardenbergh, 1908; Renovation and addition: Venturi, Scott Brown and Associates, 2000; Landscape: Andropogon Associates

McCosh Health Center
Day and Klauder, 1925

Jones Hall (formerly Fine Hall)
Charles Z. Klauder, 1931

In the last years of the twentieth century Palmer Hall and the surrounding open space underwent a metamorphosis from the former home of the Department of Physics to the Frist Campus Center. For most of its history Princeton had been a step behind the expanding living and social requirements of its students. In the early days of the College of New Jersey, the American Whig Society and the Cliosophic Society were founded to meet pressing needs that were not being addressed by college administrators, including access to an adequate library. Later, toward the end of the nineteenth century, the Prospect Avenue eating clubs arose in response to the lack of dependably good food and opportunities to socialize. Under President Shapiro's leadership in the late twentieth century, an all-campus social, dining, and activity space, first proposed by students in the 1920s, was finally realized.

When Frist Campus Center opened it was the first time that Princeton had a state-of-the-art social facility for all undergraduate and graduate students, as well as a common meeting place for faculty, staff, alumni, and visitors. The siting of Frist acknowledged that the center of the campus was no longer Cannon Green. In fact, Cram's 1925 master plan anticipated this growth of the campus to the east and south and proposed a University Club for upperclassmen on the northeast corner of Prospect Avenue and Washington Road, where the Woodrow Wilson School of Public and International Affairs stands today.

The Venturi, Scott Brown and Associates redesign recognizes the importance of Frist as the anchor of the south end of the green also bordered by 1879 Hall to the east, McCosh Walk to the north, and Woolworth Center to the west. From the north the green follows the slope of the land and steps down to the main entrance of the Campus Center. The architect's affection for well-defined front doors—oblique ones in this case—is realized here through the creation of a free-standing limestone and brick arcade, approximately seventeen feet tall, designed to frame and focus the entrance. The arcade does not run the full length of the front, but begins on the east side of the west pavilion and runs past the eastern edge of the building. What may seem arbitrarily off-center in plan is understood when approaching the entrance from the north across the green. A careful viewer will see the name of the Frist Campus Center formed from shapes along the top edge of the arcade, a subtle response to a restrictive sign ordinance.

With the exception of that arcade and major addition on the south side facing Guyot Hall, the design strategies primarily address interior architecture to accommodate the building's entirely new program. The upper levels include a lecture hall, classrooms, a film/performance theater, the McGraw Center for Teaching and

Frist Campus Center, commons level

Frist Campus Center, south facade

Cherry trees at McCosh Health Center

Learning, and the renowned East Asian Library (located in Palmer Hall and the top floor of the interconnected Jones Hall prior to the renovation). Offices for undergraduate student government; the Women's Center; the Lesbian, Gay, Bisexual, and Transgender (LGBT) Center; and the Pace Center for Civic Engagement are here as well. Below the building's original ground floor, down an expansive open central staircase, is the Frist Center's commons area. The commons functions as an enclosed village with four "streets" and is home to a convenience store, a coffee bar, mailboxes, a ticket office, a game room, a TV lounge, and other services that change over time as needs arise. This is also the location of Café Vivian— named for Dr. Vivian Shapiro, wife of the past president—and a welcome desk where student-led Orange Key campus tours originate on weekends. Because the land slopes steeply, the next floor down is dining space that opens out to the south lawn stretching toward Guyot Hall. This lawn is a site for reunions and other outdoor campus events. From there, a view back toward the upper levels of the building reveals the university shield subtly imprinted on the glass. (The facade was used to depict the fictional hospital in the television series *House*.) The lowest level contains a subdividable multipurpose room and reception lobby.

The three-story Tudor Gothic building Henry Janeway Hardenbergh designed for the physics department had historically been distinguished for the Nobel Prize winners who have worked and taught inside its efficient and practical spaces. A pair of statues that flank the main north entrance reflect that innovative spirit. They were sculpted under the direction of Daniel Chester French, best known for the seated Abraham Lincoln in the Lincoln Memorial, and depict two outstanding American scientists, Benjamin Franklin and Princeton's own Joseph Henry.

McCosh Health Center is adjacent to the southwest corner of Frist. Day and Klauder's Collegiate Gothic design and brick-and-limestone exterior complement Hardenbergh's design for Palmer Hall. The building opened in 1925, replacing an earlier infirmary building from 1892. Both were named in honor of Isabella McCosh, wife of President McCosh, who tended to students' infirmities as well as to campus grounds. On the south side of the building is a little-known sunken garden and an allée of cherry trees, spectacular during the springtime bloom and thought to have been planted by Beatrix Farrand.

52   Center for Jewish Life
Robert A. M. Stern Architects, 1993

The Center for Jewish Life (CJL) is located on the site of a former eating club at 70 Washington Road. Created to serve the university's Jewish community, the building is owned and maintained by the university through the Office of the Dean of Religious Life in partnership with Hillel. The building contains two auditoriums for prayer services, academic, and social events; a kosher kitchen and dining rooms; a library; Beit Midrash (Hebrew for "house of learning"); a game room and lounge; a computer cluster; and offices.

The university and CJL selected Robert A. M. Stern—then professor of architecture at Columbia University and currently dean of the Yale University School of Architecture—to design a building suited to the needs of the Jewish community and to relate to the domestic scale and styles of the neighboring eating clubs. Stern's portfolio of domestic architecture demonstrates his knowledge of—and ability to design in—a wide range of historical styles. For the CJL he chose an Arts and Crafts aesthetic that is well suited to the site and environs. The asymmetrical massing responds to the Washington Road and Ivy Lane frontage and to the pedestrian paths north and east of the site. Stern set the main mass of the building back from the traffic of Washington Road, but projected the octagonal form of the main floor auditorium at an angle. He designed the south side that faces Ivy Lane with a terrace and pergola overlooking a lawn, a strategy developed by architects of eating clubs on the south side of Prospect Avenue. The sloping site allows the lower level of the three-story building to receive daylight and gain direct access to the lawn.

Center for Jewish Life

Stern chose cement plaster as the primary exterior wall material. While not common on the university campus, the Arts and Crafts College Road apartments (1922) and Prospect Avenue apartments (1925) had also been built with cement-plaster exterior walls. Stern selected a warm beige paint color for the plaster in contrast to the dark window frames and metalwork, characteristic of Arts and Crafts design. His use of slate roofs and mullioned windows also acknowledges traditional campus architecture.

53 Prospect Avenue Eating Clubs

Ivy Club, 43 Prospect Avenue
Cope and Stewardson, 1898; Addition: Demetri Porphyrios with James Bradberry Architects, 2009

Cottage Club, 51 Prospect Avenue
McKim, Mead and White, 1905

Charter Club, 79 Prospect Avenue
Mellor and Meigs, 1913

Although they are among the most distinguished groups of buildings in Princeton, the eating clubs do not have a formal relationship with the university. Nevertheless, no survey of campus architecture would be complete without looking at several exemplary club buildings. Eating clubs provide meals for their members, as well as venues for parties and other social and campus life activities. While all undergraduates are members of a residential college, juniors and seniors may choose to join an eating club. Some clubs admit members on a selective basis (known as *bicker*), while others have an open admission policy (known as *sign-in*).

During most of the college's first 150 years many Princeton students were dissatisfied with housing and dining provided by the college. Some students lived in rooming houses and ate their meals there or in restaurants. In 1880 a group of students rented an off-campus building, hired a cook, and formed the first eating club, Ivy Club. Following their lead, other students formed clubs, purchased lots on Prospect Avenue, and constructed clubhouses designed in Georgian, Gothic, colonial, and other eclectic residential revival styles.

Despite varied architectural styles, the club buildings on Prospect Avenue share a common parti. The buildings are set back from the street with either low masonry walls or hedges separating the sidewalk from the expansive front lawns. Elaborate entrances are set in the two-story (sometimes three-story) formally composed front facades. Club buildings on the south side of Prospect Avenue take advantage of the downward-sloping topography. The rear facades are taller and less formal, with terraces and garden rooms that overlook club-owned recreational space and, in some cases, parking lots. Club buildings on the north side of Prospect

Avenue—only two remain as eating clubs—enjoy the same street-front amenities as club buildings across the street, whereas their rear yards are small and now border academic buildings. Interior spaces generally include a dining room, kitchen, lounge, library, tap room, game room, and several bedrooms for club officers.

The choice of historical styles and the deft execution of the design for the clubs included in this walk instantly convey a sense of permanence and long-standing tradition, remarkable when one considers that the clubs themselves were barely decades old when their buildings were constructed.

Ivy Club closely resembles Cope and Stewardson's Constitution Hill in Princeton, the home of Ivy Club member Junius Morgan (Class of 1888). It was also reputedly modeled on Peacock Inn, a seventeenth-century building in Derbyshire, England. In the year Ivy retained Cope and Stewardson (1896), the firm was at work on Blair Hall, the first Collegiate Gothic structure on campus. The club building is a skillful exercise in domestic Tudor Gothic architecture using dark rough red brick—laid in a Flemish bond pattern with rose-colored mortar—interspersed with black-and-forest-green headers, with a stone stringcourse separating floor levels. Each element contributes to the evocation of a centuries-old manor house: the grouped perpendicular-style brick chimneys rising above the gabled green-slate roof, the dark-green trim of the recessed leaded windows framed in red sandstone, the three finials that crown the entry doorway, and the irregular massing suggesting growth over time. The more informal rear elevation includes a large wing housing the dining room and kitchen and a recent three-story wing containing a great hall and library (2009). Demetri Porphyrios (PhD 1980) designed the addition while he was working on the university's Whitman College.

Ivy Club

Cottage Club; Charter Club

Cottage Club is the second-oldest eating club and is listed on the National Register of Historic Places. Cottage followed Ivy Club's example and built its own house on Prospect Avenue in 1905. It is a distinguished Georgian Revival structure designed by McKim, Mead and White that resembles the firm's Harvard Union. The firm had also designed the impressive FitzRandolph Gate in front of Nassau Hall. The footprint of Cottage traces a U-shaped plan, with the arms of the U extending south toward the rear garden. The Prospect Avenue face of the building is an essay in balance and symmetry. The wide entrance pavilion and broad end bays make modest steps forward from the facade. The elliptical shape of the entrance pavilion roof is echoed in the shapes of flanking dormers, an elliptical oculus in the pediment, and the rounded transom of the elaborate entry. The facade is enriched with Georgian architectural ornament: white quoins edging the projecting bays, a stringcourse separating the first and second floors, keystones centered above the first-and-second-floor windows, diamond-patterned brick in the pediment, and a roof of gray-and-red-slate tiles crowned by a widow's walk.

Constructed in 1913, Charter Club was also designed in the Georgian Revival style—this version in stone and created by the architectural firm of Mellor and Meigs, which was known for private residences and clubs in the Philadelphia area. Architectural historians Constance Greiff and William Short describe the club as "a prime example of the Colonial Revival movement in the style of a stone eighteenth-century Philadelphia Georgian mansion such as those in Fairmont Park." Among the many architectural elements that distinguish this structure are the schist facade (the same material used for turn-of-the-century Princeton dormitories), the elaborate entry with broken pediment and cartouche surmounted by a Palladian window, and the gently flared red-and-green-slate roof.

54   Prospect Avenue University Uses

Campus Club, 5 Prospect Avenue
Raleigh C. Gildersleeve, 1909; Renovation: Nalls Architecture, 2009

Fields Center, 58 Prospect Avenue
Raleigh C. Gildersleeve, 1901; Addition and renovation: Ann Beha Architects, 2009

172-90 Prospect Avenue
Aymar Embury, 1925

Not all eating club buildings along Prospect Avenue remain as operating clubs. Since the 1930s seven clubs have closed due to declining membership and financial hardship. Over time, the university purchased these properties and repurposed them for university uses. Among these are two buildings on Prospect Avenue supporting campus life activities: Campus Club and the Fields Center. Also included in this portion of Walk Five, but not a former eating club building, is 172–90 Prospect Avenue (faculty apartments). Other university uses in former eating clubs include the Bendheim Center for Finance (formerly Dial Lodge at 26 Prospect Avenue), Bobst Hall (formerly Key and Seal Club at 83 Prospect Avenue), and 91 Prospect Avenue (formerly Court Club, now university administration).

Members of the former Campus Club donated their clubhouse to the university in 2006. After renovations the building reopened in 2010 as a gathering

Campus Club; Fields Center, existing and addition

space for undergraduate and graduate students. Given the building's prime location at the head of Prospect Avenue, Campus Club can be seen as an extension of Frist Campus Center both programmatically and geographically. An advisory board and a programming board composed of students under the auspices of the vice president for campus life operate the facility "by students, for students." The facility contains a library, TV lounge, billiards room, cafe, and space for both formal and informal gatherings. The front and rear lawns are also used for social events.

172–90 Prospect Avenue

The Carl A. Fields Center for Equality and Cultural Understanding, founded as the Third World Center in 1971, moved in 2009 to the former Elm Club building from its previous location in the Osborn (Athletics) Clubhouse. The move provided the Fields Center with modern facilities, some housed within the restored 1901 clubhouse designed by Raleigh C. Gildersleeve and some in a new addition. The addition and renovation, designed by Ann Beha Architects, contain large and small multipurpose rooms, a lounge, cafe, visual arts gallery, and seminar room, and on the third floor a tutoring center for Community House, where university undergraduate volunteers tutor local disadvantaged middle-school and high-school students. The addition is an exemplary case of bridging one hundred years of architectural history while maintaining the integrity of both the original and the new.

President John G. Hibben (1912–32), like his predecessor Woodrow Wilson, expanded the faculty, creating the need for housing near campus. In addition to Broadmead—where the university built single-family homes for professors starting in 1907—Hibben's administration built faculty apartments, first on the west side of campus at College Road (1922) and then on the east side at 172–90 Prospect Avenue (1925).

The Prospect Avenue apartment building at the corner of Harrison Street is adjacent to Broadmead. Designed by Aymar Embury, who in the late 1940s designed Dillon Gym and the Class of 1915 dormitory, 172–90 Prospect Avenue contains ten units in a two-story row-house configuration that stretches almost three hundred feet along Prospect Avenue. The end units form bookends to the eight middle units, which are differentiated by slightly projected and recessed planes. Embury set the building back from Prospect Avenue, allowing for trees, a front lawn, and sidewalks leading to individual entrances. He located a common rear yard, service drive, and garages on the north side of the building. He designed the exterior walls in an Arts and Crafts style, similar to the earlier College Road apartment building. The walls are surfaced with smooth beige-painted cement plaster with dark-brown painted casement windows and frames. A stringcourse of brick between the first and second floors, and a pitched slate roof with several dormers, add texture to the composition.

55   Princeton Stadium and Weaver Track Stadium
Rafael Viñoly Architects, 1998

Pair of Topiary Tigers
Ruffin Hobbs, 2000
Gift of William Weaver Jr. (Class of 1934)

Without question one of the crown jewels of the athletic neighborhood is Princeton Stadium, which replaced Palmer Stadium in 1998. Palmer Stadium, designed by Henry Hardenbergh and constructed in seven months during 1914, was shaped like a Roman circus, but open at the south end. A hybrid of early twentieth-century construction technology (reinforced concrete), classical in spirit, and Gothic in detail with buttresses, turrets, and a pointed arch facing the main approach from Roper Lane, Palmer rapidly acquired the aura of sacred ground. It also had need for constant repair, probably a legacy of the rush to completion. Ultimately the unthinkable prevailed: Palmer Stadium had to be replaced. It is a testament to architect Rafael Viñoly's achievement that the replacement he designed was immediately embraced by students, athletes, and alumni alike as if Palmer Stadium had risen transfigured from the mud of the construction site.

One of Viñoly's singular accomplishments was to create a greater sense of intimacy while setting the new stadium in Palmer's horseshoe footprint. He did this in part by locating the track, which had been inside Palmer Stadium, immediately to the south, where it is joined to the stadium by back-to-back stands. This relocation, enhanced by the sunken field, has the effect of placing the spectator closer to the action on the field. Viñoly closed the south end with a track grandstand over locker facilities. In 2007 the grass surface of the stadium was replaced with FieldTurf—a porous cushioned surface composed of synthetic fibers and granular materials—and named Powers Field.

The broad concourse at the south end of the stadium offers elevated views of Frick Chemistry Laboratory, Weaver Track Stadium, and Jadwin Gym. The concourse also functions as a campus walkway linking parking to the east with the Natural Sciences neighborhood to the west and providing access to the track grandstand. The grandstand is protected from the sun by a tensile fabric canopy stretched into a series of hyperbolic paraboloids supported by cantilevered steel frames.

Princeton Stadium, Powers Field; Weaver Track Stadium

The outer wall of the new stadium is constructed of load-bearing structural concrete panels with a sandblasted aggregate surface. The aggregate is made up of bits of stone whose palette runs from amber to green and small flecks of black, producing a hue compatible with the granite of nearby Fine Hall. A press box, ticket booths, offices, restrooms, concessions, and conference rooms are located within the inner and outer walls, which are pierced by a regular rhythm of large openings. The alternating pattern of masonry and sharply incised voids evokes

Princeton Stadium north portal

the colonnade of Palmer Stadium. The grandstands hang from the colonnade, supported by a system of trusses. The widened section at the north end of the ground-level concourse—where there is no upper seating—is called Palmer Pavilion because it contains a relic of the cast inscriptions that once announced the formal entrance to Palmer Stadium. However at Princeton Stadium spectators enter through the two north portals onto Coleman or Caldwell Plazas. Flanking the entrance to Princeton Stadium, two stainless-steel tigers were installed with the intention that ivy would grow through their hollow mesh bodies. Sculptor Ruffin Hobbs sanded the legs in order to create patterns that suggest the stripes of a tiger in the glistening sunlight.

To the east of Princeton Stadium are Clarke Field (varsity baseball), Strubing Field (recreational baseball), Finney and Campbell Fields (multipurpose), Sexton Field (multipurpose), and FitzRandolph Observatory (1933).

56 Jadwin Gym

Steinman and Cain, 1969; Landscape: Princeton University Office of Physical Planning, 2002

Bill Bradley
Harry Weber (Class of 1964), 2014; cast bronze
Princeton University

Jadwin Gym marks a definitive stage in the evolutionary process that had its origins more than a century earlier on the grass of Cannon Green. Jadwin is like nothing else on campus, and it is so big that it is only from the air that one can appreciate its unique, three-part roof and geodesic construction covered with stretched rubberized fabric. Jadwin is a product of an era in which communities and campuses across the country were constructing mega multipurpose facilities that could quickly and efficiently squeeze in a wide range of spectator sports, from tennis to baseball and from basketball to track. Such multipurpose facilities tend to be engineering marvels rather than aesthetic delights.

However, Jadwin's objective is to accommodate practice, performance, and participation. It does all three quite well, providing state-of-the-art facilities for basketball and track and field on the main level and fencing, squash, wrestling, and

Class of 1935 Green; Frelinghuysen Field, with Jadwin Gym (right) and DeNunzio Pool (left)

tennis on subterranean levels. In 2009 the university named the main level game floor "Carril Court" in honor of Pete Carril, who coached the men's basketball team to thirteen Ivy League championships during his twenty-nine-year tenure as head coach (1968–96). The main level provides up to 7,500 seats with a fixed grandstand on one side, and various combinations of retractable bleachers and loose seating for rock concerts, major convocations, senior proms, and other events. The landscaped space on the north side of Jadwin, the Class of 1935 Green, extends the lobby and links other public spaces from DeNunzio Pool and Caldwell Field House to the east and Sciences Green to the north. On the green is a statue of William Warren "Bill" Bradley (Class of 1965). Among his many accomplishments: Rhodes Scholar, American Hall of Fame basketball player, Olympic gold medalist, and three-term U.S. Senator from New Jersey.

Against the west wall of the lobby is a bronze statue that commemorates an earlier chapter in Princeton's history. Variously called the *Christian Student* or the

Christian Athlete, the statue is the work of Daniel Chester French. It memorializes W. Earl Dodge Jr., a founding leader of the Intercollegiate Young Men's Christian Association. Initially located (appropriately) near Dodge Hall on the main campus, the *Christian Student* was the target of student pranks, until the university removed this source of aggravation by lending it to the Chester French museum, Chesterwood, in Stockbridge, Massachusetts. The office of a Princeton alumnus secured its return and installation in Jadwin, where it presumably has come to permanent rest.

57 DeNunzio Pool and Caldwell Field House

DeNunzio Pool
Cesar Pelli and Craig Mullins, 1990

Caldwell Field House
Steinman and Cain, 1963; Addition: Wurmfeld Associates, 1999

The apparently straightforward design of DeNunzio Pool deserves a second glance. It shows how a creative architect can use the simplest gestures to break up what is essentially a box that contains an Olympic-size pool and bleachers that accommodate 1,300 spectators. The shape of the copper downspouts and their arrangement across the three planes of the front elevation suggest ascending rows of colonnades. The three planes break up the basic rectangle and give the structure a vertical thrust. The architect uses color, both as a field or background

DeNunzio Pool

(red brick at the lower stories, teal at the top) and as visual punctuation (the groupings of dark-red tile by the downspouts and the rich copper of the downspouts themselves). These are simple but deft applications that make all the difference. Inside there are structural gymnastics at play. One would expect a structural engineer to span the short dimension of the roof structure with regularly spaced beams. Instead, Pelli and his engineer spanned the length of the building over the pool with two deep trusses, providing space for a diving platform and accentuating the orientation of the pool lanes.

Caldwell Field House provides locker rooms, training facilities, and storage for athletes competing and practicing in DeNunzio Pool, Jadwin Gym, Weaver Track Stadium, and other nearby venues. The university expanded the original building in 1999 by placing additional locker rooms on the south side under a paved plaza and connected to Jadwin and DeNunzio. A recessed glass-enclosed lobby at the northeast corner of the plaza provides access to the lower level, and a linear skylight along the north edge of the plaza provides daylight to the expanded lower level. The above-grade portions of the building are clad in red brick that relates to the high wall surrounding the track.

58   South Drive Athletic Fields

Class of 1952 Stadium
Wurmfeld Associates, 1995

Bedford Field
Marble Fairbanks, 2013

Roberts Stadium
Anderson Architects, 2008; Landscape: Quennell Rothschild and Partners

Cordish Family Pavilion
Dattner Architects, 2010

Recreation Tennis Courts
Global Sports and Tennis, 2005; Landscape: Quennell Rothschild and Partners

The athletic facilities section of Walk Five continues across Washington Road by traversing Streicker Bridge from Princeton Stadium. Pardee and Poe Fields— just west of the bridge ramps—are used for recreational sports and other leisure activities. To the south on lower ground lie stadiums, fields, and tennis courts used primarily for varsity athletics. These state-of-the-art facilities—set in a landscaped park organized along a central spine named South Drive—replaced a loose collection of grass playing fields, parking lots, and service areas. South Drive is landscaped with cryptomeria trees and beds of laurel and spirea.

South Drive Athletic Fields tennis pavilion; Roberts Stadium, Myslik Field

The Class of 1952 Stadium provides facilities for lacrosse teams and spectators. The stadium's Sherrerd Field is surfaced with FieldTurf. In 2013 the university constructed Bedford Field Stadium, just west of 1952 Stadium, for field hockey. The playing surface is the latest generation of AstroTurf, providing the smooth flat surface preferred for field hockey. Bedford's grandstand backs up to 1952's grandstand, forming an A-shaped concourse that contains home and visiting team rooms, restrooms, and a concession stand. The lacrosse and field hockey complex is framed by woodlands to the south and stately dawn redwood trees to the west.

Roberts Stadium for soccer opened in 2008. Spectator seating—surrounding Myslik Field on three sides—is built into the existing slope of the site. Plummer Field, the practice field, adjoins Myslik. Planners set the elevation of the fields—and thereby the height of the stadium—to preserve views of the woodlands from the Ellipse. The game field's playing surface is natural grass, while the practice field is FieldTurf. Team and spectator facilities are housed in three pavilions around the perimeter of the stadium. The pavilions' walls are built with ground-faced concrete block and the roofs with laminated timbers. West of the stadium, Soccer Walk is graced with zelkova trees and links the stadium's entrance plaza to South Drive and other campus walkways.

Farther west are 1895 Field for softball and the Lenz Tennis Center. Lenz provides eight hard courts for varsity tennis and spectator seating. The Cordish Family Pavilion replaced an outdated building and contains locker rooms, meeting rooms, coaches' offices, public restrooms, and covered viewing decks open on three sides. The two-story building is wrapped in carefully detailed cedar siding and metal roofing. Fifteen recreational tennis courts—relocated from the site of Whitman College—straddle South Drive south of Roberts Stadium. The iconic 1963 tennis pavilion (known as the pagoda) was dismantled and reerected between two groups of courts.

59 Baker Rink

Coy and Rice with engineer George W. Glick Jr., 1922; Addition: Harrison Fraker, 1985

Baker Rink is home to the university's ice hockey teams and an amenity for recreational skaters. In the early twentieth century athletic fields filled the campus open space south of University Gymnasium. Until the 1960s the fields, gym, and rink formed an athletics neighborhood. The former boiler house and Baker Rink exteriors were designed to provide a grand Collegiate Gothic vista across the playing fields. At the time steam was required to produce "indoor ice"—steam drove

Baker Rink

compressors to chill brine, which circulated through pipes below the rink surface to freeze water into ice. The first central steam-producing boiler house was built next to Baker Rink. Steam is no longer required for ice production, and the boiler house—now known as 200 Elm Drive—was decommissioned after the university began producing electricity and steam at the cogeneration plant in 1996 (see Lower Elm Drive feature in Walk Eight).

Baker Rink is named for Hobart "Hobey" Baker (Class of 1914), an exceptional football and hockey player who died while serving in the air force during the First World War. After the war fellow athletes from thirty-nine colleges donated funds to erect a hockey rink in his honor at Princeton. Baker Rink is one of the first indoor collegiate hockey rinks in the United States, built some ten years after the first rink using mechanical refrigeration to produce ice was built in Canada.

Spectator seating descends to the rink from a slightly elevated entry. The gable ends are solid masonry detailed in a simplified Collegiate Gothic style and the long sides are pierced with arched openings giving access to the seating. In 1985 the university added enclosed side aisles to the original building to facilitate spectator circulation and to better control temperature and humidity within the rink for optimum ice conditions.

60 Lake Carnegie and Shea Rowing Center

Lake Carnegie
Howard Russell Butler, 1906

Shea Rowing Center
Pennington Satterthwaite, 1913; Addition: ARC/Architectural Resources Cambridge, 2000

Lake Carnegie is perhaps Princeton's most extensive design project, one that is three and a half miles long and up to eight hundred feet wide. The tale of its inception was delightfully told by the designer, Howard Russell Butler (Class of 1876), in *Princeton University Land: 1752–1984*, by Gerald Breese. Upon graduation Butler took up a career as a portrait painter. Talent and social connections opened doors to some of the wealthiest elite of the Gilded Age, including Andrew Carnegie, then living in Manhattan. Having been invited by Carnegie to join him on a trip to Princeton to visit former U.S. president Grover Cleveland (who had settled there after leaving Washington), Butler shared a dream he had since his days at Princeton. As a student, he'd been an avid member of the school's rowing team; at the time, there was no place to row other than the nearby Delaware and Raritan Canal, a dangerous undertaking since the canal was busy with barge traffic. Butler's dream was to "clean out" the marshes (today's "wetlands") at the southern edge of the campus and dam the Millstone River at nearby Kingston. The resulting lake would at last provide a satisfactory venue for a winning rowing team.

Carnegie was taken by the idea (he was no stranger to creating lakes) and told Butler to work out the cost. Butler first organized the Princeton Lake Committee, chaired by Moses Taylor Pyne. He then sought the advice of a professional engineer and provided Carnegie with what he believed to be a fair estimate. Carnegie in turn gave his assent to the project, with one stipulation: that Howard Butler should be personally in charge of building it. Woodrow Wilson, who at this time was looking to Carnegie to underwrite the university's intellectual needs, had to be content instead with a lake.

By the 1990s rowing at Princeton had become the university's largest athletic program, with over two hundred students participating. In 2000 the outgrown Class of 1887 Boathouse—built shortly after the lake was completed—was expanded and the complex renamed the Shea Rowing Center. The T-shaped wing added to the original building's west end houses new rowing tanks and boat storage racks on the ground floor with airy training spaces above. The entrance was moved from the campus side to the base of the tower on the lake side. Stairs lead to locker rooms and a wood-paneled corridor-gallery with views of the lake. The original "Ballroom" space was restored, revealing its massive timber trusses and stone fireplace, and was repurposed for meeting and study space. The architects designed painted cement-plaster exterior walls with buttress-like columns and wood windows to harmonize with the original boathouse. The transformed rowing center was home to the U.S. Men's Rowing Team from 2000 to 2008 and is currently home to the U.S. Women's Team.

The story of the building of Lake Carnegie—a story of strong wills, large fortunes, and vision—also provides a snapshot of a remarkable moment in history and helps explain how Princeton was able in a single generation to transform itself from a regional college into an international university. Without its lake, the graceful bridges, the surrounding open countryside, and the boathouse buildings, Princeton would be a different, more barren place.

Shea Rowing Center

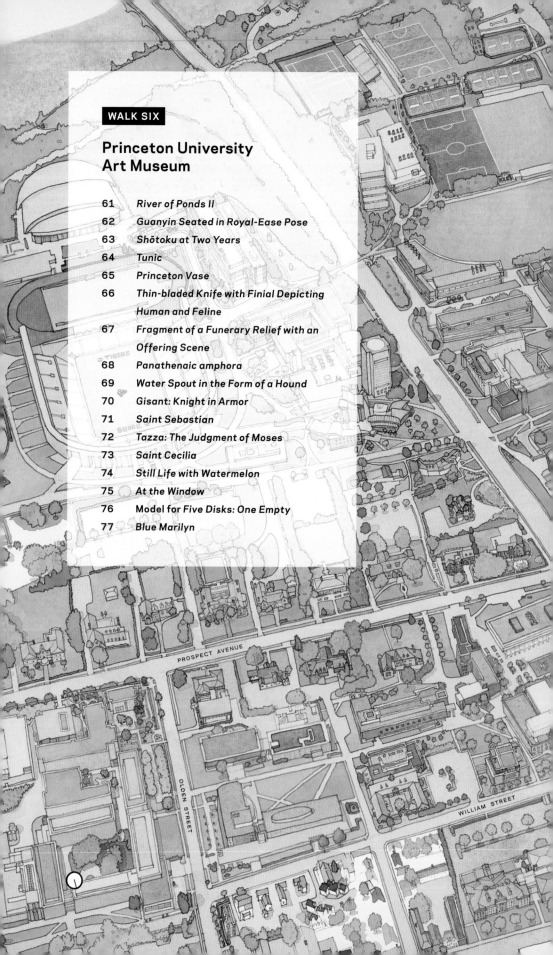

WALK SIX

Princeton University
Art Museum

61 - 77

ELM DRIVE

WASHINGTON ROAD

NASSAU STREET

Princeton University Art Museum

PRINCETON UNIVERSITY ART MUSEUM COLLECTION HIGHLIGHTS

The origins of Princeton's art collections date to the 1750s, just a few years after the founding of the university itself, when New Jersey colonial governor Jonathan Belcher bestowed upon the fledgling college the gift of "my own Picture at full length in a gilt frame." Over the course of the next century this and other portraits were augmented by objects of natural history and ancient architectural fragments to form a sort of "museum of the Enlightenment."

In 1882 the Princeton University Art Museum was officially established in conjunction with what is now the Department of Art and Archaeology, the fine arts library, and the School of Architecture. From the beginning the museum was meant to serve a dual purpose: to provide exposure to original works of art and to teach the history of art across disciplines through an encyclopedic collection of world art. The collections today number more than ninety-two thousand objects, ranging chronologically from ancient to contemporary art and spanning the globe.

This tour provides a brief introduction to this growing and ever-changing museum, which continues to add a few hundred works of art to its holdings each year. The museum's galleries are continually refreshed with new acquisitions and changing highlights from the collections (no more than 5 percent of the

McCormick Hall entrance to Princeton University Art Museum, from McCosh Walk

The Mary Ellen Bowen Gallery of American Art, Princeton University Art Museum

collections are on view at any given time), including the integration of prints, drawings, and photographs into the galleries of European and American art, as well as exceptional long-term loans and temporary exhibitions. The works of art highlighted here are but a small sampling of the museum's extensive holdings. They encourage visitors to explore the range of world cultures on display and to discover hidden treasures on their own. Some of the highlighted works may occasionally be off view.

The Museum is located in McCormick Hall (see Walk Seven). The main entrance to McCormick Hall is located on a plaza accessed from McCosh Walk. From the building lobby, visitors to the museum enter through Marquand-Mather Court, named in honor of the museum's first two directors, who, in succession, shepherded the development of the museum and its collections for its first half century. The gallery features works of modern and contemporary art.

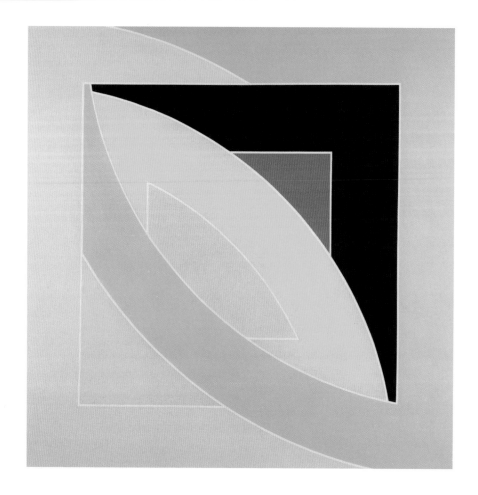

61   Frank Stella
American, born 1936
River of Ponds II, 1969
Acrylic on canvas, 306 × 307 cm
Gift of Paul W. H. Hoffmann, Class of 1947, and Camille Oliver-Hoffmann
© Frank Stella / Artists Rights Society (ARS), New York

Frank Stella's monumental *River of Ponds II* belongs to the artist's *Protractor* series, works characterized by their strong palette, large scale, and forms inspired by tools used for measuring angles and curves. Here he used a range of unmixed acrylic paints to create a sense of optical play, with some elements appearing to project and others to recede from the plane of the canvas. As an undergraduate at Princeton in the mid-1950s, Stella took classes in studio art but majored in history. After graduating, he moved to New York, where he began the works that would launch his career. His innovative use of flat, ready-made colors, simple shapes, and deductive compositions exerted a formative influence on minimalist sculpture.

Proceed to the lower galleries, which house the arts of Asia, Africa, the ancient Americas, and the ancient Mediterranean region. The galleries at the bottom of the stairs are devoted to the arts of Asia. Princeton was the first American university to offer courses in Asian art history and has outstanding holdings in Chinese and Japanese art, including bronzes, tomb figures, painting, and calligraphy.

62   Chinese (Southern Song dynasty, 1127–1279)
Guanyin Seated in Royal-Ease Pose, ca. 1250
Wood with traces of blue–green, red, and gold pigments on white clay underlayer with relief designs, height approx. 110 cm
Museum purchase, Carl Otto von Kienbusch Jr., Memorial Collection

One of the great treasures of the Asian collections is this sculpture of the Chinese Buddhist deity Guanyin, the Bodhisattva of Infinite Compassion. A bodhisattva is an enlightened being who rejects salvation in nirvana to remain in the earthly realm to allay suffering and help others attain enlightenment. Bodhisattvas have technically transcended the physicality of gender, and this sculpture can be read as either male or female, indicating the deity's universal and inclusive nature. The "royal ease" pose, with raised leg and casually draped arm, did not become associated with Guanyin until the late ninth century. Here, the torso retains a sense of solidity, and the skirt draping the lower portion of the figure conforms to the shape of the body. Temple sculptures like this were periodically redecorated, and the relief designs on the skirt and scarves were probably added later.

63 Japanese (Kamakura period, 1185–1333)
Shōtoku at Two Years, late thirteenth century
Wood, crystal, and pigments, height 53 cm
Museum purchase, Fowler McCormick, Class of 1921, Fund

Prince Shōtoku (574–632) has long been celebrated in Japan as foremost among the early advocates of Buddhism, following the introduction of the religion to Japan in the sixth century. Chronicles of his life relate that at the age of two Shōtoku placed his hands together and chanted, "I take refuge in the Buddha," upon which a relic—the left eye of the Buddha Shakyamuni—appeared in his hands. By the medieval period a cult devoted to Shōtoku had been established and images commemorating events in his life proliferated. This sculpture was constructed using the multiple-block technique, in which the pieces were glued together vertically and the joints covered with a glossy black lacquer, after which the figure was painted. The eyes were set with crystal before the blocks were assembled. Such statues were resistant to cracking, and their hollow interiors could hold objects of religious significance. This one is blackened from incense smoke, although some pigment is still visible on the ear and skirt.

Continue through the Asian galleries to the arts of Africa. A vast array of peoples and cultures are represented in the Museum's collection of African art, which includes objects made of wood, metal, ivory, beads, and a variety of other materials. Historically, field collectors in Africa often neglected to record the names of the artists who created objects, or the location and precise date of their production, although it is possible to designate the people and the current name of the countries where they originated.

64 Yoruba artist (Nigeria)
Tunic, late nineteenth to early twentieth century
Glass and stone beads, fabric, and thread, approximately 101.6 × 71.1 cm
Museum purchase, Fowler McCormick, Class of 1921, Fund

This spectacularly beaded tunic was worn by an *oba*, or Yoruba king. An appliqué of an oba's head positioned beneath the V-neck and framed by small beaded crowns symbolizes the continuity of the oba's office; the pairs of birds identify the oba as a direct descendent of Oduduwa, the god of divine kingship. Numerous intertwined patterns specific to objects associated with royalty are further evidence that this was a king's tunic. The garment was painstakingly composed by a bead artist who first threaded strands of beads, then arranged the patterns by laying the strands onto a cloth foundation before they were finally attached. Numerous repairs suggest that the tunic was valued and cared for over an extended period. The presence around the neck of rare, locally produced jasper beads and the abundance of the tiniest seed beads signal that it was created in the late nineteenth or early twentieth century.

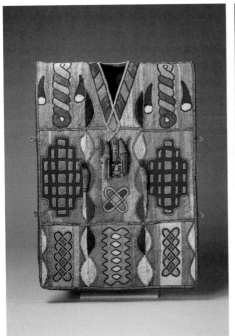

Continue to the next gallery, which features art of the ancient Americas. Princeton's collections of indigenous art from the Americas are considered to be among the finest in the world, encompassing a wide array of objects produced over some five thousand years, from Chile to the Arctic. The principal focus of the collection is on small, portable works of art in ceramic, semiprecious stones, gold, silver, and wood.

65   Maya (Nakbe region, Petén, Guatemala)
Princeton Vase, AD 670-750
Ceramic with red, cream, and black slip, with remnants of painted stucco, height 21.5 cm
Museum purchase, gift of the Hans A. Widenmann, Class of 1918, and Dorothy Widenmann Foundation

The masterful calligraphic painting on this object is the finest known example of Maya *codex style* ceramic art, so named for its similarities to Maya books, or *codices*. Graceful, confident lines painted on a cream slip present a theatrically composed mythological scene, while subtle visual devices encourage the viewer or user to turn the vessel so that the narrative unfolds over time. The formulaic texts at the upper edge serve to consecrate the vessel, to indicate that it was intended for drinking "maize tree" chocolate, and to designate its owner, a Maya lord named Muwaan K'uk'. The vase would have been used in courtly feasts similar to the scene depicted.

66 Mochica (North coast, Peru)
Thin-bladed Knife with Finial Depicting Human and Feline,
600–800 CE
Cast copper alloy, height 27.3 cm
Museum purchase, Fowler McCormick, Class of 1921, Fund

Although traditionally interpreted as scepters or coca-snuffing "spatulas," chisel-shaped objects such as this more likely served as bloodletters in sacrificial rites. Presumably, they were used to pierce the jugular vein of a sacrificial victim; the blood was then collected in a cup or bowl for consumption before the victim was decapitated. Made from a copper alloy, this piece is composed of a flat blade, a short handle, and an elaborate finial depicting interaction between two supernatural creatures.

Continue to the next gallery, where art of the ancient Mediterranean region is on view. Princeton's collections of ancient art contain more than fourteen thousand objects from many cultures and periods, and are renowned for their range and quality. Since shortly after Princeton's founding, the arts of the ancient world have played a vital role in teaching about the evolution of Western civilization.

67 Egyptian, Middle Kingdom (Twelfth Dynasty, probably reign of Senwosret I, ca. 1971–ca. 1926 BC)
Fragment of a Funerary Relief with an Offering Scene
Painted limestone, height 26 cm
Museum purchase and gift of Dan Fellows Platt, Class of 1895, by exchange

For centuries sculpted scenes of offerings to the dead were a standard feature of Egyptian tombs. In this example, a man sits before a table piled with offerings of meat and vegetables, and four columns of hieroglyphs are inscribed above him. His garments, shoulder-length layered wig, broad collar, and sash identify him as a lector priest, an important figure who recited ritual texts in religious and funerary ceremonies. Like many now monotone works from antiquity, the relief was originally brightly painted, and traces of color remain.

68 Greek (Attic), in the manner of the Berlin Painter
Panathenaic amphora, ca. 500–490 BC
Ceramic, height 62.4 cm
Bequest of Mrs. Allan Marquand

Vessels like this were filled with olive oil and awarded as prizes at the athletic competitions known as the Panathenaic Games in Athens. On one side, the goddess Athena wields a spear between two Ionic columns surmounted by cocks. Typically an inscription reading, "One of the prizes from Athens" would run alongside one of the columns; the lack of such an inscription here may indicate that the vessel was made for the commercial market rather than as a prize. The reverse of a panathenaic amphora always depicts the event for which the vase was awarded: in this instance, a charioteer holds the reins to a four-horse racing chariot. This vessel—in the style of one of the most admired yet anonymous painters of ancient Greece—was donated by the widow of the Museum's founding director.

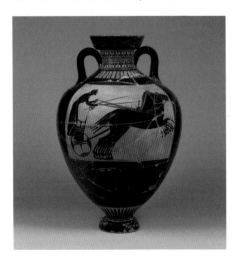

Continue through the passageway to the Roman court, which includes mosaics from the excavation at Antioch-on-the-Orontes in modern-day Turkey. Princeton played a leading role in conducting these important excavations in the early twentieth century, and the collection of mosaics displayed in the Museum, in Firestone Library, and elsewhere on campus is all but unrivaled in the United States.

69 Roman
Water Spout in the Form of a Hound, **early first century** AD
Terracotta, height 44.5 cm, length 63 cm
Museum purchase, gift of John B. Elliott, Class of 1951

The original setting of this functional sculpture is demonstrated by a number of similar spouts in private houses that were excavated at Pompeii and Herculaneum, cities buried by the eruption of Mount Vesuvius in 79 CE. Set around an opening in the tiled roof and alternating with spouts in the form of lions, these spouts channeled rainwater into a pool in the inner courtyard. The collared dog may represent a Molossian hound, a breed renowned for its bravery and ferocity and often used for household security. The hound's upright ears and focused expression show him to be a vigilant sentinel.

Take the elevator or stairs to the upper galleries, which house Western art from the Middle Ages through the present. Upon exiting the elevator, turn left and proceed to the medieval gallery, which is on the left and is lit with stained-glass windows. If you use the stairs, turn right upon entering the large gallery at the top of the stairs and follow the signs to European art of the thirteenth to eighteenth centuries. The entrance to the medieval gallery is located at the right side of the rear portion of this gallery.

70 Spanish
Gisant: Knight in Armor, ca. 1500
Stone
Gift of Baroness Cassel van Doorn

Gisant tombs, which depict the deceased in a reclining position, became a widespread type of royal tomb in the twelfth and thirteenth centuries and continued into modern times. This gisant figure is from a Spanish tomb and shows an unidentified nobleman dressed in armor. Its anomalies—for example, the gauntlets do not match—suggest that it depicts the actual armor owned by the nobleman rather than being a generic or idealized portrait. By tradition, the deceased was represented as thirty-three years old, the age of Christ when he died.

Use the left-hand doorway to exit the medieval gallery. The next grouping will be on the wall to the left.

71 **Master of the Greenville Tondo**
Italian, active 1500–1510
Saint Sebastian, ca. 1500-1510
Oil on wood panel transferred to canvas on pressed-wood panel, 76.7 × 53.4 cm
Gift of the Samuel H. Kress Foundation to the New Jersey State Museum;
transferred to the Princeton University Art Museum

Saint Sebastian was a Christian soldier in the Roman army who was sentenced to death for converting new believers. He was tied to a post and shot with arrows but miraculously survived. The saint's suffering provided Renaissance artists with the opportunity to depict youthful male anatomy within a religious context. This example is shown alongside an idealized ancient Roman torso of a nude youth, demonstrating the ways in which classical art influenced artists working in the age of Renaissance humanism.

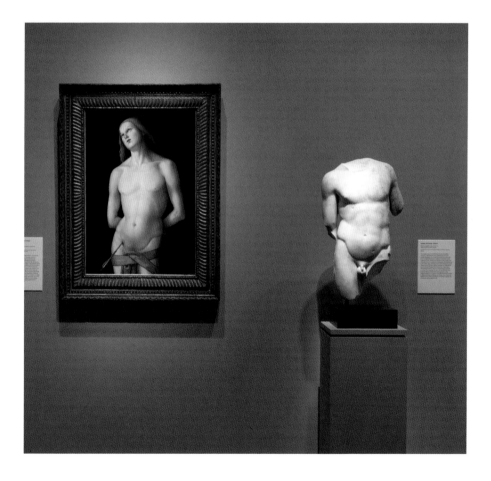

72 Pierre Reymond
French, ca. 1513–after 1584
Jean de Court
French, active 1541–1564
Tazza: The Judgment of Moses, 1546
Painted enamel on copper, height 14.2 cm, diameter 24.9 cm
Museum purchase, Fowler McCormick, Class of 1921, Fund

This footed bowl, or *tazza*, is the joint creation of Pierre Reymond, who signed and dated the foot, and Jean de Court, who initialed the bowl. The bowl's interior design is based on an illustration that was published in 1553; thus, the bowl was painted later than the foot. The scene from the Hebrew Bible depicts Moses in the camp of the Israelites, where he settled all disputes that were brought before him. His father-in-law, Jethro, stands at his side and counsels him to appoint additional judges to assist him. This episode took place just before Moses received the Ten Commandments and was an important step in the establishment of the Israelite polity, which in turn influenced Calvinist community governance during the period when the bowl was made.

Proceed back to the central gallery, which features large-scale paintings of historical, mythological, and religious subjects from the seventeenth, eighteenth, and nineteenth centuries, and enter the galleries of nineteenth- and early twentieth-century European art.

73   Sir Edward Burne-Jones
British, 1833–1898
Saint Cecilia, ca. 1900
Made by Morris & Co. (est. 1875)
Stained and painted glass, 213.5 × 75.5 cm
Museum purchase, Surdna Fund

The Gothic Revival style in architecture, which came to prominence in the 1870s, created a large market for stained glass, and Edward Burne-Jones was an enormously sought-after designer of such windows during this period. This spectacular window is one of nearly thirty versions designed by Burne-Jones on the theme of Saint Cecilia, the patron saint of music. The first was commissioned in 1875 by the organist of Christ Church, Oxford. These windows were executed by Morris & Co., the firm founded by the influential artist William Morris (1834–96), who also initiated the Arts and Crafts movement in England. Proponents of this movement believed that industrialization had corrupted art, creating a false separation between the designer and the manufacturer. They favored handmade objects and advocated for a return to the traditions of medieval craftsmen, abolishing distinctions between fine and decorative arts.

Proceed back to the central gallery and enter the gallery of American art. Princeton's distinguished collection of American art includes important examples of portraiture, Hudson River School landscape painting, American Impressionism, and folk art.

74   Rubens Peale
American, 1784–1865
Still Life with Watermelon, 1865
Oil on canvas, 48.3 × 69.9 cm
Gift in honor of Professor John Wilmerding from his friends and former students and the Kathleen C. Sherrerd Fund for Acquisitions in American Art

Rubens Peale was the son of the great American painter Charles Willson Peale, whose iconic *George Washington at the Battle of Princeton* hangs at the entrance to this gallery. Unlike his many artistic siblings, however, Rubens did not begin his artistic career until late in life: at the age of seventy-one he was taught to paint by his daughter, Mary. Peale completed *Still Life with Watermelon* at age eighty-one. It presents a finely balanced composition that echoes the quiet simplicity of his

brother Raphaelle Peale's frieze-like, neoclassical compositions, executed decades earlier, but also relates to his uncle James Peale's horizontal tabletop arrangements of indirectly illuminated fruit, including the pictorial device of a piece of fruit shown overhanging the table's edge, intended to give an added dimension of realism.

75 Winslow Homer

American, 1836–1910

At the Window, 1872

Oil on canvas, 57 × 40 cm

Gift of Francis Bosak, Class of 1931, and Mrs. Bosak

Distinct among the images of sunlit rural life that constituted the bulk of Winslow Homer's artistic production in 1872 is a group of four closely related scenes remarkable for their interiority of setting and mood. Each work depicts the same similarly attired young woman, pensively standing or seated in a darkened room before an open window that reveals a glimpse of bright countryside. One contemporary reviewer identified the woman as "a Salem girl," referring to the Massachusetts seaport, which provides a plausible underlying narrative for the paintings, as the sitter—whose distinctive black dress likely signifies mourning—becomes the bereaved companion of a sailor lost at sea. If this hypothesis is true, then these works anticipate by a decade Homer's engagement with the theme of men and the sea, which was to become a crucial part of his overarching preoccupation with man's struggle against nature.

76 Alexander Calder

American, 1898–1976

Model for *Five Disks: One Empty*, 1969

Black-painted sheet aluminum, height 56.2 cm

Gift of the artist, in honor of Alfred H. Barr Jr., Class of 1922

© *Calder Foundation, New York / Artists Rights Society (ARS), New York*

Alexander Calder is best known for his kinetic sculptures, or "mobiles," but he also imbued his stationary sculptures with a sense of movement and lightness. These "stabiles" are considered one of his greatest contributions to twentieth-century art. This work is the model for a monumental steel sculpture that Calder designed especially for the Princeton campus at the request of his friend Alfred Barr, a Princeton alumnus and the founding director of the Museum of Modern Art. The larger work, along with numerous other outdoor sculptures, is part of a self-guided walking tour of the campus art collection that can be accessed at artmuseum.princeton.edu/campus-art.

77   Andy Warhol
American, 1928–1987
Blue Marilyn, 1962
Acrylic and screenprint ink on canvas, 50.5 × 40.3 cm
Gift of Alfred H. Barr Jr., Class of 1922, and Mrs. Barr

Pop artist Andy Warhol was fascinated by celebrities and preoccupied with loss, mortality, and disaster. The death of actress Marilyn Monroe in 1962 coincided with the artist's experiments with screenprinting, a technique he used to reproduce multiple images of existing photographs, as if on an assembly line. Screenprinting tends to flatten the resulting image, both literally and symbolically. These pictures, shocking for their time, contributed significantly to the development of pop art as an ironic critique of the perceived soullessness of consumer culture. The work's donor, Alfred Barr, acquired the work directly from the artist in the year in which it was painted.

For a brief history of the Museum and an in-depth look at its collections, see Princeton University Art Museum: Handbook of the Collections, *revised and expanded edition (Princeton, 2013).*

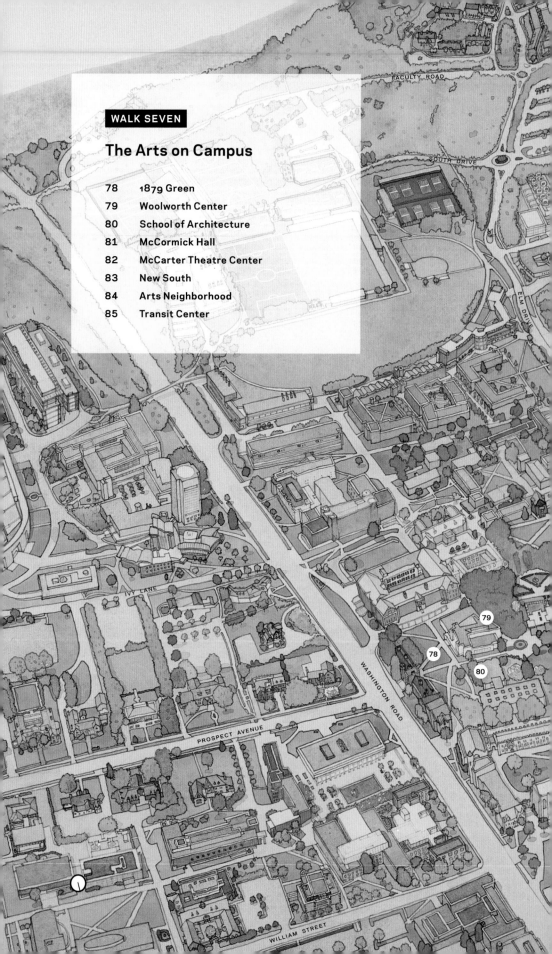

COLLEGE ROAD

DICKINSON PLACE

UNIVERSITY PLACE

NASSAU STREET

The Arts on Campus

EDGE-TO-EDGE DEPLOYMENT OF THE ARTS

"The time has come for Princeton to give greater recognition to the centrality of the arts in its teaching and research mission." President Shirley M. Tilghman (2001–13) made this commitment in her 2006 "Report on the Creative & Performing Arts at Princeton," a commitment that began to take tangible form with Peter B. Lewis's $101 million gift. This walk highlights the first steps in implementing the arts initiative and also chronicles the rich history of arts scholarship at Princeton beginning in the late nineteenth century. As Boston's "emerald necklace" links parks and neighborhoods by linear greenways, the arts buildings in this walk are linked by connective landscapes and pathways.

In 1882 President McCosh charged a committee to prepare a curriculum in the history of art, a relatively new academic discipline. His charge led to the founding of the Department of Art and Archaeology and the construction of the Museum of Historical Art in 1889. The history of art curriculum expanded to include architectural studies, leading to the founding of the professional School of Architecture in 1919. The department began offering music courses in 1934 and in 1946 the university created the Department of Music, originally housed in Clio Hall. The university began offering undergraduate instruction in the creative and performing arts in 1939. By the time President Tilghman proposed her arts initiative more than a half century later, undergraduates could obtain certificates in Creative Writing, Theater and Dance, and Visual Arts. Lewis's gift helped create an academic Center for the Arts and greatly expanded the faculty, fellows, and course offerings in these programs. While the Department of Art and Archaeology, the Department of Music, the Princeton University Art Museum, and the School of Architecture are not formally part of the Lewis Center, they collaborate academically with the center and with other humanities departments.

The curricular emphasis on the arts amplifies the vibrant activities of more than sixty-five undergraduate performing arts organizations, some of which predate the formal arts curriculum. Some organizations rehearse and perform in theater spaces—the Triangle Club in McCarter Theatre Center and Theatre Intime in Murray Theater—while others perform all over campus, from archways to residential colleges to Frist Campus Center.

Like the undergraduate performing arts organizations, curricular arts programs inhabit dispersed buildings and spaces. The Allen Committee (named for its chair, former dean of the School of Architecture, Stan Allen), which informed President Tilghman's report, cited this "edge-to-edge deployment" around campus as a positive attribute in integrating the arts with the academic and social life of the university and community. Physical linkage of these dispersed facilities is accomplished by a series of open spaces, pathways, and landscapes. The 2008 Campus Plan identified landscape projects that would

Aerial rendering of Blair Walk looking south toward Arts Neighborhood and Transit Center

strengthen connectivity between the area around McCormick Hall—the location of the Department of Art and Archaeology, the Princeton University Art Museum, and the Marquand Library of Art and Archaeology—in the central campus and the Arts Neighborhood bordered by Alexander Street and University Place. (See Landscape Walks, McCosh Walk and Blair Walk.)

1879 Green looking south

78   1879 Green

Today's 1879 Green was originally part of Prospect, the thirty-five-acre estate donated to the college in 1878. By 1908 the open space was defined by the existing Prospect House to the west and recently constructed buildings: 1879 Hall to the east, McCosh Hall to the north, and Palmer Physical Laboratory to the south. 1879 Hall, designed by Benjamin Morris as a dormitory and constructed in 1904, was the first of these buildings. Its linear, rhythmic composition of three-story end bays, two-story intermediate bays, and a central tower provided a backdrop for intramural sports on the green and separation from the increasingly busy Washington Road.

The western side of the green was appropriated for music and architecture building sites in 1962 that partially block the view of the north elevation of Palmer Laboratory, in what was characterized as "the crime of '62" by preservationists. When Palmer was converted to Frist Campus Center, architect Robert Venturi argued that the partial blockage had disrupted the symmetry of the original Palmer Hall. Hence, his asymmetrical design for the freestanding arcade that announces the building entries when seen from the north.

Around the same time as the construction of the music and architecture buildings, 1879 Hall was converted from a dormitory to academic space for the Departments of Philosophy and Religion, giving identity to 1879 Green as an academic quadrangle. The truncated green space shares several similarities with McCosh-Dickinson-Chapel courtyard to the north. They are about the same size and slightly wedge shaped, giving an exaggerated sense of perspective when viewed from the narrower end. They are bordered on the narrow end by major campus walkways and connect to open spaces and other campus walkways at

Aerial view (from top) of McCosh–Dickinson–Chapel courtyard, School of Architecture, Woolworth Center, and 1879 Green (right), 1963

the wider ends. A walkway through the southeastern archway of McCosh-Dickinson-Chapel courtyard connects to 1879 Green, thereby encouraging diagonal movement from 1879 Green to Firestone Plaza. There are memorable building facades fronting the open space: the south elevation of University Chapel in McCosh-Dickinson-Chapel courtyard and the north elevation of Frist Campus Center in 1879 Green.

Contributing to 1879 Green's porosity is the archway below the tower of 1879 Hall and the walkway between the music and architecture buildings. The archway frames an axial vista eastward toward Prospect Avenue from a promontory at the level of the green. In the opposite direction the landscaped walkway between the music and architecture buildings leads to the front lawn of Prospect House. Both the music and architecture buildings have transparent, floor-through lobbies that visually connect 1879 Green to Prospect. Today 1879 Green is a tree-lined, slightly sloping green space traversed by pathways and, in favorable weather, shaded and sunlit for relaxation and outdoor gatherings.

79 Woolworth Center

Moore and Hutchins, 1963; Addition and renovation: Juan Navarro Baldeweg with Wank Adams Slavin, 1997

The Woolworth Center—the original building and the addition—exhibits a dual personality. When looking at the original building, it is easy to dismiss it as a blocky brick box set on top of a fieldstone shelf. But then one looks slightly to the north to Juan Navarro Baldeweg's addition; inside and out, this side of Woolworth is luminous. Perhaps the most striking exterior details are two great light scoops that perch on the roof like an enormous metal-and-glass butterfly about to take flight. The scoops bring light from the north and south into the depths of the building. By thrusting up and out from the flat plane of the roof, they return visual interest to a part of a building that for many modernists was simply a way to keep out the rain.

Inside the entrance atrium, which ties the two personalities of Woolworth together, one discovers a glass clerestory and roof that diffuse daylight into the below-grade McAlpin Rehearsal Hall. The trapezoidal rehearsal hall may be subterranean, but the architect designed the space to be a well of light. Paved with the

Woolworth Center; Woolworth Center interior

same brick as the outside stairs and terrace, the atrium uses a range of design strategies to break down the boundaries between the interior and exterior. Rising from the main level is the rounded clear-glass wall of the three-story Mendel Music Library—named for Arthur Mendel, chairman of the department (1952–67)—which projects into the space to showcase students doing their research. The visual interest of the music library is echoed on the opposite side by flights of stairs that appear to be carved out of the wall. Glass guardrails create balcony-like spaces that look into the atrium with a view of Prospect Gardens to the west. These and other gestures result in a great interior room that celebrates geometry and light.

80   School of Architecture
Fisher, Nes, Campbell, and Partners, 1963; Auditorium Renovation: Alan Chimacoff, 1980; Addition: Architecture Research Office, 2006

One of Princeton's three professional schools, the School of Architecture was founded in 1919 and occupied space in McCormick Hall. The new School of Architecture building, designed and built around the same time as the Engineering Quadrangle (E-Quad), is evocative of its time—the rectilinear forms, the lack of ornament, the hard edges, the flat roofs, the regular repetition of the windows lined up in such a way (directly over one another) to give the horizontal building some vertical thrust, the relative absence of wood to lend warmth and texture to the interiors, and the use of brick. However, it is the way in which the architects of the School of Architecture use brick that suggests how, despite a common aesthetic vocabulary, they are more successful than the architect of the E-Quad. The design team at the architecture school specified brick that had been fired unevenly, to create variations to the basic reddish-brown color. Compared to the monochromatic tones in the E-Quad bricks, the effect is subtle but significant.

There are also larger gestures, the most important of which is the attempt to break up the volumes to create a more human scale. In part this is dictated by the site, which infringes on the grounds of Prospect. The architects could neither occupy a large footprint nor build too high, which would have been visually intrusive. The result is two modest wings set at right angles to one another to form a T, the stem of which is somewhat off-center from the bar. The longer, east–west bar is three stories and complements the height of McCosh Hall, its neighbor to the north, while the south wing is two stories in apparent deference to 1879 Hall to the east. The bar contains studios and classrooms. In 1980 Alan Chimacoff renovated the ground-floor lobby, exhibition space, and Betts auditorium. The south wing contains the architectural library and administrative offices. Labs, equipment, and other shared resources are located in the basement level.

Originally the two wings were bridged by a narrow, somewhat restrictive two-story link that served as the entrance to both wings. In 2008 it was replaced by an expanded three-story link, facilitating flow between the wings. Architecture Research Office (ARO)—Adam Yarinsky (MArch 1987), Stephen Cassell (Class of 1986), and Kim Yao (MArch 1997)—clad the new addition in a skin of partially fritted glass, enhancing its transparency. The link contains circulation and social space: an elevator and glass-enclosed stair serve all floors, including the two-story lobby, a ramped balcony at the second floor, and a student lounge on top. The see-through quality of the addition effectively reopens the view between 1879 Green and the grounds of Prospect House (Sherrerd Green), a historically significant visual connection.

Reference to the Architecture School's neighbors suggests why this building is better integrated with the campus fabric than the much larger E-Quad was at the time it was built. However, the E-Quad had no nearby university buildings to relate to and it was too far east to benefit from the gravitational pull of Cram's campus

School of Architecture

plan. As an infill building, this was not the case for the School of Architecture. The design team addressed constraints of site and surroundings, which shaped everything from the footprint of the building and the manipulation of the facade to the decision to use the materials familiar to this precinct of the campus—brick and limestone trim.

81   McCormick Hall

Cram and Ferguson, 1923 (partially demolished 1964); Addition: Francis A. Comstock, Frederic D'Amato, and Sherley W. Morgan, 1928 and 1935 (demolished 1964); Addition: Steinman and Cain, 1966; Museum addition: Mitchell/ Giurgola, 1989; Library addition: Shepley Bulfinch Richardson and Abbott, 2003; Landscape: Princeton University Office of Physical Planning, 1998

Cubi XIII
David Smith, 1963; stainless steel

Human Condition
Rudolf Hoflehner, 1960; cast iron
Gift of Stanley J. Seeger Jr. (Class of 1952)

McCormick Hall houses the Department of Art and Archaeology, the Princeton University Art Museum, and the Marquand Library of Art and Archaeology. Since the origins of the art history curriculum in the 1880s, these three academic entities have been inextricably linked. To the dismay of some who believed architecture

McCormick Hall north and east facades

"Cubi XIII," by David Smith, 1963

should remain a purely scholarly pursuit rather than a professional course of study, the School of Architecture and its library moved from McCormick to a new building in 1963. Today's building complex is a three-dimensional jigsaw puzzle that reflects the interrelationship of its occupants.

This tour of the building's exterior begins on McCosh Walk and continues in a counterclockwise direction. Standing on McCosh Walk and facing the building, a seasoned visitor might wonder what happened to the concrete sculpture, *Head of a Woman*—attributed to Pablo Picasso but executed by artist Carl Nesjar—that once announced the museum to the public. The sculpture was moved to a new location south of Spelman Halls to make way for a 2003 underground addition to Marquand Library. The facade of the building, clad in brown sandstone with travertine trim, was part of a major addition completed in 1966. The library wing—the portion of McCormick Hall closest to McCosh Walk—features a three-story, north-facing, glass curtain wall that brings daylight into the library and provides readers with a view of the historic core of the campus. Perched on top of the library wing is part of the 2003 library expansion, which contains classrooms and assigned carrels. On the lawn north of the library wing is *Cubi XIII*, part of David Smith's final and most famed series of sculptures. Smith polished the stainless steel so that it would reflect the changing colors of its surroundings, especially when placed outdoors among trees. Although the burnished surface is constructed of basic geometric shapes, it also reveals a painter's sensibility.

West of the library wing and around the corner to the south is a pathway that descends a flight of stairs and dips under an elevated portion of the westernmost wing. This wing, also part of the 1966 addition, contains the Department of Art and Archaeology's teaching spaces and faculty offices. While preserving the ground-level walkway, the design blocks an axial vista—first envisioned by Frederick Law Olmsted in his never-implemented 1893 campus plan—from Nassau Street to the archway in the north side of Brown Hall. Before descending the stairs one can see a sculpture on the sloping lawn. Made in 1960, *Human Condition* fuses elements of man and machine, expressing the artist Rudolf Hoflehner's—and the era's—concern with the symbiotic yet fraught relationship between the social and industrial worlds. The artist did not coat the iron: he intended the work to rust, demonstrating that even this cyborg is vulnerable to the ravages of time.

McCormick Hall, 1923 and 1989 buildings

Facing the pathway beyond the west wing underpass is the remaining portion of the original School of Architecture building designed by Cram and Ferguson between 1917 and 1921, and completed in 1923. Cram's choice of northern Italian Gothic for the building's exterior was a departure from the English Gothic style that he used for the Graduate College and University Chapel. The architects of the 1966 addition demolished the north section of Cram's building, the original 1889 Museum of Historic Art, and the 1928 and 1935 additions that contained the drafting room and other teaching spaces for the School of Architecture. South of the Cram building is the 1989 museum addition that retains elements of both the historic style of Cram's design and the modern style of the 1966 addition, a strategy characteristic of postmodern architecture. The tour continues around the south end of the complex and up a winding path amid a wooded area of Prospect Gardens that screens the mainly blank plaster walls of the 1989 and the 1966 museum additions. Before turning left onto the landscaped plaza that leads to the main (north) entrance of the complex, note the ground-level skylights that provide daylight to the reading areas of the underground library addition. See Walk Six for a tour of the Princeton University Art Museum collection highlights.

82 McCarter Theatre Center

Taylor and Fisher, 1930; Addition: Grieves Associates, 1991; Addition and renovation: Hardy Holzman Pfeiffer, 2003

Triangle Club, an undergraduate musical-comedy performance group founded in 1883, performed in temporary quarters until building the wood-framed Casino in 1895 on the site of today's Dillon Gymnasium. The building was moved twice to make way for university buildings and in 1924 it was destroyed by fire. Triangle then built the brick-and-stone McCarter Theatre across from the historic campus on University Place. While Triangle continues to perform at McCarter and other venues on campus and around the country, the building and the management have changed over the years. When an addition was built in 2003 the complex was renamed McCarter Theatre Center, and the main eleven-hundred-seat theater in the original building was renovated and renamed Matthews Theatre. The McCarter Theatre Company operates as an independent regional producing theater that also books over two hundred musical and dance events produced by touring companies and performing artists. The addition, used extensively by the university's Programs in Theater and Dance, includes the 360-seat Berlind Theatre, a large rehearsal room and flexible performance space; a classroom; and offices.

Former Triangle Club member D. K. Este Fisher (Class of 1913) designed the original building's exterior in the prevailing Collegiate Gothic style. Construction was completed just before the Great Depression and the Second World War halted major building projects and unleashed the forces of modernity. The massing of the exterior follows the three-part organization of a traditional proscenium stage theater: lobby, auditorium, and stage/fly loft. The handsome, relatively unadorned lobby pavilion is domestically scaled and set back from College Road and the residential neighborhood to the north. The steeply pitched slate roof is bracketed by tall chimneys on the gable end and pierced by four dormers on the main facade.

McCarter Theatre Center lobby window

McCarter Theatre north facade, ca. 1930–50

The dormers contain high stained-glass windows detailed with stone tracery that give prominence to the balcony lobby. One enters the main floor lobby and box office through three arched openings trimmed in limestone.

Fisher took advantage of the sloping site to align the orchestra seating in the direction of the slope and to place the high fly loft on the downhill side. The enclosing walls of these elements are clad in the same randomly coursed building stone as the lobby piece. To relieve the solid walls, Fisher recessed brick panels topped with Gothic-inspired arches. A tower on the University Place side provides access to the rigging platforms in the fly loft, water storage tanks for the fire suppression system, and prominence to the building when viewed from the southeast. Audiences grew as the theater attracted pre-Broadway tryouts and touring music and dance companies, overwhelming the capacity of the lobby. In 1991 lobbies were appended to the east and west sides, providing space for socializing during intermission and before and after performances.

McCarter Theatre Center, Berlind Theatre

The university commissioned Hugh Hardy (Class of 1954) to design an addition to McCarter Theatre Center for the undergraduate academic Program in Theater and Dance (now two separate programs) and the professional theater company. Previously this program made do with a small dance studio and flat floor performance space in a renovated public school building at 185 Nassau Street. Hardy, well known for his theater designs in New York City and elsewhere, placed the Berlind Theatre stage back-to-back with the McCarter stage. Berlind has stadium seating, a proscenium, and a fly loft. The first-floor rehearsal studio and the second-floor lobby are located on the south side of the building, with large windows that provide daylight to the studio and—at the time—views from the lobby toward the train station. In 2017 the view from the lobby windows will feature a new home for the performing arts at Princeton, the Lewis Center for the Arts. Construction of the Berlind Theatre, together with the existing McCarter Theatre, established a cornerstone of the Arts Neighborhood in this part of campus.

83   New South

Edward Larrabee Barnes, 1965; Alteration: Wurmfeld Associates, 1981; Renovation: James Bradberry Architects, 2010

By the 1960s Nassau Hall could no longer accommodate enough office space for the expanding administration. The solution was to construct a purpose-built office building in a campus location remote from Nassau Hall. Edward L. Barnes designed an office tower on a site south of Pyne Hall and Dillon Gym, but the building's modern design was deemed incompatible with its Collegiate Gothic neighbors. The university moved the building location farther south without allowing Barnes to adapt the design to the new site conditions. In the process, the building gained the name "New South" in reference to "Old North," as Nassau Hall was colloquially known. Ironically, ten years later, the university built the modernist Spelman Halls on a site even closer to Pyne Hall.

Many observers criticize New South for its bulk and its corporate appearance. For the original site Barnes had designed an open, slightly raised podium between the below-grade floors and the upper floors to preserve vistas and to reduce the visual mass of the building at eye level. Due to a steep grade change on the relocated site there is a two-story precipice on the south side. A 1981 alteration that filled in the tall first floor to create additional office space eliminated this awkward situation but exacerbated the building's bulky appearance.

In the twenty-first century the site is no longer remote but pivotal between Whitman College and the Lewis Center for the Arts. As some administrative offices moved to locations in West Windsor Township, space in New South was repurposed for Lewis Center programs. In 2010 James Bradberry Architects renovated the double-height first floor to accommodate dance and theater rehearsal studios and converted the sixth floor to offices and seminar rooms for creative writing. Bradberry also redesigned the north entrance to the building with a full-height

New South north facade, date unknown

glass wall that opens onto a green. The landscape plan by Michael Van Valkenburgh Associates integrates the grade, plantings, and pathways of this green with the Arts Neighborhood and beyond. The plan also mitigates the precipice on the south side by adding a retaining wall and landscaped berm to screen a service area for both New South and the Lewis Center.

Lewis Center for the Arts model

84 Arts Neighborhood
Urban design: Beyer Blinder Belle Architects and Planners with Michael Van Valkenburgh Associates and Vanasse Hangen Brustlin, 2014

Lewis Center for the Arts
Steven Holl Architects with BNIM Architects, scheduled completion 2017

Redevelopment of twenty-three acres of land around the New Jersey Transit station—the terminus of the Dinky—was the most ambitious project undertaken by President Tilghman's administration. By expanding space for the undergraduate curriculum in the creative and performing arts, the Arts Neighborhood at long last will provide a major gateway from the south to the town of Princeton and the university's campus along Alexander Street. The project consists of a new building complex to house the performing arts, as well as a number of other components: a new transit center with a new train station and convenience store; adaptive reuse of former station buildings for a new restaurant and cafe; new landscaped green spaces, pathways, and streetscape; traffic improvements, including a new round-about at the intersection of Alexander Street and University Place, and an access road from Alexander Street to the West Garage; and sites for future arts and academic buildings.

Upon the project's completion in 2017 the Programs in Theater and Dance will relocate from 185 Nassau Street to the Lewis Center for the Arts in keeping with the 2008 Campus Plan. The Department of Music will also gain rehearsal space in the Lewis Center. In 2010 the Program in Creative Writing moved from 185 Nassau Street to New South, where new dance and theater rehearsal studios have also been constructed. The Program in Visual Arts will remain at 185 Nassau Street, benefiting from space vacated by other Lewis Center programs.

For the Lewis Center Steven Holl and Michael Van Valkenburgh collaborated to create a dynamic relationship between buildings and landscapes that maximizes porosity. Porosity, as envisioned by the designers, means both interconnectedness with established pedestrian circulation routes and transparency of the buildings' exteriors. Three buildings—one for theater and dance, one for music, and one for a vibrant mix of Lewis Center faculty, fellows, and administrative offices—will interconnect at a lower-level forum. The forum will give access to a black-box theater, dance theater, instrumental rehearsal and performance room, gallery, and collaborative project space. At the arts plaza level above the forum, the buildings will spatially define a landscaped courtyard and provide passages that connect with paths to Forbes College to the west, Blair Walk and McCarter Theatre Center to the north, Tilghman Walk to the east, and the transit plaza to the south. "Skylights" submerged in the plaza's shallow pool will bring daylight and water current patterns into the forum.

The buildings will be clad in stone similar in color to Nassau Hall's Stockton stone. However, detailing will reflect twenty-first-century technology: smooth texture, large panels, thin joints, and sharp corners. Large expanses of transparent and translucent glass will provide glimpses of the buildings' activities from the outside and framed views of the campus from within. To help achieve the university's sustainability goals for reduced carbon emissions and energy consumption, heating and cooling for the buildings will be provided from geothermal wells. The constant temperature of the earth mitigates summer and winter temperature ranges to maintain comfortable environmental conditions within the buildings. Green roofs and rainwater harvesting will help achieve the university's goal to retain and reuse storm water on site, rather than discharge it into local streams.

85   Transit Center

New Jersey Transit Station and Wawa Store
Rick Joy Architects, 2014–16; Landscape: Michael Van Valkenburgh Associates

The transit component of the site redevelopment includes a new multimodal transportation center and rehabilitation of the existing train station buildings: a new train station, a twenty-four-hour convenience store, public and campus bus service, bicycle parking, commuter parking, and access to the West Garage from a signalized intersection on Alexander Street. The forum level of the Lewis Center for the Arts is also accessed from the transit plaza, and is entered through a grove of multistemmed gingko trees on the north side of the plaza. Rick Joy Architects designed the new train station and convenience store. The train station building features walls and columns of precast concrete, a steeply pitched roof of blackened stainless steel, and an entrance portico that is visible to pedestrians arriving from

Transit Center rendering

the arts plaza and Blair Walk to the north, as well as vehicles traveling on Alexander Street. The convenience store features a blackened stainless-steel facade and a sustainable green roof. A landscaped courtyard shaded by honey locust trees is located between the train station and convenience store, and provides access to both buildings and to the train platform, as well as a delightful waiting room in good weather. Michael Van Valkenburgh Associates—in collaboration with Beyer Blinder Belle Architects and Planners, Rick Joy Architects, and Steven Holl Architects—was responsible for other components of the transit center landscape, including the transit plaza, the Lewis Center entry court, parking lots, and the streetscape. Located along the extension of Blair Walk that connects the original walk to the new transit plaza, the two station buildings constructed in 1918 are being rehabilitated by Rick Joy Architects and repurposed as a restaurant and a cafe. The cafe is located in the former north station building and the restaurant is located in the former baggage handling facility, expanded with a new wing. With the completion of the Arts Neighborhood project, and the continuing expansion of teaching and research in the arts, Princeton will realize the aspiration articulated in 2006 by President Emerita Shirley M. Tilghman.

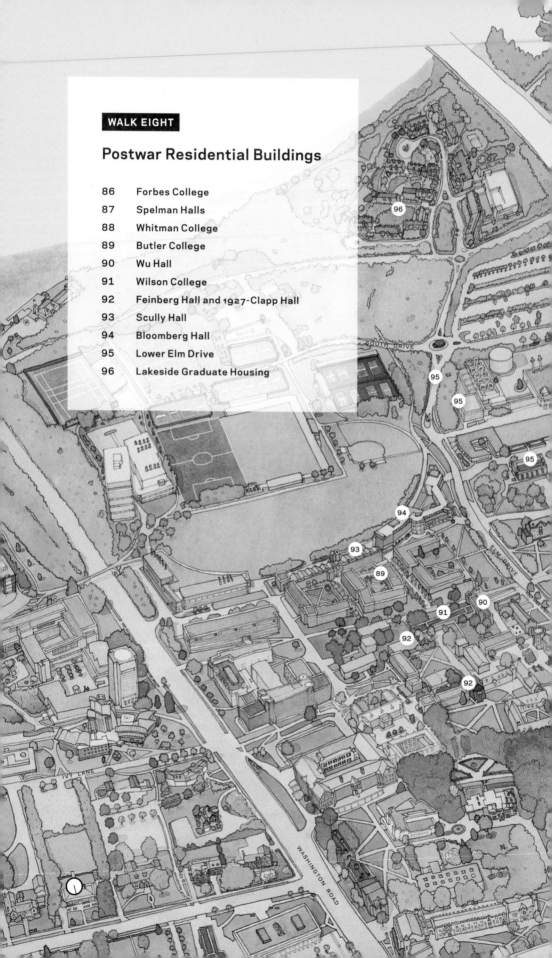

COLLEGE ROAD

DICKINSON PLACE

UNIVERSITY PLACE

Postwar Residential Buildings

THE RESIDENTIAL COLLEGE SYSTEM

The expansion of Princeton's residential college system from a two-year to a four-year plan in the early 2000s was a further step in the university's commitment over the past century to provide on-campus housing for all undergraduate students, on-campus dining for all freshmen and sophomores, and dining options for juniors and seniors in addition to the private eating clubs. The residential colleges are viewed as the nexus for the integration of the academic and nonacademic aspects of student life at Princeton. While Harvard and Yale developed residential colleges in the 1920s and 1930s, Princeton did not create its first residential college—named for Woodrow Wilson—until 1968 and did not begin to create a residential college system until 1982. Princeton's system placed all freshmen and sophomores in residential colleges, which were composed of then-existing dormitories; dining halls; and social, recreational, and study spaces. The system required only one additional facility, Wu Hall, in Butler College. Dormitories not assigned to residential colleges served then, and now, as housing for juniors and seniors. Most juniors and seniors continued to join eating clubs, although other dining options were made available to them.

In 2000 the trustees authorized a 10 percent increase in the undergraduate student body—from 4,700 to 5,200—and in implementing that plan, the university expanded from five to six residential colleges and designated three of them as four-year colleges. The new arrangements required construction of one

Aerial rendering of Butler College environs

new and one rebuilt residential college, renovations to existing colleges and dormitories, and pairing of four-year colleges with two-year colleges (Mathey with Rockefeller, Butler with Wilson, and Whitman with Forbes).

Walk Eight features four of the six residential colleges, two upperclass dormitories—Spelman Halls (also known as Spelman Hall) and Scully Hall—and one graduate student housing complex, all built or acquired since the end of the Second World War. The buildings that make up Rockefeller and Mathey Colleges—built in the early twentieth century as dormitories and dining commons and later aggregated into the residential college system—are featured in Walks Two and Three.

Forbes College facing Alexander Street

86   Forbes College
Andrew Jackson Thomas, 1924; Addition: Hillier Architecture, 1971; Renovation: Venturi, Rauch and Scott Brown, 1985

To accommodate an increase in student population precipitated by the admission of undergraduate women in 1969, the university needed additional dormitory space. The entire inaugural class of women lived in Pyne Hall. In 1970 the university purchased Princeton Inn on Alexander Street and converted the main building and annex to a dormitory. The annex formerly housed the hotel employees. An addition designed by J. Robert Hillier—a native Princetonian and graduate of the university's School of Architecture (MFA 1961)—connecting to the main building was then built to provide more rooms. In 1984, shortly after the university implemented the two-year residential college system, Venturi, Rauch and Scott Brown renovated the entire complex, which was renamed Forbes College. Today Forbes is paired with the four-year Whitman College. In addition to dorm rooms and dining facilities, the college contains the Norman Thomas 1905 Library, a digital media lab, and performing and visual arts studios.

The building's west terrace affords views of the Graduate College across the Springdale Golf Course. The current eighteen-hole golf course, which replaced a course built by the Princeton Golf Club around 1900, was constructed in 1915 on land donated to the university in 1909. The course is leased to a private club and also is used by university golf teams. It was reconfigured in 2007 with the construction of a new clubhouse at its southern end.

The 1924 Princeton Inn is designed in a Dutch Colonial Revival style. The east front, set back from Alexander Street, features a central three-story section with dormers in the sloped slate roof. End bays with a gambrel roofline are built with

Forbes College facing golf course

rough brick, while the central bay features a two-story portico with white-painted wood columns and recessed wood-clad walls. Two-story wings extend both north—in a meandering L-shaped configuration—and south, where the later addition forms an enclosed courtyard with bluestone pavers and plantings. The central section of the west facade is spanned by a two-story white-painted wood portico along its entire length. Tall windows in the first-floor public rooms provide views of the stone terrace, lawn, golf course, and Graduate College.

87   Spelman Halls
I. M. Pei & Partners, 1973

Head of a Woman
Designed by Pablo Picasso, 1962; Executed by Carl Nesjar, 1971
Cast concrete, granite, and quartzite

At Spelman Halls the classical preference for axial compositions and rational planning reach an unexpected apotheosis in the work of the renowned modern architect I. M. Pei. Pei and partner Harold Fredenburgh reinterpreted the familiar vocabulary of Princeton's quadrangles in a progression of linked triangles. The triangle is a geometric figure that has fascinated Pei most of his creative life; the East Building of the National Gallery of Art in Washington, D.C., and the glass pyramid outside the Louvre Museum in Paris are two well-known examples. Constructed of modern materials, including great expanses of concrete and glass, each of the eight buildings is similar to the next. Variety is achieved not by any change to the shape, but by aligning six dormitories on preexisting pedestrian paths and setting another pair among existing trees.

Spelman Halls

The university hired the firm in 1969 to study development opportunities on the southwestern corner of the campus, to better integrate the Princeton Inn—later Forbes College—with the historic campus to the east. Of the options studied, only student apartments were built at the time, Spelman Halls. Other elements of Pei's interim plan were later realized: relocation of the train station and construction of a theater, garage, and arts center. To achieve the desired integration the architect reinforced an existing diagonal path from Dillon Gym to the train station and the Princeton Inn by placing buildings on either side of the pathway. Openings between the buildings provide framed vistas and also align with existing building and site features, including an archway on the south side of Pyne Hall and an east-west pathway on the south side of Dillon Gym. The buildings are set within a grove of trees and are open to lawns on the north and south. In 2002 the concrete sculpture *Head of a Woman* was moved from McCormick Hall to a location just south of Spelman on axis with the north entrance of New South. Norwegian artist Carl

"*Head of a Woman*"

Nesjar executed Pablo Picasso's *Head of a Woman* in 1971 from a twelve-inch maquette that Picasso had completed in 1962. The huge sculpture was poured and then sandblasted on-site.

The program for Spelman Halls— apartments for 220 coeducational students, including six married couples— varies from traditional upperclass dormitories and provides an alternative to eating clubs. Each of the fifty-eight apartments is a complete domestic unit with living and dining areas, outside balcony, full kitchen, bath, and four bedrooms. The entry stairway, which is glazed for the full height of the building and skylighted, opens to the diagonal path and forms the dominant architectural element around which each building is organized. Here Pei designed an updated version of the Princeton entryway system (rather than a system of units connected by long corridors). Both in form and function, the shape of the buildings signals that a corner has been turned—a precise, hard-edged corner. If the Collegiate Gothic architect attempted to give the illusion, if not the reality, of hand-wrought materials, Pei leaves no doubt that what one sees are 979 precast floor and wall panels weighing up to thirty-eight thousand pounds each.

Contemporary construction techniques yielded certain savings for Spelman Halls. For instance, construction time, compared with traditional masonry construction, was cut in half from twenty-four to thirteen months. Also, the abstract geometric forms are undeniably arresting amid the organic ebb and flow of the surrounding landscape. The impact is amplified by the white color of the exterior walls that emphasizes the hard-edged geometry of the buildings' mass and contrasts with the natural setting and stone walls of the nearby Collegiate Gothic buildings. The inside concrete walls of each entry stair tower are painted a different bright color and further identified by a supergraphic numeral in the same color. Walking in, around, and under the buildings, the pedestrian level seems dramatic but also vaguely alienating in comparison to Spelman's Collegiate Gothic predecessors. Nevertheless, by consciously working within Princeton's older design tradition, Pei opened a door that architects such as Venturi and Scott Brown and Kliment and Halsband would walk through a decade later. Awarded the Pritzker Architecture Prize in 1983, Pei was the first of four Pritzker Laureates who have designed buildings for Princeton to date (Frank Gehry, Robert Venturi, and Rafael Moneo followed).

88 Whitman College (Fisher, Wendell, Lauritzen, Baker, 1981, and Hargadon Halls; Murley-Pivirotto Family Tower)

Porphyrios Associates with EYP Architecture and Engineering, 2007; Landscape: Quennell Rothschild & Partners; Landscape: Michael Van Valkenburgh Associates

Stardust

Bhakti Ziek, 2014; silk, Tencel, and metallic yarns
Princeton University

Whitman College is Princeton's first residential college built specifically for the four-year residential college system. Whitman is paired with the two-year Forbes College. The site, south of Dillon Gymnasium and most recently occupied by tennis courts, was large enough to accommodate a two-hundred-seventy-five-thousand-square-foot complex. The site plan fits seamlessly with the surrounding buildings, taking advantage of the topography—the site slopes north to south—and reinforcing existing pathways and vistas. The complex consists of six linked

Whitman College, Community Hall

buildings forming three-sided courtyards on two levels, a tower on the west, a great hall on the east, and a welcoming green space as foreground. The tennis courts, which supplanted the nineteenth-century Brokaw Field in the late 1950s, and the historic viewing platform were reconstructed near the Lenz Tennis Center in 2004, the latest stop in a ninety-year migration.

The choice of the Collegiate Gothic style of architecture and selection of Demetri Porphyrios (PhD 1980) as the design architect revealed a desire to connect with the defining characteristics of the era of Woodrow Wilson and Ralph Adams Cram (see Walk Three). However, returning to traditional architecture presented challenges for the designers and builders of Whitman College. Princeton's early twentieth-century Collegiate Gothic buildings—like their contemporaries at Yale, Penn, and elsewhere—were themselves a reinterpretation of medieval design and construction methods. By the early twenty-first century, building trades, codes, and lifestyles had changed. The traditional entryway system—with stairwells serving a limited number of interior rooms or suites—did not readily provide a second means of egress as required by current building and fire codes. The interior floor plans were therefore organized with corridors linking rooms and suites, resulting in fewer fire stairs and exterior doors and a wider building footprint. Compare the ground-level facades of Whitman College's dormitory buildings with those of nearby Cuyler Hall. In medieval masonry construction exterior walls are monolithic and support the floors and the roof. In contemporary construction masonry back-up walls or steel frames support the floors and roof, while the exterior masonry is a non-load-bearing veneer, set apart from the back-up or frame with a cavity containing insulation and air and vapor barriers. At Whitman both the back-up wall and the exterior masonry

Whitman College west facade and tower

are loadbearing, providing the mass and appearance of traditional masonry construction while incorporating the cavity necessary for climate control. However, elaborate stone-carved detail found in medieval and Gothic Revival buildings is limited in Whitman.

The project team considered various types of building stone for the exterior walls but finding a source presented challenges. Cope and Stewardson used the relatively uniform gray stone from Pennsylvania (Wissahickon schist) for early Collegiate Gothic dormitories, such as Blair Hall. Day and Klauder used a more variegated stone (Lockatong argillite) for later dormitories, such as Holder Hall. The project team concluded that no quarry could supply adequate quantities of either material for a project requiring six thousand tons of stone. Ultimately Porphyrios selected five varieties of bluestone from two different quarries, one in upstate New York and the other in central Pennsylvania. Masons blended the varieties off-site, producing a palette that resembles argillite. Porphyrios used Indiana limestone to clad Community Hall and several prominent arcades, as well as for trim around windows, corners, rooflines, and elsewhere on the building. Limestone's light uniform color, smooth surface, and visually minimal joints serve to distinguish those elements from ones clad in bluestone.

Inside, Community Hall is a spacious, high-ceilinged dining hall with a stone floor, wood-paneled walls, a timber-framed ceiling, and a fireplace reminiscent of the former freshman and sophomore Commons at Madison Hall. However, the servery is up-to-date, as are the food offerings, in keeping with renovations to food service facilities in the other residential colleges. In 2014 *Stardust*, a six-panel jacquard tapestry handwoven by fabric artist Bhatki Ziek, was installed on the north wall in

Community Hall. Created on her Vermont loom over the course of ten months, each of the sixteen-foot panels is woven with silk, Tencel, and metallic yarns. The other common spaces are fitted with furniture and finishes reminiscent of traditional residence halls and eating clubs, while providing contemporary conveniences, such as flat-screen TVs, wireless data transmitters, and air-conditioning. Other spaces include a sixty-five-seat theater with lighting grid and stepped seating, a library, and a suite for the Writing Program entered directly from Tilghman Walk.

The landscape, designed by Michael Van Valkenburgh Associates, integrates the complex into the campus as if it had always been there, with several three-sided quadrangles similar to earlier Collegiate Gothic dormitory buildings, large broad lawns facing Elm Drive and Butler College to the east, and an extension of the stream valley woodlands along the west side. Large cedar of Lebanon trees, craned into place after building construction was complete, enhance the illusion of a centuries-old complex.

89   Butler College (Yoseloff, Wilf, Bogle, 1967, and 1976 Halls)
Pei Cobb Freed & Partners, 2009; Landscape: Michael Van Valkenburgh Associates

Up and Away
Odili Donald Odita, 2009; acrylic latex wall paint
Princeton University

Across Elm Drive from Whitman College is a recent complex of dormitories and common spaces belonging to Butler College. The complex replaced dormitories called the "New New Quad," designed by Hugh Stubbins in 1964. (The "New Quad"

Butler College with Butler memorial stele in foreground

Butler Memorial Courtyard

was the informal name of the 1960 Wilson College buildings.) The initial Butler College was dedicated in 1983 as one of the new two-year residential colleges. With the advent of the four-year residential college system in 2007, the university replaced the forty-year-old dormitories of the "New New Quad" with ones better suited to new program and student preferences.

Henry Cobb, senior partner in the firm Pei Cobb Freed (PCF), designed the new Butler College dormitories. (PCF is the successor firm to I. M. Pei & Partners, architect of Spelman Halls.) Cobb's design is confidently contemporary, but the site plan, materials, and details recall the variety and intimacy of Princeton's Collegiate Gothic precedents. The site plan—developed in concert with landscape architect Michael Van Valkenburgh Associates (MVVA) and the Campus Plan team—responds to various preexisting conditions and constraints. On the north Wu Hall and Wilson College face Goheen Walk, which intersects Washington Road at an oblique angle. Cobb and other architects working in this area take advantage of this geometric anomaly to align their buildings or different wings of their buildings with one or the other axis, creating interesting juxtapositions. The eastern section of the Butler College dormitories nestles into the open L-shaped courtyard of Scully Hall. The western section relates to Bloomberg Hall on the south.

Cobb's design consists of five buildings varying from two to four stories above grade linked by a common lower level. He expressed the larger suites of rooms on the upper floors with projecting, curvilinear bays on the exterior and reinforced the horizontal motion suggested by the bays with elongated bricks (twelve inches rather than the conventional eight) and horizontal bands of limestone trim. The trim is flush with the brick and placed at seemingly random intervals.

Sunken courtyards bring light into the lower level, where the college's main common spaces—a studio, cafe, lounge, gallery, and several classrooms—are located, and provide outdoor green spaces for building occupants. Inspired by the design and purpose of Butler College, Odili Donald Odita's mural *Up and Away* spans two floors in the main entry area for the common spaces. Angular abstractions of bright colors bring dynamism to otherwise static white walls and suggest an energy rising through the building. The below-grade placement of the large contiguous common area allows the above-grade levels to have the scale of individual buildings with many portals. New academic buildings, including the Andlinger Center for Energy and the Environment and the Lewis Center for the Arts, use a similar site and massing strategy.

The east courtyard—named Butler Memorial Courtyard in honor of individual donors and classes who provided funds for the "New New Quad"—is in the form of a Greek theater intended to evoke ancient ruins that have merged with the landscape over time. PCF and MVVA designed the theater with larch trees, grass terraces, stone retaining walls, and ramps leading to a circular patio paved with bluestone from the former buildings' courtyard.

90   Wu Hall
Venturi, Rauch and Scott Brown, 1983

Wu Hall houses the social and dining facilities for Butler College. The need for such a facility arose from the 1982 implementation of the residential college system. President William G. Bowen (1972–88) wanted Wu Hall to demonstrate a renewed commitment to architectural design excellence at Princeton. Advised by Provost Neil Rudenstine and Dean Robert Geddes of the School of Architecture, who both shared his vision, Bowen recommended Venturi, Rauch and Scott Brown (VRSB) for the commission. At the time VRSB was at work renovating the dining halls and dormitories of Rockefeller and Mathey Colleges, two of the first residential colleges in the new system, and Blair Hall. Wu Hall was the firm's first new construction project at Princeton, followed by many additions and freestanding buildings over the next twenty years.

The site for Wu Hall includes a narrow frontage on Goheen Walk and a long extension northward between Wilcox Hall and 1915 Hall. A north–south walkway, which connects Cuyler and 1913 Halls with Goheen Walk, descends along the west side of the site. VRSB's design for the building exploits these site constraints and opportunities. The architects attached the east side of the building to Wilcox, utilizing the existing kitchen for Wu Hall's servery and dining hall. They eased the northern part of the east side to expand a small courtyard set among other Wilson College buildings. On the Goheen Walk frontage they projected a two-story bay window that asserts the building's presence while maintaining pedestrian flow. They placed the main entrance on the west side accessed by a widened portion of the descending north–south walkway. Opposite the juncture of the walkway and

Wu Hall

Goheen Walk, they placed a brick-and-limestone stele—a freestanding, flattened column inscribed with a memorial to Lee D. Butler (Class of 1922)—with a cartoon tiger perched on top and a sundial on the south side. To provide service access to Wu and Wilcox Halls, they created a ramp from Elm Drive, under the entrance plaza, and screened it with a brick-faced retaining wall.

VRSB clad the structural frame of the building with a brick-and-glass curtain wall. The architects display this strategy on the first floor of the west side, where freestanding interior columns are set back from a lightweight metal-and-glass exterior wall. In a gesture to traditional university masonry buildings, they detailed the bay window facing Goheen Walk with substantial limestone piers and framed the multipaned windows with thin, gray-painted mullions. The most striking—and photographed—element of the composition is the dark-gray-granite-and-white-marble panel over the west entrance. Here, VRSB translated its knowledge of architectural history into a flattened, abstracted, overscaled pattern of circles, rectangles, and triangles, based on the representation of a sixteenth-century, two-story, three-part gate.

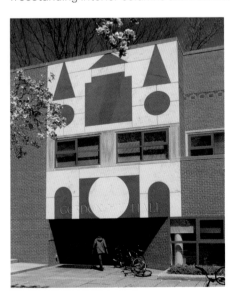

Wu Hall entrance

The firm combined an expression of contemporary construction methods with traditional university masonry construction and historical European precedents to create a new aesthetic: postmodernism.

The interior likewise blends contemporary and traditional spaces and materials. The dining hall on the main level features solid oak tables, wainscoting, banquettes, and chairs modeled after ones found in the early twentieth-century Commons in Madison Hall. However, the custom-designed pendant light fixtures are unlike any other fixture seen at Princeton. The main entrance opens to a spacious tile-floored lobby that gives access to the dining hall on the right and a broad wood stair to the left. The stair has conventional treads and risers as well as overscaled ones that create platforms for informal seating. At the landing is a bay window that echoes the one facing Goheen Walk. The stair leads to lounges, study areas, and college offices on the second floor.

Wu Hall was pivotal, both for the careers of Robert Venturi and Denise Scott Brown, and for architectural design at Princeton University. It was also pivotal in its site strategy, demonstrating how thoughtful site planning can fill in amorphous spaces, relate stylistically diverse buildings, and connect pathways and green spaces. The building received a national AIA Honor Award in 1984.

91   Wilson College
(Wilcox, Dodge-Osborn, Gauss, 1937, 1938, and 1939 Halls)
Sherwood, Mills, and Smith, 1961; Addition and renovation: Michael Graves and Associates, 2009

Founded in 1968, Woodrow Wilson College is the oldest of the six residential colleges and houses more than five hundred students. Designed by the modernist firm Sherwood, Mills, and Smith, the complex initially encompassed five dormitories and common areas that included a dining hall. In the 1980s the university added Feinberg Hall and 1927-Clapp Hall to Wilson College, as well as Walker Hall, designed in 1930 by Charles Z. Klauder.

Lester W. Smith (Class of 1930) and his firm were charged with employing a style other than Collegiate Gothic for the first residential–dining hall complex the university had built in more than forty years. The manner was to be modern with a nod to the traditional. Consistent with this precinct, the construction would be brick with limestone trim around the windows. In plan the scheme for what came to be called the "New Quad" looked to Ludwig Mies van der Rohe's 1940 master plan for the Illinois Institute of Technology (IIT) campus, including repetitive rectangular slabs and flat roofs but without the Miesian exposed steel-frame structural system. The IIT scheme had been widely published and hailed as the first truly modern campus design. However, at Princeton the architects arranged the buildings in a more relaxed, open quadrangle, responding to the sloping terrain and the presence of existing buildings. In the years since its dedication, nature and Princeton's deservedly famous landscaping have softened the raw edges of the "New Quad."

The "New Quad" offered the first dining hall conveniently located on the south side of the campus (Wilcox Hall). Michael Graves—the internationally known Princeton-based architect—designed a new entrance to Wilcox Hall in 2009, as well as the renovation of the dining hall and servery. (Graves, a longtime professor at the university's School of Architecture, was ineligible to receive campus building commissions until his transfer to emeritus status.) The three-story entrance with a new elevator and stair provides a companion piece to Wu Hall's rounded bay window on Goheen Walk and a focal point to Lourie-Love Walk that leads from the Ellipse through Butler College to the entry to Wilcox Hall.

Wilson College, Wilcox Hall addition

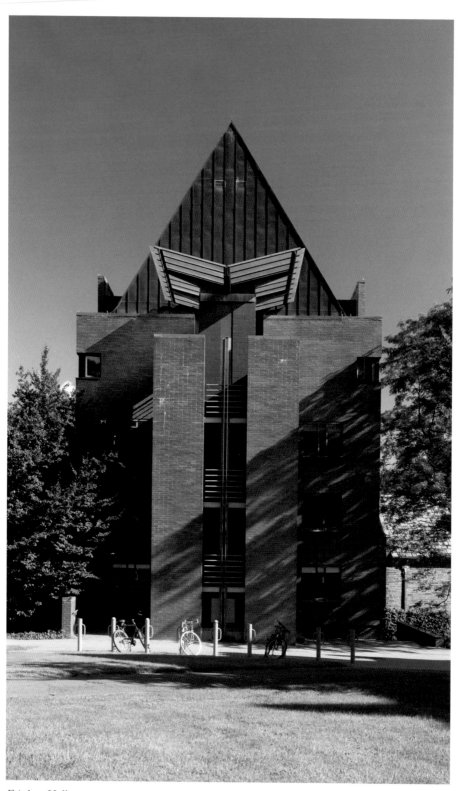

Feinberg Hall

Feinberg Hall
Tod Williams Billie Tsien Architects, 1986

1927-Clapp Hall
Koetter Kim and Associates, 1987

Feinberg Hall and 1927-Clapp Hall shift back into the world of the vertical. Both starkly define as well as stand apart from the rest of the "New Quad" with its repetition, parallel lines, and right angles. Feinberg architects Tod Williams (Class of 1965) and Billie Tsien used towers, steeply pitched gable roofs, light, and shadow— a Gothic if not Victorian sensibility—to create a building that acts as a wayfinder, like Holder and Blair towers. By constricting the pedestrian passage from the upper campus down into the Wilson College court, Feinberg reinterpreted in strictly contemporary imagery the movement through a Collegiate Gothic archway, from one outdoor room to the next.

Two stair towers reinforce the perpendicular. The prefabricated interior stair system, with green Vermont slate treads, spirals around a narrow shaft of space connecting the ground floor to a skylight. The exterior north stair is a small tower unto itself, encircling an elevator shaft and topped by an inverted steel-and-wire glass canopy, which mimics the steeply pitched roof. The tower is tied back to the building at the landings. It provides an alternate circulation path as well as back porches to the student suites. The effect is visually interesting, accommodates the social needs of the occupants, and imaginatively fulfills the requirements of the state fire codes.

Eighty feet tall, the forty-by-forty-foot building features brick and block bearing-wall construction with wooden floors on concrete planking. There is a marked interest in the texture of exterior materials and details. For instance, the brick is overscaled and the color is a rich plum, or aubergine, with iron spotting. The joints are raked horizontally to help give the primarily vertical building a sense of weight. Windows are steel and glass, and the steeply inclined roof is a steel frame clad in standing-seam copper. In Feinberg it is clear that in the hands of a creative architect, mass-produced materials can be made to yield a sense of craft. In 1988 Feinberg Hall received an AIA Honor Award for design excellence.

Like Feinberg, 1927-Clapp fills a gap between existing dormitory buildings and creates a transition between upper- and lower-level courts. While Williams and Tsien placed Feinberg at an angle to the orthogonal grid of Wilson College, Koetter Kim followed the grid. While Williams and Tsien placed the stair connecting the courts to one side of Feinberg, Koetter Kim created an archway near the midpoint of the building and placed the stair and building entries within this enclosure. 1927-Clapp completes the south edge of a large courtyard defined by the original Wilson College dormitories. The north facade facing this courtyard is scaled to align with

1927-Clapp Hall north facade

the existing buildings, while the south facade—because of the sloping site—is one story higher and features a gable that accentuates the vertical effect. Despite 1927-Clapp Hall's stylistic departure from Feinberg Hall and the original Wilson College buildings, Koetter Kim's choice of exterior materials (red brick with limestone trim, slate, and gray metal) and details (multipaned windows, stringcourses) is similar to traditional campus buildings, as well as Venturi, Rauch and Scott Brown's reinterpretation of these.

93   Scully Hall

Machado and Silvetti Associates, 1998; Courtyard landscape: Louise Schiller; Ellipse landscape: Quennell Rothschild & Partners

Scully Hall follows in the tradition of dormitory buildings forming the edge of campus, like Blair, Buyers, and Little Halls. Entrances and courtyards face the campus side and a wall-like facade faces the world beyond—represented here by the Ellipse. In its 1995 campus plan the architectural and planning firm Machado and Silvetti Associates proposed reshaping Poe and Pardee Fields into an elliptical form, framed by future buildings, with a continuous perimeter walk. This simple but powerful concept became the armature for siting new buildings over the next generation of southward expansion. The firm designed Scully Hall to establish the geometry of the Ellipse and form the southern edge of campus. (This southern edge continued to shift south within a generation of the Ellipse's construction.) With its stern, square tower and saw-toothed gables faced in slate, the elongated south wing of Scully evokes the historic Collegiate Gothic models of campus.

Scully Hall south facade

Scully played several strategic roles in the development of campus. Not only did it define an edge; it also provided much-needed swing space as Princeton upgraded and modernized its large stock of older residential facilities in the first decade of the twenty-first century. Upgrading included everything from wiring for data transmission to compliance with new fire and accessibility codes. But it also signified reorchestrating the interior architecture of existing dormitories to advance a changed view of what dormitory life should be. Thus, Scully became a prototype for later twenty-first-century dormitories.

The design revolution led by Scully Hall was largely internal or programmatic. This meant comfortable shared living of the sexes; access for people with disabilities; a revision to the traditional system of entries so that residents have an alternate escape route in the event of fire; internet access and private bath space; rooms for advisors; and more public spaces, such as libraries, laundries, and conference rooms. Compare this to the domestic rigors endured by Princeton's first students. For the first one hundred years students had to look after their own needs. The unwritten contract only required the college to provide an education. However, students at the beginning of the twenty-first century expect the university to accommodate residential as well as social needs, often under one roof. It is this expectation that has driven and shaped Princeton's growth in residential facilities.

Nothing quite so revolutionary happens on the exterior. Machado and Silvetti continued Venturi's practice of drawing on Princeton's design history by adopting and adapting a number of its defining characteristics, including the great tower and arch (note Princeton's shield above the arch). Variety of texture is achieved not by Gothic handcraftsmanship, but by the manipulation of machine-made materials,

Scully Hall north courtyard

including brick of varying sizes and patterns and, on the south side, striated precast concrete V-shaped panels with inset aluminum casement windows. A landscaped setback from the Ellipse walkway designed by Quennell Rothschild & Partners—densely planted with euonymus, laurel, and wild roses—softens the concrete facade and provides privacy for ground-floor dorm rooms. The common room of each of the three Scully wings is painted in a brilliant saturated color—red, blue, or green—that glows in the night. The three sides of Scully form the latest in the ongoing series of Princeton's great outdoor rooms, with plantings designed by landscape architect Louise Schiller.

94 Bloomberg Hall

Michael Dennis and Associates, 2000; Landscape: Quennell Rothschild & Partners

Wall Drawing #1134, Whirls and Twirls (Princeton)
Sol LeWitt, 2004; acrylic paint
Princeton University, gift of the Bloomberg family

Built as an upperclass dormitory in 2004, Bloomberg Hall became part of Butler College with the implementation of the four-year residential college system. The architect Michael Dennis conceived the dormitory when the "New New Quad" dormitories of Butler College were still standing. He designed Bloomberg in the context of old Butler, and Henry Cobb subsequently designed the new Butler College dormitories in the context of Bloomberg Hall. They fit together seamlessly.

Dennis's site plan for Bloomberg Hall also helps to define the Ellipse. Bloomberg is one of three buildings fronting the north side of the Ellipse (the others are Scully Hall and Icahn Laboratory). Although the building follows the geometry of the Ellipse, Dennis indented the central section to create a large three-sided courtyard. The partly paved, partly planted courtyard is prime space for people-watching and sunbathing, given its southeast orientation toward Poe Field. From Elm Drive one enters the courtyard, a section of Tilghman Walk, through a two-story archway. On the ceiling is a work by Sol LeWitt. A leading proponent of minimalism, LeWitt would prepare guidelines and diagrams for his murals, then outsource the labor to others. The instructions for *Wall Drawing #1134, Whirls and Twirls (Princeton)* not only indicated the width of the color bands but also specified that no colored section may touch another section of the same color.

The P-rade, the annual alumni reunions procession, which starts at Nassau Hall and proceeds south on Elm Drive, passes through this archway on its way to

Bloomberg Hall

Poe Field. (The P-rade once followed a route from Nassau Hall through the 1879 Hall archway, along Prospect Avenue, and through Ferris Thompson Gateway to the former university field—now the E-Quad—where the annual Princeton-Yale baseball game was played.) Another one-story passage connects the courtyard to the pathways of Butler College and beyond. The meandering plan configuration, punctured by archways, is reminiscent of the Collegiate Gothic Blair, Buyers, and Little Halls.

The building's design reflects the university's residential programs and responds to external cues. Bloomberg comprises a range of single bedrooms with shared bathrooms, singles with hall baths, and three- and four-bedroom suites with shared baths; a mix of common rooms—study lounges and social spaces; student organization spaces—the campus radio station, WPRB; and rehearsal studios for a cappella singing groups and dance groups. Dormitory rooms are located on all four floors, accessed by corridors on the upper three floors and a modified entryway system on the ground floor. The four-story facades have a base clad in gray-slate panels, two intermediate floors clad in red-orange brick and limestone, and an upper floor clad in gray-slate shingles. This pattern is interrupted by strongly articulated

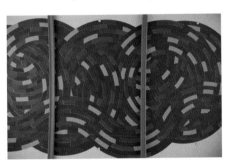

full-height, metal-framed window walls that correspond to common rooms, stairwells, and in some cases residential suites. The shingles and projecting V-shaped window bays relate to Bloomberg's neighbor Scully Hall, and the brick shade and bond pattern are reminiscent of early twentieth-century buildings like 1879 Hall and Jones Hall.

"Wall Drawing #1134, Whirls and Twirls (Princeton)"

95   Lower Elm Drive
Landscape: Michael Van Valkenburgh Associates, 2008

West Garage
Enrique Norten of TEN Arquitectos with Walker Parking Consultants, 2004

200 Elm Drive (former Boiler House)
Day and Klauder, 1925; Renovation: Clarke Caton Hintz, 2005

Chiller Plant Addition
Leers Weinzapfel Associates, 2005

Visitors and members of the campus community are likely to enter campus from the south via Elm Drive. This shift from the historic eighteenth-century entrance on Nassau Street—memorialized by FitzRandolph Gate—and the nineteenth-century train station at the foot of Blair Hall reflects the automobile's role as the twentieth century's dominant form of transportation. Elm Drive, which terminates at Nassau Street on the north and Faculty Road on the south, is the only north–south vehicular route through the historic campus. Today the university maintains a pedestrian-friendly environment by parking cars at the periphery and encouraging walking and alternative modes of transportation, including shuttle buses and bicycles, to circulate on campus. The West Garage, designed by Enrique Norten of TEN Arquitectos with Walker Parking Consultants and built in 2004, serves parking needs on the western part of campus. The long and narrow garage parallels the railroad tracks; the west side forms a backdrop to the transit plaza buildings and the north side faces an arrival plaza. Norten designed a stainless steel scrim to enliven the north and west facades of the garage.

Woodlands, a stream corridor, and gently sloping terrain provide a welcoming setting for the Elm Drive entrance to campus. Michael Van Valkenburgh Associates enhanced the stream valley landscape by adding dense plantings along the drive, effectively linking Lake Carnegie woodlands to Whitman College, and reconstructed pathways east to the playing fields and south to graduate student housing. Nearby the university's landscape team thinned the woodlands west of Bedford Field, revealing a row of mature redwood trees previously obscured by undergrowth. Additional redwoods were planted and a new path through the grove connects to an older path, Butler Walk, south of Faculty Road that leads to the Shea Rowing Center.

On the west side of Elm Drive, across from the South Drive athletic fields, are the university's central energy plant and other Facilities Department buildings. Energy conservation and reduction of greenhouse gas emissions are key components of the university's 2008 Sustainability Plan. The energy plant—which generates electricity, steam, and chilled water for campus buildings—evolved from the first central, coal-fired boiler plant to today's multibuilding complex, including

Lower Elm Drive looking north; Walk to Boathouse

a cogeneration facility, chillers, cooling towers, and thermal storage. The boiler house, designed by Day and Klauder and built in 1925, was decommissioned in 1996. A 2005 renovation by Clarke Caton Hintz removed an addition on the east side of the building, exposing an intact Collegiate Gothic facade that features a three-story arched window wall. Public Safety and the Office of Design and Construction occupy the renovated boiler house, now known as 200 Elm Drive. The cogeneration facility generates electricity from burning natural gas and produces steam as a useful by-product. While many energy plant facilities appear utilitarian, the 2005 addition to the chiller plant fits beautifully into its natural surroundings. The architectural firm Leers Weinzapfel Associates enclosed the equipment on two sides with stone masonry (schist) walls and the ends with all-glass curtain walls, which—depending on ambient light and orientation—reflect the landscape or reveal the machinery within.

The university is also developing renewable energy sources to help achieve its energy conservation and emissions reduction goals. Geothermal wells augment heating and cooling systems by using the moderate temperature of the earth (between 45 and 54 degrees) to offset extremes of winter cold and summer heat. The university constructed geothermal wells at the Lawrence Apartments on the south end of the golf course, Lakeside Graduate Housing, and the Lewis Center for the Arts. In 2012 the university installed an array of solar collectors on the West Windsor fields—at the time the largest installation on any campus in the United States—that supplies approximately 5 percent of campus electricity usage.

96   Lakeside Graduate Housing
Studio Ma, 2015; Landscape: Hoehn Landscape Architecture

As its name suggests, Lakeside Graduate Housing borders Lake Carnegie. The area includes woodlands that recall the extent of forest that used to exist in this area along the Stony Brook and Millstone River. The Hibben and Magie faculty and staff apartments, constructed in phases on the site in the early 1960s, were demolished to allow redevelopment for graduate student housing. The 2007 Housing Master Plan envisioned building new housing to supplement the Graduate College, Lawrence Apartments, and other graduate student housing. The plan also envisions additional faculty and staff housing in downtown Princeton on the redeveloped Merwick and Stanworth properties. Once these projects are complete, the university plans to demolish the Butler Tract housing (post–Second World War barracks that were converted to graduate housing).

Lakeside provides a mix of two- and three-story townhouse units and four- and five-story apartment buildings set among existing and newly planted trees, a woodland path, an outdoor commons area, and rain gardens. Architectural firm Studio Ma sited the new buildings to maximize vistas toward the lake and to optimize solar orientation. The new buildings are located on the footprint of the former apartment buildings and parking lots to minimize impact on the woodlands. The buildings create a sense of community by focusing activity on streets and courtyards, and by a massing that provides variety and intimacy. In this regard Lakeside is similar to traditional student housing, such as the Graduate College, and to contemporary undergraduate housing, such as Butler College. A five-level parking garage, screened by trees and housing, replaced a paved surface parking lot.

The landscape architecture firm Hoehn Landscape Architecture preserved important woodland groves and added new plantings appropriate to the site's varied

Lakeside Graduate Housing rendering

ecological zones. Grasses and perennials occupy lowland meadows, while ferns and native shrubs form the understory of upland woods. Existing woodlands were supplemented with several hundred new trees. Rain gardens and subsurface detention manage storm water to prevent flooding and improve water quality before the storm water flows into the lake. Hard surfaces of cul-de-sacs and breezeways are constructed with permeable paving to allow water to percolate into the ground, rather than flow into the storm-water system.

With the four-year residential college system for undergraduate students in place, and the Housing Master Plan guiding development of graduate student, faculty, and staff housing, the university is now well positioned to accommodate housing needs for members of the university community for the foreseeable future.

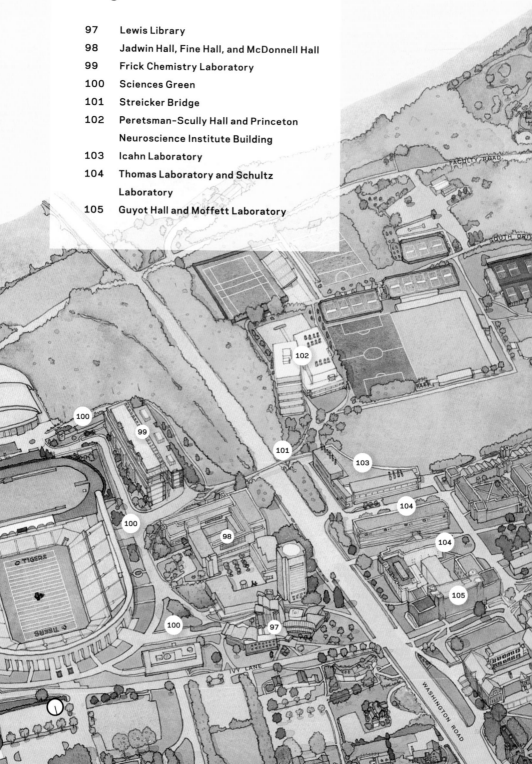

WALK NINE

Natural Sciences Neighborhood

ELM DRIVE

Natural Sciences Neighborhood

CONTEMPORARY SCIENCE LABORATORIES IN A NATURAL SETTING

Natural science laboratories at Princeton have historically clustered along Washington Road. Starting in the 1870s President McCosh erected a series of specialized laboratory buildings on both sides of Washington Road south of Nassau Street (see Walk Four) to elevate the academic standing of teaching and research in the natural sciences. The first, the John C. Green School of Science, stood on the site of present-day Firestone Library. Although the building's masonry exterior walls appeared indestructible, the floors and roofs were made of combustible materials and the building was destroyed by fire in 1928. The Class of 1877 Biological Laboratory was constructed on an adjacent site and remained until demolished for Firestone Library in 1946. Succeeding administrations built additional laboratory buildings on the east side of Washington Road— Aaron Burr Hall (chemistry), Frick Chemistry Laboratory, and Green Hall (engineering)—and further south on the west side, Palmer Hall (physics and math) and Guyot Hall (geology and biology).

Beginning in the 1960s—spurred by an influx of federal funding for scientific research and the obsolescence of the first generation of laboratory buildings—and continuing to the present, the university gradually relocated natural science facilities from the north end of Washington Road to the south,

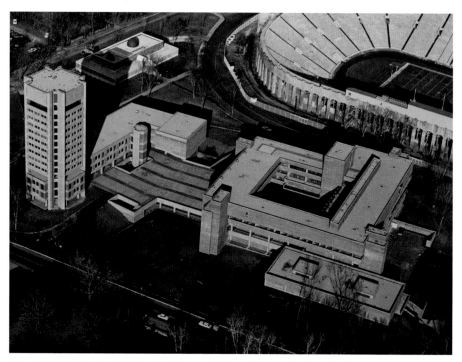

Fine Hall (left), Jadwin Hall (right), Peyton Hall and Palmer Stadium (top)

below Guyot Hall at Ivy Lane. The physics and mathematics departments moved
from the former Palmer Hall and Fine (now Jones) Hall to the Jadwin-Fine
complex in 1969; the chemistry department moved from old Frick to new Frick
in 2010; and the psychology department moved from Green Hall to Peretsman-
Scully Hall in 2013. Engineering moved east from Green Hall to the Engineering
Quadrangle in 1962. Relocation of these departments from their original homes
has provided an opportunity to adapt these older buildings to new uses. Also
during this time the university constructed new buildings for emerging scientific
disciplines, including astrophysical sciences (Peyton Hall), molecular biology
(Thomas and Schultz Laboratories), genomics (Icahn Laboratory), and neuroscience (Princeton Neuroscience Institute). Lewis Library consolidated natural sciences departmental libraries into a new building.

The 2008 Campus Plan envisioned a Natural Sciences Neighborhood
flanking Washington Road, integrating existing and planned buildings with
improved landscape, pathways, and roadways. As Washington Road slopes south
toward Lake Carnegie through this neighborhood, natural woodlands and the
character of the stream corridor become more prominent. This stream valley
was one of the original main entries to the town and campus and was heavily
wooded until modern times. A major goal of the campus plan has been to restore
the stream and adjacent woodlands in order to enhance the watershed and the
contemporary experience of this gateway. Existing walks have been restored
and new walks constructed. A new pedestrian bridge joins the two halves of the
Natural Sciences Neighborhood, while also connecting residential facilities west
of Washington Road with athletics facilities east of Washington Road. The
sloping topography, restored woodlands, and new campus landscapes minimize
the impact of the large footprints and bulk of contemporary science laboratories
and enhance the experience of entering campus and town from the south.

97   Lewis Library
Gehry Partners, 2008; Landscape: Quennell Rothschild & Partners

Lewis Library is the natural sciences' counterpart to Firestone Library, the research center for the humanities and social sciences. Historically the natural sciences libraries had been housed within individual departments, such as the math-physics library, the largest of the specialized libraries, which was located in the Jadwin–Fine–McDonnell complex. An open site just north of Fine Hall proved to be an ideal location to consolidate the dispersed science libraries. The site performs several strategic functions and acts as an anchor of the Natural Sciences Neighborhood as it develops to the south along both sides of Washington Road. It also provides a pathway between the Frist Campus Center and Princeton Stadium through the building, and common ground between the Engineering Quadrangle and the Natural Sciences Neighborhood linked by the walkway connecting Prospect Avenue and Ivy Lane.

While Lewis Library houses some traditional library functions—compact book shelving, collaborative and individual study spaces, and librarians' offices—it primarily provides access to electronic resources and digital maps and is also home to a computational science and engineering research institute; a high-performance data center; a media center; and an array of classrooms, seminar rooms, group study rooms, and informal gathering spaces. As part of the media center, a video recording studio links the university to network and cable news stations, and increasingly serves professors who record their lectures and conduct video conferences for on-campus and online distribution.

Lewis Library (left) and Fine Hall (right)

Architect Frank Gehry's avant-garde design for Lewis Library contrasts radically with Demetri Porphyrios's Collegiate Gothic design for Whitman College completed the year before. Princeton had abandoned Collegiate Gothic and adopted modern architecture as the preferred style for new buildings after the Second World War. While some excellent examples of modern architecture were realized,

Lewis Library atrium

there were also several mediocre examples, prompting some trustees and alumni to urge a return to traditional styles. A detente between modernism and historicism emerged in the late 1970s, largely through the vision of long-serving university architect Jon Hlafter (Class of 1961, MFA 1963) and the practice of Venturi, Scott Brown and Associates. Princeton had room for both, and cared about both. While some observers prefer one style over the other, both Gehry's and Porphyrios's designs are characteristic of Princeton, each in its own way.

The tall central portion of Lewis Library mediates between Fine Hall tower and the residential scale of Ivy Lane. The building entrance from the corner of Ivy Lane and Washington Road is located on a diagonal path that passes through the building's central space and leads to Peyton Hall and Princeton Stadium. The arched intersecting roofline of the two-story wing facing Washington Road, affectionately known as the "turtle" or "tree house," contains a wonderful space that is in high demand by students as well as event planners. The central open space is alive with natural light and vibrant color. A delightful characteristic of Gehry's design aesthetic is the ability to see through his buildings, from the interior of one element to the exterior of another. One can experience this delight from the central space and from other transitional spaces in the building.

98   Jadwin Hall, Fine Hall, and McDonnell Hall

Jadwin Hall
Hugh Stubbins and Associates, 1970; Renovation: Payette Associates, 2008

Fine Hall
Warner, Burns, Toan, and Lunde, 1969

McDonnell Hall
Gwathmey Siegel and Associates, 1998

Five Disks: One Empty
Alexander Calder, 1970; painted mild steel

Construction in the Third and Fourth Dimension
Antoine Pevsner, 1962; cast bronze

Sphere VI
Arnaldo Pomodoro, 1966; polished bronze

The Department of Physics and the Department of Mathematics were among the vanguard of natural science departments to move from upper Washington Road to the area south of Ivy Lane in the late 1960s. Peyton Hall, the home of the Department of Astrophysical Sciences, and Moffett Laboratory, appended to

Guyot Hall, anticipated these moves in the early 1960s. Physics had been located in Palmer Hall since 1908 and mathematics had been located in the original Fine Hall, designed by Charles Z. Klauder and built in 1931 as an addition to Palmer. Since the Fine name—in honor of Henry Burchard Fine, first chair of the Department of Mathematics (1904-28)—moved with the building, the original Fine Hall was renamed Jones Hall. In the late 1990s, when planners repurposed Palmer Hall for the Frist Campus Center, they moved the remaining physics lecture and demonstration halls, teaching laboratories, and classrooms to a new building named McDonnell Hall at the Jadwin-Fine site.

The composition of these buildings, designed by three different architects over a span of thirty years, reflects a geometric anomaly: the intersection of Washington Road and Nassau Street is not a right angle but an acute angle, offset by seventeen degrees. Goheen Walk—the east-west walkway that connects the Jadwin-Fine-McDonnell complex east of Washington Road to Elm Drive in the center of the historic core—is parallel to Nassau Street. Fine Hall is parallel to Goheen Walk, Jadwin Hall is parallel to Washington Road, and McDonnell Hall takes a hybrid approach: the base is aligned with Jadwin and the upper stories are aligned with Fine Hall. These alignments may not be significant to the casual observer, but in architectural terms they are. However, characteristic of many of the campus's large science buildings of this era, more attention was paid to maximizing research space than to integrating the structures into the campus landscape. The campus's traditional emphasis on vistas and pathways, so formative in the shaping of buildings in the historic core of campus, was absent from areas developed in the mid-twentieth century.

Fine Hall (left), McDonnell Hall (center), and Jadwin Hall (right)

As with site planning, the massing of the buildings expresses different approaches. Fine Hall is a ten-story tower with a small floor plate set on a three-story base, whereas Jadwin is a six-story, horizontally banded building with a large footprint. The two buildings are joined by upper and lower plazas over a lower level that provides lobby and circulation space for lecture halls and connects below grade with Lewis Library and Frick Chemistry Building. The lobby contains a sculpture by Arnaldo Pomodoro. Pomodoro's *Spheres* series of the 1960s was characterized by forms partially eaten away by internal erosion. Princeton University has one of the earliest examples of Pomodoro's new spheres, known as *Rotanti* (Rotors) and distinguished by their potential mobility. McDonnell Hall fills in the Washington Road

McDonnell Hall

frontage, providing closure to the lower plaza and a focal point at the end of Goheen Walk. The Fine Hall tower is the eastern counterpoint to Holder Tower in the historic core and Cleveland Tower at the Graduate College to the west.

The site planning and massing of the buildings derive from their various functions. Fine Hall contains faculty offices and seminar rooms for teaching mathematics and theoretical research. Jadwin Hall contains large laboratories and a high-bay block that formerly housed a cyclotron (particle accelerator) and now houses low-vibration apparatuses and clean rooms. In 2008 the department converted part of the upper floor of Jadwin from underused graduate study space to the Center for Theoretical Science. Designed by Payette Associates, this space is expressed on the north facade—visible from the lower plaza—and east facade by a window wall that replaced the original windowless brick wall. The physics lecture and demonstration halls are embedded in the lower level of McDonnell. The upper levels contain teaching laboratories facing Washington Road and classrooms facing the lower plaza.

The architectural design of Jadwin and Fine can be characterized as mid-century modern—a style derived from the International Style of modernism developed in Europe in the interwar period, but with an expanded range of forms, palette of colors, and articulation of surfaces. McDonnell serves as a generational link between the modernist buildings of the mid–twentieth century and early twenty-first-century modernism as seen in the adjacent new Frick Chemistry Laboratory. The architects of Jadwin and Fine used a limited palette of brick-and-granite for exterior cladding. Fine Hall is predominantly granite with brick infill, while Jadwin is predominantly brick with granite trim. McDonnell continues the brick and granite coloration in the base, but introduces metal in the walls and roof of the laboratory piece. The zinc material is assembled with standing seams and shingles, both traditional means for constructing metal roofs.

The lower plaza features a mobile by Alexander Calder. Calder designed this monumental sculpture especially for Princeton. For a short time the disks were painted orange to honor Princeton's colors, but the artist gave instructions to have them blackened after his visit to campus in 1971. Most famous for his kinetic sculptures, or "mobiles," he also imbued his stationary "stabiles" (a term suggested by the artist Hans [Jean] Arp) with a sense of movement and lightness. Despite the sculpture and the distinctive profile of Fine Hall's Taplin Auditorium, the lower plaza has never become a gathering space in the tradition of other academic courtyards. However, it does provide a transitional space between Goheen Walk and Sciences Green. The upper plaza—an enclosed courtyard providing access and daylight to Jadwin Hall—features a sculpture by Antoine Pevsner. Pevsner, along with his brother Naum Gabo, helped found the constructivist movement in Russia with a 1920 manifesto stating that art should be active in four dimensions, including time. In this sculpture Pevsner exploited the contortion of flat metal planes, theoretically capable of indefinite projections. The striations on the surface also suggest the possibility of the infinite.

99 Frick Chemistry Laboratory
*Hopkins Architects with Payette Associates, 2010; Landscape: Michael
Van Valkenburgh Associates*

Washington Road Stream Valley Restoration
Vanasse Hangen Brustlin, 2010

Resonance
*Kendall Buster, 2010; powder-coated steel and knitted PVC shade cloth
Princeton University*

Continuing the migration of natural science laboratories from upper to lower
Washington Road, the Chemistry Department not only moved its operations from
old Frick Laboratory (see Walk Four) but also the building's name. As the field
expanded beyond physical chemistry into organic and synthetic chemistry,
the department was constrained by obsolescent facilities. In spite of the 2008
economic crisis the project proceeded, enabled by funding from royalties from
a patent held by Professor Emeritus Edward C. Taylor (1954–97). The atrium
commons and the auditorium are named in his honor.

The program translated into a building of over two hundred sixty thousand
square feet, more than double the size of Icahn Laboratory. A functionally and
physically obsolete Armory building and parking lot were demolished to create
a site for chemistry, and Armory occupants, including ROTC, were moved to other
locations. In the process of preparing the 2008 Campus Plan, the planning team
worked with the architects on siting the building and integrating it into larger

neighborhood planning strategies.
The site was large enough to accommodate the program and also offered
an opportunity to restore the wooded
stream valley as a setting for the new
building. Michael Van Valkenburgh and
Associates enhanced the woodlands
and natural habitat of the stream
corridor, designed rain gardens to
manage storm water, and created a new
woodland path along the edge of the
valley. The stream itself was restored,
with the return of its natural meander
and flood plain in a project designed by
the engineering firm Vanasse Hangen
Brustlin (VHB). The design of both projects represents the larger landscape
strategy to improve the watershed, to

Washington Road restored stream and woodlands

Frick Chemistry Laboratory

restore the woodland character of the stream valleys as entries to campus and the town, to enhance campus connections and spaces of the eastern part of the Natural Sciences Neighborhood, and to strengthen links between disciplines and with other areas of campus by interconnected landscapes, including Sciences Green.

The design premise, executed by London-based Hopkins Associates, clearly reflects Princeton's mission to combine science teaching and research under one roof. The building is composed of four laboratory floors on the east and four faculty office and conference floors on the west. The floors are connected by bridges, open stairs, and a main-floor social space, Taylor Commons, in a full-height atrium. The teaching labs are on the main floor, visible from Taylor Commons through glass windows. A cafe, cleverly named Ca Fe (for the chemical elements calcium and iron), is located in the commons. A sculpture commissioned for the building from Kendall Buster is suspended in the atrium space. *Resonance* reflects the artist's training in both art and micro-biology. Suspended from the ceiling by steel aircraft cables, six clusters of

"Resonance"

semitransparent orbs span the atrium, suggesting clouds or cells seen through a microscope. Lighting and point of view dramatically change the appearance of the work. A lab for vibration-sensitive, shared research equipment—visible from the main floor—and the auditorium are located on the lower level. The building is connected by a tunnel to Jadwin's loading dock and provides continuous enclosed circulation between Frick, Jadwin, McDonnell, Fine, and Lewis Library.

The laboratory wing forms a backdrop for Weaver Track Stadium to the east, and the office wing engages with the natural environment to the west. The main entrance to the building is from the vehicular and pedestrian plaza and Streicker Bridge to the north. The east and west exterior walls are clad in aluminum panels and sunscreens with high-performance clear glazing. Stone is substituted for aluminum in the panel system for the north and south walls. Hopkins' detailing of the panel system is modular and minimal, characteristic of his preference for high-tech design and appropriate for a modern science building.

Hopkins and Payette's expertise in designing with sustainable building technologies is evident throughout the building. The atrium provides daylight to the interior of the office and labs, as well as the main atrium level and visible portions of the lower level. The glazed roof is shaded by a louvered sunscreen with photovoltaic panels that generate electricity for use in the building. To conserve energy consumed by air handling equipment, ventilation air from the offices is circulated through the atrium and supplements outside air to supply the laboratories. Conditioned fresh air introduced at the floor of the atrium is also used to supply the labs, rising naturally, rather than forced by fans from above. Laboratory experiments require fume hoods that change air supply and exhaust several times an hour. While there are substantially more fume hoods in the new chemistry laboratory than in the older one, the fume hood and air supply design is more energy-efficient, resulting in less energy consumption. Before lab exhaust air leaves the building, heat is extracted and the energy is used to mitigate heating demands.

100 Sciences Green
Michael Van Valkenburgh and Associates, 2010

Architecture Laboratory
Jean Labatut and Robert S. Taylor, 1951

The Hedgehog and the Fox
Richard Serra, 2000; Corten steel
Princeton University, gift of Peter T. Joseph (Class of 1972 and Graduate School Class of 1973) in honor of his children, Danielle and Nicholas

Michael Van Valkenburgh Associates designed Sciences Green to unify exterior spaces and buildings of different eras and qualities while providing an engaging, pedestrian-scale campus social space. The site is located south of Western Way between the sciences buildings along the east side of Washington Road and Princeton Stadium. An initial phase of construction adjacent to Frick Chemistry Laboratory and Jadwin Hall has been completed and future phases will address the northern section. Sciences Green represents a new landscape typology on the Princeton campus: the robust scale and character of the open space and plantings balance the large scale of the modern science buildings and establish a very different relationship between building and landscape from the Collegiate Gothic quadrangles of the historic core. While the historic area of the campus is charac-terized by low-scale building ensembles that frame open space and are organized around vistas and pathways, the areas near Lake Carnegie are structured primarily by the woodland landscape. There, buildings are of relatively massive scale and were designed as semiautonomous structures. The mid-twentieth-century site planning strategy for lower Washington Road cleared woodlands to make space for these large science buildings, with little regard to the creation of exterior campus spaces and vistas, or pedestrian connections to other areas of campus. The current planning strategy integrates new and existing science buildings into the restored natural landscape of the Washington Road stream valley and makes strong pedestrian connections to other areas of campus.

Four primary east–west pathways lead to Sciences Green. One through the atrium of Lewis Library continues a diagonal pathway that starts from Rockefeller-Mathey College and crosses Washington Road at Ivy Lane. Another, through the paved lower courtyard of Jadwin–Fine–McDonnell Halls, is an extension of Goheen Walk. Another, through the plaza on the north side of Frick Chemistry Laboratory, continues Tilghman Walk across Washington Road over Streicker Bridge. A fourth, through a portal to Princeton Stadium, connects the athletic fields east of the

Sciences Green looking north

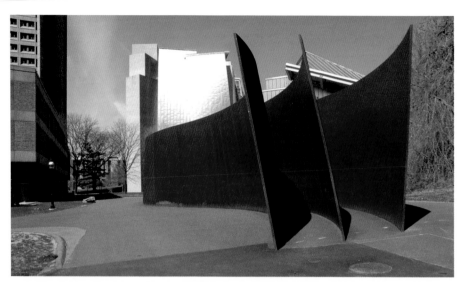

"The Hedgehog and the Fox"; Architecture Laboratory

stadium with Streicker Bridge and Tilghman Walk west of Washington Road via
a raised concourse between the grandstands of the football and track stadiums.
An asphalt roadway—bordered on one side by a granite curb and on the other
by a granite-paved walkway—provides service access and an accessible pedestrian
path from Ivy Lane on the north to Washington Road and Jadwin Gym–Class of 1935
Green on the south.

At the north end of Sciences Green—on the diagonal path from Lewis Library toward Princeton Stadium—is a Richard Serra sculpture. Industrial yet sensual, this massive sculpture invites visitors to walk through its steel curves in order to experience art, space, and environment in a physical way. The title, taken from an Isaiah Berlin essay, quotes the Greek poet Archilochus, "The fox knows many things, but the hedgehog knows one great thing." Serra extends this proposition as a question to students—will you be a fox or a hedgehog?

At the south end of the green is the Architecture Laboratory. Its most prominent feature is a high-bay glass cube—designed by Jean Labatut, who was director of graduate studies in architecture at Princeton—used for research of building components and systems and for studying design mock-ups and models. Built before the School of Architecture moved from McCormick Hall to its current building on 1879 Green, the lab hosted distinguished visitors from the architectural and engineering professions, including Frank Lloyd Wright, Buckminster Fuller, and Pier Luigi Nervi. Princeton engineering professors also use the lab for research, including David Billington, who tested bridge designs, and Robert Mark, who analyzed the structure of Gothic cathedrals. In 2013 the school installed a robotic arm—previously used on an automobile assembly line—to experiment with computer-aided design and computer-aided manufacturing.

101 Streicker Bridge

Christian Menn with HNTB, 2010; Landscape: Michael Van Valkenburgh Associates

An elegant pedestrian bridge, designed by the eminent Swiss engineer Christian Menn with Theodore Zoli (Class of 1988) of HNTB, rises from the woodlands bordering Washington Road. The bridge connects the east and west sides of the Natural Sciences Neighborhood, as well as the undergraduate residential buildings to the west with the varsity athletic facilities to the east. Crossing the bridge from east to west one sees Cleveland Tower of the Graduate College rising in the distance. On the west the bridge ramps land on Tilghman Walk between Peretsman-Scully Hall and Icahn Laboratory. On the east the ramps land on a plaza between Frick Chemistry Building and Jadwin Hall.

Several proposals by alumni and other interested parties have been made to bridge over, or tunnel under, Washington Road between Nassau Street and Faculty Road to enhance the connection between the east and west sides of campus. Streicker Bridge, however, is located where the natural grade allows a gradual and seamless transition without depressing the roadway or steeply elevating the bridge. Menn designed the ramps with a gradual slope to provide access for people in wheelchairs, bicycles, small service vehicles, and the ubiquitous golf carts.

David Billington, emeritus professor of civil and environmental engineering, was a strong advocate for bringing Menn to campus. Menn and Zoli designed the bridge with a main span and four approaching ramps, so-called legs. Structurally

Streicker Bridge ramps, looking west

the main span is a deck-stiffened arch and the legs are curved continuous girders supported by steel columns. The legs are horizontally curved and the shape of the main span follows this curvature. The arch and columns are weathering steel, and the main deck and legs are posttensioned concrete. In lieu of conventional guard-rails, the sides are protected with stainless-steel wire mesh panels. Billington's criteria that a structure exhibit "elegance, efficiency, and economy," as well as serve "symbolic, scientific, and social" purposes, is evident in Menn's design: the treelike structural supports of the bridge allude to the natural woodlands setting; the bridge enables research and teaching through data collected by movement and temperature sensors cast into the structure; and the bridge brings together various segments of the campus fabric and community.

102   Peretsman-Scully Hall and Princeton Neuroscience Institute Building
José Rafael Moneo Vallés Arquitecto with Davis Brody Bond, 2013; Landscape: Michael Van Valkenburgh Associates

As one approaches from the east after crossing Streicker Bridge, or from the west after traversing Tilghman Walk around the Ellipse, the building complex housing the Department of Psychology and the Princeton Neuroscience Institute rises from the embankment at the edge of Pardee field. The taller building, Peretsman-Scully Hall, houses the Department of Psychology. The lower building, with a set-back mechanical penthouse and lower levels visible from the fields below the embankment, houses the Princeton Neuroscience Institute. The buildings are programmatically and physically joined.

The Princeton Neuroscience Institute, established in 2006, evolved from cross-disciplinary research among psychologists, molecular biologists, and faculty members from other disciplines. The institute's labs and offices—and those of its predecessor, the Center for the Study of Mind, Brain, and Behavior—were first located in Green Hall, the former home of the Department of Psychology. The institute also attracted faculty from engineering, physics, and chemistry, and soon space in Green Hall became inadequate. An expansion program was developed during the 2008 campus planning process, resulting in the decision to move both the department and the institute from Green Hall to a new site in the Natural Sciences Neighborhood. This dual move of related but separate academic units follows the path south led by the Departments of Mathematics and Physics to Fine and Jadwin Halls in the late 1960s.

Spanish architect Rafael Moneo, winner of the 1996 Pritzker Architecture Prize, teamed with Davis Brody Bond, with whom he had established a successful partnership on a previous project at Columbia University. Moneo deftly satisfied Princeton's mandate to create separate identities for each academic unit by creating unique forms for each, but unifying the complex by using similar materials and detailing for the exterior walls. There are two types of aluminum exterior curtain-wall systems utilized on the building, a single-wall and a double-wall system. The single-wall system—the weather wall—is a conventional high-performance panelized system consisting of bands of tinted vision glass and pearlized glass spandrel panels (opaque and nonreflective). The weather wall maintains optimum temperature and humidity within the building and serves as an air and moisture barrier. The double-wall system uses a similar panelized weather wall, but here Moneo places a layer of serrated glass panels approximately twenty-four inches in front of the weather wall and replaces the spandrel panels with vision glass. The serrated glass panels—custom-made in a factory in Spain—diffuse the natural light

Peretsman–Scully Hall (left) and Princeton Neuroscience Institute Building (right)

Princeton Neuroscience Institute,
glass curtain wall

that enters the building to allow for reduced reliance on artificial light during daylight hours. The precast concrete panel–clad penthouse over the Princeton Neuroscience Institute building conceals mechanical equipment and portions of the exhaust stacks. The entrance from Tilghman Walk on the Pardee Field level leads to the main lobby that provides access to both Peretsman–Scully Hall and the Princeton Neuroscience Institute. In addition to laboratory facilities, the buildings contain classrooms, an auditorium, and common areas on the first level below grade. Interior materials include bluestone flooring, stainless-steel railings, and varnished white oak panels with a profile similar to the serrated glass panels on the building's exterior. Below the Pardee Field embankment are two floors with views of the South Drive athletic facilities. The woodlands along Washington Road provide shaded views from within Peretsman–Scully Hall. As with most buildings on campus, these structures were designed to be seen on all sides and to be integrated into a campus landscape of adjacent buildings, fields, streets, and natural features.

103 Icahn Laboratory
Rafael Viñoly Architects, 2003; Landscape: Quennell Rothschild & Partners

Horse-Head Conference Room
Frank Gehry, 2002; lead over plywood
Princeton University, gift of Peter B. Lewis

The university created the Lewis–Sigler Institute for Integrative Genomics in the late 1990s and developed a plan for a genomics laboratory building. Integrative genomics, an interdisciplinary field emerging from the federal government's Human Genome Project, requires flexible laboratory and support spaces for molecular biology, computational biology, computer science, chemical engineering, chemistry, and physics, among other disciplines. Furthermore, scientific research at Princeton combines theoretical and experimental approaches complemented by an under-graduate teaching component (the integrated science curriculum). The site of the genomics laboratory building is bordered on the north by Thomas Laboratory and a service drive, on the east by Washington Road and a woodland buffer, on the west by a wing of Scully Hall, and on the south by the Ellipse and Pardee Field. The objective was to design a building on a constrained site that would enhance collaboration among scientists and interactions between faculty and students.

Rafael Viñoly—the Uruguayan architect who successfully replaced Palmer Stadium with the new Princeton Stadium and Weaver Track—was selected for this equally challenging commission. First, Viñoly determined that in order to facilitate the desired collaboration and interactions, the building should be two stories above grade, rather than three stories, as envisioned in planning studies. To accommodate the larger building footprint, he convinced university planners to enlarge the site by reconfiguring the geometry of the Ellipse (moving the radii farther to the south). Then he aligned the north wing of the building to parallel Thomas Laboratory and aligned the east wing to parallel Washington Road, creating a dramatic entrance at the northeast corner where the wings intersect. He placed flexible, daylighted laboratories, offices, and conference rooms in these two wings. The laboratory floors are almost twenty feet high to allow for an accessible utility zone above the suspended ceilings. He located support spaces and teaching laboratories in the basement, connected to Thomas Laboratory by a tunnel. The tunnel promotes shared use of teaching labs and imaging core facilities located in both buildings. Finally, he placed a two-story atrium in the portion of the building facing Tilghman Walk.

Among the most striking features of the building's design are rotating louvers on the exterior and a walk-in sculpture in the atrium space. Viñoly opened the building corridors to the atrium and opened the atrium to the playing fields, creating an environment conducive to informal interaction among researchers and students, as well as formal dinners and symposia. The cable-supported glass wall

Icahn Laboratory

that encloses the atrium space faces south, requiring extraordinary measures to reduce heat transfer. Viñoly's solution—a phalanx of forty-foot-high, computer-controlled metal louvers that adjust with the sun—is both functionally and aesthetically elegant. The primary exterior building material of the laboratory wings is ribbed precast concrete, tinted to harmonize with the brick shades of the adjacent Scully Hall and Thomas Laboratory.

Tilghman Walk at Icahn Laboratory; Icahn Laboratory atrium

The Horse-Head Conference Room was designed by noted architect Frank Gehry as an exploration for a house he designed for former university trustee Peter B. Lewis (Class of 1955). The house was never built, but the project gave Gehry the opportunity to explore a new language of architecture, one that would be fully developed in his designs for the Guggenheim Museum at Bilbao. Viñoly placed the sculpture–conference room in the atrium along with two other freestanding objects: a cafe servery and an oval wood-clad auditorium.

104 Thomas Laboratory and Schultz Laboratory

Thomas Laboratory
Venturi, Rauch and Scott Brown with Payette Associates, 1986

Schultz Laboratory
Venturi, Scott Brown and Associates with Payette Associates, 1993

Thomas Laboratory and Schultz Laboratory are considered two parts of a single vision, programmatically and aesthetically. They are the products of the same design team and represent a major commitment by the university in the 1980s to establish an international presence in molecular biology.

The first structure, the four-story, one-hundred-ten-thousand-square-foot Thomas Laboratory, honors the eminent medical researcher, administrator, and author Lewis Thomas (Class of 1933). The scale, rhythm, and proportion of the facades are determined by the specific requirements of program and interior layout. The two long elevations of the first three stories are characterized by a consistent rhythm of identical window bays that echo the rhythm of the lab-office modules inside. The top floor, which houses the mechanical plant, is wrapped in brick and cast stone. On either end of the building are lounges fronted by large bay windows that look out to the campus. The lounges are not the only gesture toward encouraging human interaction: the corridors are wide, ceilings are relatively high, and glass walls between the labs and internal support spaces bring in natural light and afford views across the building's width. If light and transparency are gestures that humanize the environment, Venturi, Rauch and Scott Brown (VRSB) underscored their intent by a liberal use of oak on wall rails, doors, furniture, and casework. The non-load-bearing internal partitions can be reconfigured easily to accommodate evolving needs.

Robert Venturi (Class of 1947, MFA 1951) and Denise Scott Brown, who popularized the concept of the "decorated shed," applied their art to give variety to what might otherwise be a long, inert rectangle. Their exterior design strategies focused primarily on patterns and colors of brick and cast stone, most notably the diamond-patterned brickwork on the long walls and the checkerboard pattern on the end walls. But for practical reasons, VRSB went beyond decoration. For example, the windows on the south side are recessed to reduce the heat and glare

Thomas Laboratory

of the sun. This also helps mitigate some of the flatness of the long south elevation. In a witty allusion to Princeton's long tradition of Collegiate Gothic architecture, the main north entrance is topped by a somewhat flattened ogee arch. In a building that has surface decoration dominated by rectangles, squares, and diamonds, this unexpected sinuous line over the front door is a welcome surprise. The project so impressed the architectural community that it received a national AIA Honor Award in 1987.

Seven years later the same team designed Schultz Laboratory, an addition to Moffett Laboratory on the north side of Goheen Walk, a major east-west pedestrian axis that traverses this sector of the campus from Washington Road to Elm Drive. As is the case with Thomas Laboratory, Venturi, Scott Brown and Associates (VSBA) used color and pattern to break up the mass of the basically rectangular laboratory building. On the south entry facade, bands of brick alternate with bands of limestone and windows. The stone casing on either side of the windows imparts texture and some vertical lift; stone is also the dominant material on the exterior of the first floor and around the entrance, evoking traditional brick and limestone patterns. The architects also rounded and inflected the south wall and splayed the north wall where the building joins Moffett.

Venturi again paid homage to the Collegiate Gothic style that was most familiar on the campus during his Princeton undergraduate years in the 1940s and as a graduate student. VSBA used green slate for the walkways and floor of the lobby, for example, as echoes of the older tradition. The single large limestone column, which is cut into the facade at the entrance, revives the importance of ceremonial front doors. The gray granite band that runs just below the top of the column suggests a classical capital. The entrance, tucked under the second story, recalls the porches of Collegiate Gothic and Victorian buildings. The oblique angle

Shultz Laboratory

of the entry door allows the porch to have more depth than would otherwise be possible on a tight site. The manner in which the entrance is designed also allows for the play of light and shadow, by day and night. The window glass is divided into panes, suggesting leaded mullions. Facing Goheen Walk, full-height windows framed by stone and brick piers provide views into the public space of the monumental staircase and wood-wainscoted walls of the ground floor.

105 Guyot Hall and Moffett Laboratory

Guyot Hall
Parish and Schroeder, 1909; Laboratory additions: O'Connor and Kilham, 1960 and 1964; Library addition: Mitchell | Giurgola, 1981; Renovation: Payette Associates, 2006

Moffett Laboratory
O'Connor and Kilham, 1960

Guyot Hall was the last academic building constructed during Woodrow Wilson's presidency, fulfilling a commitment made years earlier by President McCosh to elevate Princeton's reputation in the natural sciences. Nineteenth-century scientists, such as Joseph Henry (physics) and Arnold Henry Guyot (geology) at Princeton, commonly worked in primitive facilities. But by the mid-nineteenth century new scientific and technical schools provided modern accommodations for technical education. If Princeton was to attract succeeding generations of outstanding talent, a priority had to be first-rate labs, classrooms, and offices for faculty and students.

Designing and building them, however, was not the same thing. Architects were challenged by their clients to chart new territory, since there were few precedents. The study of theoretical and applied sciences is a radically different kind of education from the traditional classical curriculum. A curriculum grounded in experimentation and close observation of the physical world demanded a new way of building—for example, the ability to quickly vent foul-smelling and perhaps even deadly gases from a chemistry lab. Long before the twentieth century Princeton's Joseph Henry noted in a speech to his colleagues that the architecture of science "should be looked upon more as a useful than a fine art...In building, we should plan the inside first, and then plan the outside to cover it." In other words, his ideal was an architecture that would be practical and flexible.

The original Guyot Hall is a fraction of what it was intended to be. The architects had planned a large quadrangle whose dimensions would have been 288 feet by 256 feet. In fact only the north wing was built, a four-story structure 288 feet long and 60 feet deep, which yielded nearly two acres of laboratory, class, office, and exhibition space. Functionally the building is programmed in two parts: biology in the east; geology in the west. Both programs are announced on the exterior by a wonderful parade of carved limestone gargoyles, two hundred in all: living species are represented on the biology wing to the east; extinct species are on the geology wing to the west. Field glasses are recommended, since the animals cavort high up at the roofline. The gargoyles are a welcome touch of whimsy on a structure in which the dark brick, flat roof, squared-off symmetrical towers, buttresses, and sheer size convey gravitas.

The two crenellated towers at the front or north side identify the main pedestrian entrances and internal stairways. The companion towers at the rear

Guyot Hall north wing

house elevator shafts. Until 2000 the first floor exhibited dinosaur skeletons and other specimens in a natural history museum. The museum—founded by Professor Guyot in 1856—was located in what is now the Faculty Room of Nassau Hall from 1874 through 1904. The collection was moved to Guyot Hall when the building opened but is no longer displayed, with the exception of an Allosaurus skeleton that was too large to move and a smaller exhibit, "Leaping Tiger and Saber Tooth," which is on view on the commons floor of the Frist Campus Center.

As geology has evolved into geosciences and overlapped with other ecological and environmental studies, it is not surprising that Guyot has witnessed several additions and a number of extensive interior renovations. In 1960 Moffett Biological Laboratory, designed by O'Connor and Kilham, was added on the east side along Washington Road. Also in 1960 and again in 1964, additions for geosciences were added on the west side, south of the original building. In 1981 an addition to house the geosciences library and map collection, designed by Mitchell|Giurgola, was inserted into the courtyard between the east and west wings. In 2006 when the library moved out, Payette Associates converted the addition to teaching laboratories. In 1993 Schultz Laboratory was added on the south. With these additions, the size of Guyot Hall today closely approximates the ambitious plans of its original architects.

Over a forty-five-year period, beginning with Jadwin and Fine Halls in 1970, the university built over 1.5 million square feet of research and teaching space in the area south of Guyot Hall. At the beginning of this transformation the disciplines of genomics and neuroscience did not exist. If the rapid pace of discovery and the emergence of new disciplines continue, Princeton will again see growth in this neighborhood.

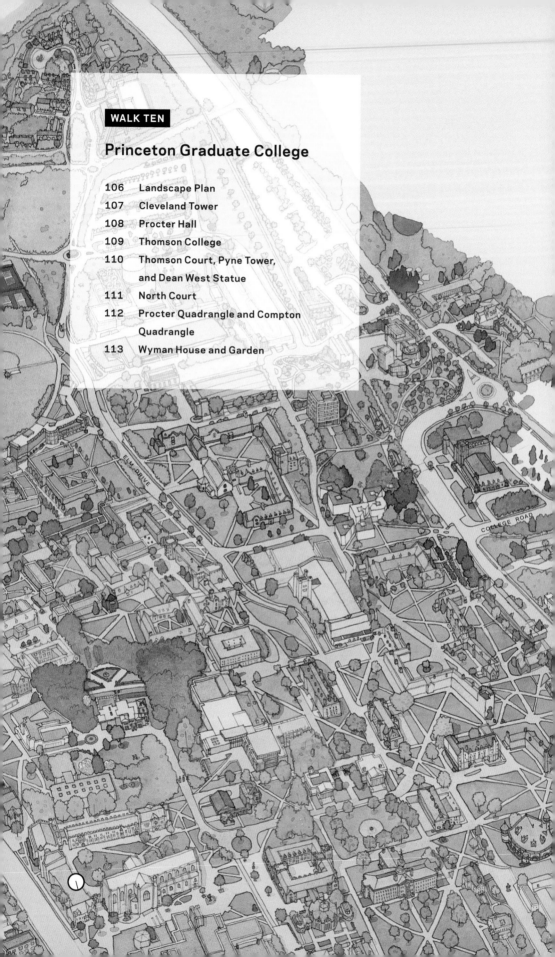

WALK TEN

Princeton Graduate College

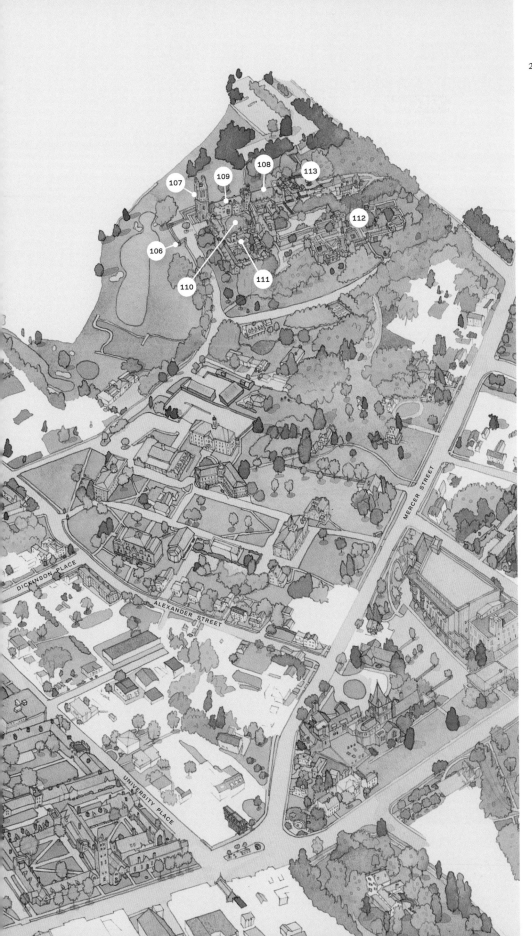

Princeton Graduate College

Bonus intra, melior extra (Enter good, leave better)
—Anonymous, Latin motto, ca. 600 CE, inscribed on the mantel above
the great fireplace in Procter Hall

ORIGINS OF THE GRADUATE COLLEGE

Princeton's Graduate College was created from the dust of a failed friendship. In most accounts, President Woodrow Wilson played the role of progressive hero who wanted to site the Graduate College on the grounds of the undergraduate campus to enrich the intellectual life of the students, while his antagonist, Graduate School Dean Andrew Fleming West (1901–28), assumed the part of imperious separatist intent on building his campus on a site located one mile from Nassau Hall. It is an engaging drama, but the facts are more complex.

The university's trustees officially voted to establish Princeton's Graduate School on December 13, 1900, with West as its first dean. The idea for a graduate program was first broached a century earlier, but it was not until Princeton's Sesquicentennial in 1896 that the concept gained ground. That year, the trustees decided a graduate school would place Princeton on equal footing with the world's great universities. The Graduate School would require physical space for graduate students and faculty masters to live, dine, and socialize, i.e., the

Aerial view looking east, Graduate College in foreground, ca. 1920–25

Graduate College. The Philadelphia firm of Cope and Stewardson, which had just completed the widely popular Blair Hall, was commissioned to draw up plans. Published the following year, the firm's concept envisioned an irregular quadrangle entered through an archway similar to that of Blair Tower.

President Wilson and Dean West agreed that the Graduate College would be a self-contained residential community; there would not be a separate faculty; the style of the architecture would be Collegiate Gothic; and the college would be built in the middle of the undergraduate campus, most likely on a recently acquired parcel north of Prospect House called the Academy Lot. President Wilson then made an unexpected move: he unilaterally appropriated the Academy Lot for another favored project, the preceptorial program. What was built on the Academy Lot was not Cope and Stewardson's Graduate College, but McCosh Hall, the classroom building in which Wilson's innovative program was launched. West was stunned; he felt betrayed and realized that by pursuing a site on campus, he and the Graduate College would remain subject to Wilson's priorities. While Wilson continued to advocate for a site in the "geographical heart of the university," known as the Prospect site adjacent to 1879 Hall, West began to look elsewhere for a new site and funds to construct the buildings.

Throughout much of the controversy, consulting architect Ralph Adams Cram backed Wilson. His 1909 master plan showed the proposed Graduate College on the Prospect site. But Cram, along with some alumni and trustees, eventually switched sides in support of an off-campus site, which had the additional advantage of being a blank slate for his High Church theories of architecture. Cram took on the project with a passion born from a conviction that the Graduate College would be one of the works he would be judged by: "I have taken enormous pride in this particular building and have tried to make it not only the best thing we ourselves have ever done, but the most personal as well, and also, if it might be, the best example of Collegiate Gothic ever done in this country." So confident was he about the importance of this project that he made no attempt to downplay the costs. To the contrary, the steep budget attested to the nobleness of this great enterprise. The Graduate College, he boasted, "shall not cost less than $5,000,000," an enormous sum in the early years of the twentieth century.

Nothing quite prepares one for the first encounter with the Graduate College. Approaching from the historic campus along College Road, past the golf course, and up the gentle rise to Cleveland Tower, one reaches the ceremonial front door, soaring 173 feet above the green and rolling countryside. The complex is less an academic precinct than an English abbey, and the emotions evoked during a walk in and through it are more likely to be religious than pedagogical—which is what Dean West and his architect intended. If one happens to be there when the sixty-seven-bell carillon sounds, the spirituality of the place can be overwhelming.

The brick, limestone, and argillite of Cleveland Tower and the rest of the original ensemble of buildings, known as the Old Graduate College, are the embodiment of deeply held beliefs about the interrelationship between education and architecture. Winston Churchill once observed that we shape architecture and architecture in turn shapes us. Both Dean West and Cram would have agreed. In the course of designing and building the Graduate College, they worked together as an inspired team in pursuit of a common purpose; "The joy of surroundings that keep [the student] buoyant," West wrote, "means doubling and trebling his power." When they disagreed—which they did—it was over the color of the stone in Wyman House or which craftsman was best suited to produce the stained glass of Procter Hall or the pace of construction on Cleveland Tower. Their disagreements were never about the importance of the work or the relationship between architecture and education. Both men expected the stones—in their beauty, civilizing influence, and spirituality—to aid in the education of generations of gentlemen scholars.

Cram and West had both traveled through England and had been deeply inspired when developing both the original campus and the graduate campus. What West saw in the leafy quadrangles of Cambridge convinced him that architecture could affect action and thought; the medieval towers and great halls of Oxford confirmed for Cram that Gothic was the style in which the highest moral values resonated. In an age of rampant materialism and mechanical standardization, both men saw the Gothic style as an expression of and

Old Graduate College (top) and New Graduate College (bottom), 1963

inspiration for spirituality. It harkened back to medieval Paris and Oxford, when the universities in both cities were, in West's phrase, "the eyes of Christendom." For both men Gothic architecture was more a principle than a style of design. Like his great medievalist contemporaries in England and France, Cram did not see himself as an antiquarian, but as the standard bearer of a tradition that once brought back to life could equal, if not surpass, achievements of the past.

While the original ensemble of buildings and landscape continues to represent the most intact demonstration of the collaboration between Ralph Adams Cram and Beatrix Farrand, over time increasing Graduate School enrollment has required expanded facilities. In the 1960s when enrollment passed one thousand students, two new quadrangles, known as the New Graduate College, were added to the existing ones. Since then, the graduate student population has increased (exceeding two thousand students by 2005) and diversified (e.g., married students, women, and international students). To address these changes, the university constructed different types of residential life buildings on other campus sites. These include the Lawrence Apartments (1965 and 2002) and Lakeside Graduate Housing (see Walk Eight). Cleveland Tower, Procter Hall, Thomson College, and North Court are collectively known as the Old Graduate College. Procter and Compton Quadrangles comprise the New Graduate College.

106 Landscape Plan
Beatrix Jones Farrand, 1912

Approaching the Graduate College from the east, one ascends a gently curved roadway and walkway that slows the pace to emphasize the picturesque. The view of Cleveland Tower is constantly changing to emphasize its dynamic thrust to the sky. The tower appears, disappears behind trees, then reappears again, a deliberate metaphor for the scholar's halting pursuit of truth. The grove of evergreen trees on the north side not only serves as a windbreak, but also eases the considerable changes of grade. The trees and shrubs do not crowd the foundation or hide the outlines of the architecture, but in fact focus the viewer's attention on the buildings. At the top of the hill the land is leveled to form an entrance court defined by a low wall of native stone that continues in front of Cleveland Tower, in the words of Beatrix Farrand "making a broad terrace, out of which Cleveland Tower will rise, and giving a quiet base to the line of buildings." Cram, incidentally, was against a terrace at the foot of Cleveland Tower; he favored a sloping lawn. Over the years the consensus is that Farrand was correct in her vision.

Farrand's thirty-one-year association with Princeton began in 1912 with the Graduate College, an area of campus that offers insight into her philosophy and practice. What she designed around Cram's architecture remains essentially intact, including the two great cedars of Lebanon in Thomson Court, given to Dean West by Farrand's former teacher and director of Harvard's Arnold Arboretum, Charles Sprague Sargent. It was at the Graduate College that Farrand first tested landscape strategies that would distinguish the Princeton campus. These included

Procter Hall exterior, with Beatrix Farrand, 1931

Cleveland Tower

the creation of the campus's distinctive character primarily through the use of trees and grass; exploitation of existing topography to create landscape spaces that guide circulation and orientation; plantings arranged to best show the architecture of buildings; maximum open space in courtyards; and a vista from every dormitory room window. Her palette prioritized plants, native when possible, that would bloom during the academic year. At the Graduate College she planted clusters of deciduous shrubs to add color (varieties of dogwood, masses of forsythia) to groves of evergreen trees and used vines and espaliered plants to add texture to facades and to frame entries—trademarks that came to characterize her work on the campus over the course of her tenure at Princeton.

One may discover the essence of the Graduate College in the dialogue between the architecture (intended to inspire) and the landscape (intended to soothe), between stone and leaf, and between the rational and the romantic.

107 Cleveland Tower
Cram, Goodhue, and Ferguson, 1913

Although Cleveland Tower is easily Princeton's most prominent landmark, it is surprising to learn that this great edifice was not part of Cram's original design. The tower was added at the eleventh hour as a tribute to Grover Cleveland, twenty-fourth president of the United States, an influential university trustee, and a close friend of Dean West. To pay for the 173-foot-high tower West opened the project to public subscription; no gift was too small, including the pennies of schoolchildren from across the land. The Class of 1892 gave the five-octave carillon, installed in 1922 and later restored in 1994 with an additional eighty tons of bells.

Echoing in broad outline Oxford's Magdalen Tower, Cleveland Tower is a striking composition of originality. It seems to disobey the law of gravity; stone rises as if it were lighter than air. The shaft is not a single piece, but divided into four distinct tiers. Horizontal limestone stringcourses define the first two divisions. The shaft tapers as the tower gains altitude, progressively eroding each section and altering the stone from the rough, darker argillite to the smooth, pale limestone.

The lowest section of the tower is a block of almost solid argillite, save for a single arched limestone-framed window on each exposed face. The four surfaces of the next section are broken by long and deep limestone incisions; these windows are taller and narrower. The third level, or belfry, is distinguished by an abundance of delicately carved limestone. At the very top an imaginary rectilinear solid has been largely cut away, leaving only the four pale limestone pinnacles. Perhaps the most impressive feature of Cleveland Tower is that for all its size and height, it does not feed, house, or provide study space for students. It is instead a memorial to Cleveland and the ceremonial front door of the Graduate College.

108 Procter Hall
Ralph Adams Cram, 1913

The jewel of the Graduate College is the great Procter Hall. From Cleveland Tower one can access the dining hall by walking through Thomson Court to the southwest corner and entering a vestibule in the base of Pyne Tower. Alternatively, one can walk through the common room to the same vestibule. For Dean West, Procter Hall was the armature of the Graduate College around which his educational theories revolved.

A great hall for the graduate students to gather in every night offered the opportunity for a Christian message in a secular space. There was a High Table—literally on a level higher than the rest of the dining hall—and prayers before every meal. There were also inspirational talks from the dais to the students in their bachelor's robes. Yet the full force of spiritual instruction would not be carried by prayers or lectures, but by the architecture and the related arts—music, painting, wood carving, and most notably stained glass. Cram and West were successful in designing a spiritual space, as indicated by an event that occurred a few years after the dedication. Industrialist Henry Clay Frick, invited to dinner by West, groused to his host that the space "looked too damn much like a church—all it needs is an organ!" Far from being offended, West leaped at the opportunity to solicit from his guest funds to underwrite the installation of a four-manual organ in the gallery. The organ, completely overhauled in the 1960s, is today one of the university's hidden treasures.

The effect Procter Hall casts speaks for itself. West believed that history was the story of great men. Portraits of heroes of the Graduate College—Professor Howard C. Butler (the first master of the Graduate College), Francis L. Patton (Princeton's president from 1888–1902, when the concept of the Graduate School was approved by the trustees), and Dean West—hang near the High Table as the place of greatest privilege. Nearby to the left of Butler is Moses Taylor Pyne, chairman of the Graduate School Committee. Conspicuously absent is a portrait of Woodrow Wilson, an early supporter of the Graduate School.

Procter Dining Hall

The art of portraiture continues high above in the vaults of the carved wooden ceiling. Here one sees a series of wooden hammer-beams projecting horizontally from the wall to relieve the weight of the roof. They serve an aesthetic function as well: the end of each beam is carved into a human likeness. What these anthropomorphic carvings represent has long been a subject of debate. With no written proof, tradition has it that they represent the trustees at the time Procter Hall was built; the key to the mystery is the object that each holds in his outstretched hands. For example, the figure that holds what appears to be a bar of soap appears to represent trustee William Cooper Procter (of Procter and Gamble).

The magnificent stained-glass window behind the High Table is by the Philadelphia artisan William Willet, a protégé of Dean West; to the left, in the bay at the southwest corner, is the work of Cram's protégé, Charles J. Connick, a stained-glass artisan from Boston. Under West's guidance the figures Willet designed convey the message that classical muses and Christian saints are members of the same mystical family, and there is no inherent conflict between religious and secular education, because scholarship ultimately leads to knowledge of God. If a scholar were to succumb to the sin of pride in these glorious surroundings, West would have him be ever mindful of the Latin admonition that figures prominently in the glass: *Nec vocemini magistri quia magister vester unus est Christus*, which West translated: "And be ye not called masters, for one is your master, even Christ."

Connick's window in the south bay continues and expands on West's gospel that true scholarship is a quest for enlightenment, illustrated by the legend of the Holy Grail. As told by the fifteenth-century author Sir Thomas Malory, the legend chronicles the search for the cup Christ used at the Last Supper and its final attainment. The lower lancets depict the first appearance of the Holy Grail to Sir Galahad, who is surrounded by the Knights of the Round Table. At a formal dinner in Procter Hall the night before the dedication ceremonies on October 22, 1913, one of the invited foreign dignitaries, Professor Arthur Shipley of Christ's College, Cambridge, remarked as he entered the hall that "this room was three hundred years old the day it opened." Whether Professor Shipley meant his words as criticism or praise, no higher compliment could have been paid to Cram and West.

109 Thomson College
Cram, Goodhue and Ferguson, 1913

The entrance into Thomson College, the first and oldest of the Graduate College's closed quadrangles, is through the rib-vaulted passageway to the right of Cleveland Tower. Cram designed an element of surprise by placing the passageway arch off axis from the court, in the far southeast corner. Upon entering, the self-contained world of the Graduate College becomes evident. The separation or isolation from the outside world (all the entries open into the quad) is deliberate: Dean West anticipated that graduate students would arrive from different schools around the world and their fields of study at Princeton would be broad. To confine them to one place, removed from the town and the undergraduates, intentionally created a community that would breed solidarity. "These are the places where the affections linger and where memories cling like the ivies themselves," West wrote in the 1913 Graduate College prospectus, "and these are the answers in architecture and scenic setting to the immemorial longings of academic generations."

Thomson College is a memorial to Senator John Thomson (Class of 1817). Characteristic of the Collegiate Gothic style, endless variety prevails. The suites housing graduate students, each with its own fireplace, open into outdoor courts. The separate entries and stairs to the suites are connected by a spacious underground passageway around the perimeter of Thomson College. Cram intended the corridor as an unobtrusive route for staff to bring tea or firewood to the residents. The passageway has been adapted to house mechanical equipment, recreational and social spaces, bathrooms, and utilitarian services.

110   Thomson Court, Pyne Tower, and Dean West Statue

Thomson Court
Beatrix Jones Farrand

Pyne Tower
Cram, Goodhue and Ferguson, 1913

Andrew Fleming West, Class of 1874
Robert Tait McKenzie, before 1928; cast bronze
Princeton University, gift of William Cooper Procter (Class of 1883)

Thomson Court is graced with Beatrix Farrand's omnipresent wisteria. Farrand's climbing hydrangea and ivy emphasize salient angles on the walls throughout the court. Her restrained landscape design combines the upper and lower lawns with the graceful horizontal blue-green branches of the two great cedar of Lebanon trees. Gazing out to the cedars from the upper lawn is the bronze statue of Dean West. Dressed in his academic robes, West looks steadfastly toward the common room, Procter Hall, and Pyne Tower.

The crenellated shape of Pyne Tower rises above an archway at the east end of Procter Hall, which leads out to the manicured grounds of the Springdale Golf Course. Cram designed the tower to house the master of the Graduate College, Howard C. Butler (Class of 1892), who occupied rooms on the second and third floors. Today's first-floor common room served as the formal parlor where guests were received. Connick was called upon again to design the armorial medallions that appear on each of the common room windows. Dean West selected the seven coats of arms, which represent the families of men significant to New Jersey's colonial history.

Thomson College

111 North Court
Cram and Ferguson, 1927; Landscape: Beatrix Jones Farrand

North Court is both the name of the dormitory building and the courtyard enclosed by the building. The U-shaped building is an addition to Thomson College and follows the established floor plan of suites containing one bedroom and a living room, sharing a bath with an adjacent suite. Each of five entryways and stair towers provides access to four suites on each floor. The building varies from two to four floors. North Court also continues the materials (argillite, limestone, and slate) and details (gables, dormers, bays, lead window cames, and arched doorways) of Thomson College. From the cloister on the north side of Thomson Court, one can access the North Court courtyard through an open passageway near the midpoint of the arcade. At the east end of the arcade, a short flight of stairs leads to a smaller cloister and the elegant Van Dyke Library. As one enters the courtyard, the formality of Thomson Court relaxes into a charmingly intimate space. Seen from the top of the limestone steps is a slate disk with paths radiating in a sunbeam pattern to building entries around the court. The courtyard is Farrand's design, as are the proportions of the gracious stairs. A katsura tree in the northeast corner reinforces the relaxed quality that contrasts with the stately cedar of Lebanon trees in Thomson Court. Farrand, who favored keeping the quads open, placed the tree off to the side, rather than the center. The plantings along the quad are also more varied than those in Thomson Court, including the shape and color of the leaves, and the blossoms and berries. In every instance it seems that the choice is intended to complement,

North Court

rather than upstage, the architecture. "Within the quadrangle," Farrand wrote, "only creepers and wall shrubs should be used, as free standing shrubs would tend to destroy the impression of quiet which the buildings themselves give."

112 Procter Quadrangle and Compton Quadrangle
Ballard, Todd & Snibbe, 1963; Landscape: Clarke and Rapuano

Northwood II
Kenneth Snelson, 1970; stainless steel

Floating Figure
Gaston Lachaise, 1927, installed 1969; cast bronze

A passageway at the northwest corner of Thomson Court leads to Procter and Compton Quadrangles, known as the New Graduate College. In the 1960s Collegiate Gothic was out of fashion and possibly too expensive for the expansion of the Graduate College. A bold, original note might have been risky. Instead, Ballard, Todd & Snibbe, turning away from Cram's towers and pitched roofs, designed a series of staggered stone and glass cubes stacked two and three stories high that represented a modern yet contextual approach to the expansion.

The absence of ornament, expansive glass windows, flat roofs, and use of clean geometric shapes in the buildings' plans and elevations identify both quads as undeniably modern. Yet the architects took their cue from the older buildings.

Sheathed in the same argillite stone, the residences are arranged as loose quadrangles, with communal buildings in between. The stone surfaces alternate at strategic intervals with characteristically modern large floor-to-ceiling window walls, but the pronounced gray-green vertical framing members suggest traditional mullions. The Procter and Compton Quads offer variety in the massing; a deft handling of glass, metal, and stone; and a gently scaled footprint on the land.

While the architects related to Cram's buildings through the use of similar exterior materials, the floor plan they designed is decidedly different. There are single rooms in lieu of suites, corridors in lieu of entryways, and hall baths serving multiple bedrooms in lieu of semiprivate baths. The only fireplaces are located in the freestanding pavilions that serve as common rooms. Unlike Cram and Farrand's enclosed courtyards, these courtyards formed by the dormitory buildings are open on one side and feature modern sculptures. In the Procter courtyard is a sculpture by Kenneth Snelson. Deceptively simple in appearance, *Northwood II* is in fact a complex, engineered system of weights and counterweights. Three pairs of parallel steel bars identical in length are held together by wire cables, creating a delicate push-pull tension. Although the work is composed of a minimal number of components, each part is necessary for the whole to exist. In the Compton courtyard is a sculpture by Paris-born artist Gaston Lachaise, who had worked for Art Nouveau glassmaker René Lalique before moving to America, where he became associated with the leading avant-garde artists of the day. The first bronze cast of *Floating Figure* was exhibited in 1935 at the Museum of Modern Art, where it remains on view.

"Floating Figure"

Procter Quadrangle

113 Wyman House and Garden

Cram, Goodhue, and Ferguson, 1913; Landscape: Beatrix Jones Farrand, 1916; Landscape redesign: Lynden Miller, 2005

Wyman House—named after the Graduate College's primary benefactor, Isaac Wyman (Class of 1848)—is the residence of the dean of the Graduate College. Cram's Tudor-style stone and half-timbered house complements the high west gable of Procter Hall. Although modest in comparison to the design of Procter Hall, Dean West was no less attentive to detail. This is apparent in his correspondence with the contractor: "Wyman House may be less conspicuous and less obtrusive in tone when contrasted with the brighter and richer end of Procter Hall. I do not mean dark red or brown, but the bluish or purple-black and deep grey tints."

Farrand designed the Wyman House garden as a private and year-round space, which allowed her to expand her floral palette. Out of this greater freedom came a splendid walled garden on the private north side of the house. The garden, which is appreciably larger than the house, is L-shaped in plan and subdivided into three formal outdoor rooms: an enclosed lawn next to the house, an open quad next to the campus, and, in between, a formal parterre planted with seasonal flowers that originally included roses. The lawn is a crisp square split by a path that leads through a gate to the parterre, where beds of perennials and annuals are arranged into quadrants, separated by walks. An arbor of pleached hornbeam graces the east end of this space. To the west is the walled quadrangle of lawn edged in woody shrubs and shaded by a large beech and pine. Thanks to the stewardship of Dean

Wyman House garden plan, date unknown; Wyman House garden

of the Graduate School Theodore Ziolkowski (1979–92) and his wife, Yetta, the well-loved garden was restored in the 1970s to include ivy grown from cuttings from locations including Martin Luther's house in Wittenburg, University College at Oxford, and Christ's College at Cambridge. The ivy of Oxford and Cambridge are at home amid the brick walls of the garden, which incorporate original stonework from both universities.

In 2005 garden design consultant Lynden Miller oversaw reconstruction of the parterre. She raised and reconfigured the planting beds, selected a new palette of mostly perennials, and replaced the grass walks with gravel. These steps helped to ease the maintenance of the garden. At the time, the trees in the west quadrangle had grown to the point where their shade eclipsed a sundial there. Rather than remove the trees, Miller moved the sundial to the sunnier parterre, where it now stands as the centerpiece.

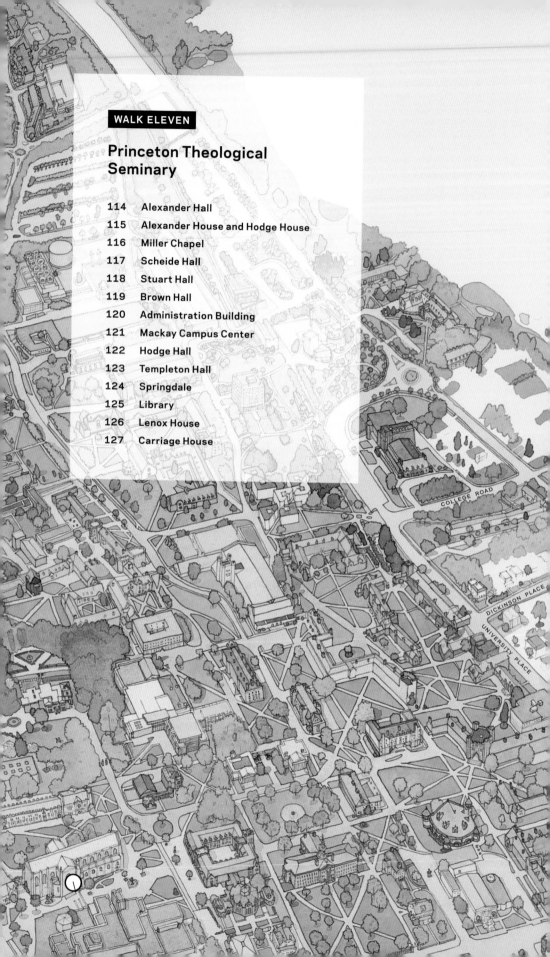

COLLEGE ROAD

DICKINSON PLACE

UNIVERSITY PLACE

Princeton Theological Seminary

A PLACE OF THEIR OWN

The Princeton Theological Seminary, or, as it was called until 1958, the Theological Seminary of the Presbyterian Church, was born out of frustration. Princeton University's founders had intended the fourth oldest institution of higher learning in the English colonies to educate Presbyterian ministers of the Gospel. But almost from the beginning the university—then the College of New Jersey—adopted a larger mission, and over the years candidates for the ministry were a declining percentage of those graduating. Many in the church's hierarchy were disappointed. In the first decade of the nineteenth century that disappointment deepened.

There was also an issue of student discipline. Even under the best conditions a large group of young men in tight quarters is a challenge. With few social outlets in a country town and in the face of outright scorn for sports—which would have served as an outlet for the young men—the ringing of bells at all hours of the night and the occasional explosion of gunpowder were an undergraduate rite of passage. When more tolerant clerics were succeeded by strict disciplinarians, pranks festered into periodic riots. The climate was so charged that conservative critics of the college blamed students for the fire that destroyed Nassau Hall in 1802.

It was about this time that influential members of the Presbyterian Church and conservative clerics within the college began to advocate for the establishment of a new theological school. The decisive move was made in 1808, in the midst of "The Great Awakening," a national evangelical surge that called for new ministers of the Gospel. In that year a minister named Archibald Alexander petitioned the General Assembly of the Presbyterian Church to establish one or more seminaries. In the brief space of four years Alexander was given the task of growing the new institution, whose mission was to increase the supply of "enlightened, humble, zealous, laborious pastors to watch for the good of souls."

When the seminary opened to three students in August 1812 the college saw it as a financial threat. The church's patronage had paid for the building of Nassau Hall. Now, with the seminary, much-needed funds would be redirected to what was, in some respects, a rival institution just a few blocks from the college campus. Those fears proved to be well grounded. Until the arrival of James McCosh in 1868, the college was somewhat adrift. Not a single new academic facility had been built since Geological and Philosophical Halls in 1803.

But in the long run the separation set in motion a series of unintended consequences. No longer required to toe the theological line of the church, the curriculum of the college was ultimately free to grow in new directions. In fact, by the terms of an understanding reached between the college and the seminary, the college was expressly forbidden to hire its own professor of theology.

Another unforeseen advantage was that the college was largely spared from strong opinions or fallout of the occasional doctrinal wars inevitable to the faith. Both would eventually burden the seminary, which was the first Presbyterian seminary in the Western Hemisphere.

For many years, though, the college remained Presbyterian at its core. At various times both institutions shared trustees, major donors, and even presidents. "Of the twenty men appointed as professors at the seminary up to 1900, they collectively included four who had taught at the college, ten who were college alumni, eleven who were its trustees, and ten to whom it awarded honorary degrees, four of whom were awarded two such degrees each," William K. Selden wrote in *The Legacy of John Cleve Green*. Both saw the rise of student eating clubs around the same time and for the same reasons; and both reserved the highest administrative position for Presbyterian ministers. Indeed it was not until 1902, when Woodrow Wilson was elected president of the university, that Princeton broke tradition and selected someone who was not a Presbyterian minister, although Wilson's father had been a clergyman.

The architecture of the seminary is a testament to this close relationship. William Appleton Potter, who figured prominently in the shaping of Princeton University's Victorian campus, did important work here. But the architecture also reflects how the institutions eventually diverged. Most significantly the seminary did not have a Collegiate Gothic phase. While Collegiate Gothic had been mandated by the university's trustees as part of a larger effort to reinvent the College of New Jersey as Princeton University, there was no similar effort at the seminary to redefine its mandate. The seminary grew increasingly tenacious in defending its image as a bastion of theological conservatism. Also, Collegiate Gothic, which speaks an Anglican vocabulary, would have been inappropriate for the no-frills Reform Christianity the seminary espoused. This was the great watershed after which the architectural histories of the seminary and university flowed in different directions. During the period of turmoil at the seminary, in the early decades of the twentieth century, some remodeling took place but there was no new construction. This yielded an unexpected irony: the visitor today looking for the architecture of the university's Victorian past can find it a few blocks to the west at the Princeton Theological Seminary.

The seminary is composed of three architecturally distinct campuses. The original, historic precinct is bounded by College Road and Alexander and Mercer Streets. Two blocks to the north and west off Stockton Street stands the Colonial Revival Tennent Campus (designed in the 1920s for the Hun School by architect Rolf William Bauhan and purchased intact by the seminary in 1943). Finally, some miles to the south between the Delaware and Raritan Canal and Route 1 is the West Windsor campus, a 1960s housing complex acquired by the seminary for married students in 1965. This walk is restricted to the original campus, which shares the greatest historic and architectural affinity with the Princeton University campus.

Alexander Hall

114 Alexander Hall
John McComb Jr., 1815; Restoration: Short and Ford, 1978

The seminary walk begins at Alexander Hall, originally called Old Seminary.
Alexander Hall exhibits a close relationship between the architecture of the seminary and of the college: the use of local stone; the slightly projecting central bay
(both at the front and back) with its oculus at the center of the pediment; the
Georgian bilateral symmetry. These design elements all harken back to Nassau Hall
as originally designed by Dr. William Shippen and Robert Smith and later remodeled
by Benjamin Latrobe after the 1802 fire. Indeed, Alexander Hall—the main building
and oldest facility of the seminary—offers a truer picture of the original Nassau
Hall (with the exceptions of the 1913 Colonial Revival cupola and the front doorway)
than the Nassau Hall one sees today, which was profoundly altered in the Italianate
style by the architect John Notman. The one entrance at the front is an original
feature, as are the two entrances at each side. The two rear doors are much
closer to the original configuration of Nassau Hall than one finds today. There are
important differences, though: Alexander Hall has a gable rather than a hip roof;
and it appears taller (four stories plus an English basement as opposed to three)
but not as long as Nassau Hall.

    Alexander Hall is currently a dormitory. When it opened in 1818 it was, like
Nassau Hall, a multipurpose building with all the seminary's functions under one
roof, from a refectory and living spaces for the seminarians to a library and a
second-floor chapel, or "Oratory." John McComb Jr., the architect, is today best
known for New York's City Hall (1803–12), which he designed with Joseph François

Mangin. That McComb looked back to an eighteenth-century Georgian precedent when he designed the seminary's first building says as much about the continuing power of Nassau Hall as a model for America's colleges as it does about the conservative tastes of his Presbyterian clients.

The selection of McComb, a New York architect, was a break from the pattern that prevailed in the area until the Civil War, when Philadelphia was the venue of choice for design talent. The turn north to Manhattan may be explained by McComb's local connections: he was the son of John McComb Sr., a builder-architect, and Hannah Stockton, a member of one of Princeton's oldest and most prestigious families, the same family that gave the original four acres for the seminary. A major renovation in 1978 by the local firm Short and Ford introduced twentieth-century amenities, such as an elevator, air-conditioning, and other system upgrades.

115   Alexander House and Hodge House

Alexander House, 58 Mercer Street
Architect unknown, 1818

Hodge House, 74 Mercer Street
John Haviland, 1825

Alexander House and Hodge House stand on either side of Alexander Hall. Like Alexander Hall, Alexander House (which the seminary built for Professor Archibald Alexander) is not built in the Greek Revival or Federal manner of the period, but looks to a Georgian past. There is no ornament or delicate detailing. Yet the symmetrical structure has dignity and is surely meant to convey to passersby a useful sense of tradition, for an institution that was so new.

By contrast, the contemporary Hodge House seems almost frivolous, perhaps because the architect had international experience and practiced in Philadelphia, then the center of American fashion. Born in England in 1792, John Haviland learned his craft in London and St. Petersburg. Arriving in Philadelphia in 1816 he made his reputation with the publication of *The Builder's Assistant* (1818), one of the earliest illustrated pattern books written and published in North America.

In the days when most buildings were designed by talented builder-carpenters, the well-used pattern books were prized possessions.

Haviland's work for the seminary's third and perhaps most influential professor, Charles Hodge, was thus an early commission. The most distinctive design detail appears above the front

Hodge House

door—the faux Palladian window that has white rays of stylized sunburst that radiate from the window arch to illuminate the center hall. Notwithstanding this striking detail, Hodge, like Alexander House, looks back to the earlier Georgian tradition, although the proportions are somewhat lighter and more sophisticated. The kitchen wing to the east, which compromises the closed rectangular shape of the house, is a later addition. The overall appearance of both houses, especially Alexander, is close to what Princeton University's Maclean House would have looked like as originally designed by Robert Smith. Both Alexander and Hodge Houses continue to serve their original purpose as professors' residences.

116 Miller Chapel

Charles Steadman, 1834; Renovation: William A. Potter, 1874; Relocation, addition, and renovation: Delano and Aldrich, 1933; Renovation: Ford Farewell Mills and Gatsch, 2000

Although Charles Steadman typically worked from the designs of others, which he readily adapted for his own purposes, he was considered to be the most talented and prolific of Princeton's native architect-builders. The seminary's Miller Chapel is Steadman's work, its bold Doric facade likely influenced by John Haviland's Greek Revival–style churches in Philadelphia. Named for the seminary's second professor, Samuel Miller, the chapel originally faced Mercer Street on a site to the east and somewhat behind Alexander Hall. The seminary, at the time more prosperous than the college, could boast that Miller Chapel opened its doors thirteen years before the college could afford its own freestanding chapel (1847), since torn down to make way for Pyne Library (now East Pyne Hall). If the seminary had followed through and

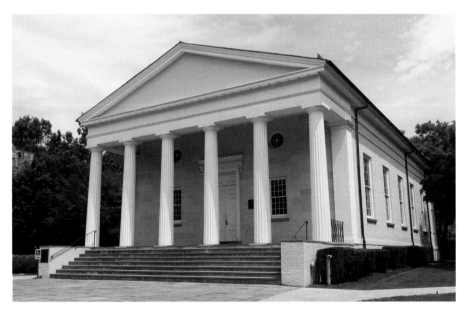

Miller Chapel

built a planned twin edifice to the west of Alexander Hall, the Greek Revival temples would have been the fraternal twins of Whig and Clio Halls on the college campus. They might have even suggested a neoclassical plan for the seminary, similar to that introduced at Princeton by Benjamin Latrobe and developed by Joseph Henry. Yet, apart from Miller Chapel, the seminary had no neoclassical phase.

The addition of Miller Chapel to the seminary, along with Alexander Hall and the two adjoining brick houses, gave this campus a compelling presence on Mercer Street. It was a formula the college would later adopt under President McCosh. By the closing decades of the nineteenth century both the seminary and college sited new buildings according to a similar pattern: academic facilities were oriented toward the community, and new student facilities faced internally.

However, in 1933 the seminary moved the building from Mercer Street to its present site. It was then enlarged and renovated by New York architect Delano and Aldrich. The new site for this major building suggests that the seminary realigned the campus to focus inward—a contemplative orientation organized around a campus green. Miller Chapel became the keystone of two loose quadrangles, defined by Alexander and Hodge Halls to the north and Stuart, Brown, and the Administration Building on the south. The chapel's 1874 renovation involved adding Victorian touches such as stained-glass windows and a polygonal-domed rear apse, and returning to what was perceived to be a more theologically and aesthetically appropriate clear glass. The reproduced hand-rolled (rather than commercially produced) glass has the delicate lavender tint of old glazing. Much of the interior, including the chancel, dates from this restoration, although the gallery parapet and the supporting columns are the original work of Steadman.

In 1995 the seminary developed a thoroughly researched and vetted architectural program for yet another renovation. The program addressed the obvious questions about what precisely is being restored when a building's history is a succession of important architects. This does not even consider accommodating heating, cooling, lighting, and security technologies unimagined when the building was first designed, as well as providing life safety and handicap access improvements. The program called for removal of the partitions, raised floor, and lowered ceiling of the chancel/choir introduced in the 1933 renovation, to effectively restore Steadman's "one-room meetinghouse" design. Paul Fritts, a West Coast organ builder, installed a new tracker organ and praised the acoustic properties of the restored interior, saying, "A great organ can't work in a bad room."

117 Scheide Hall
Ford Farewell Mills and Gatsch, 2000

The seminary programed the renovation of Miller Chapel to coincide with the construction of the adjacent Scheide Hall. Ford Farewell Mills and Gatsch (FFMG), which specialized in mixing new building design with historic renovations, created both projects. Scheide Hall houses support spaces for the chapel, including offices

Scheide Hall (left) and Miller Chapel (right)

for the chaplain and the director of music and a large choir rehearsal and recital space. Scheide Hall is named for musicologist, bibliophile, and seminary benefactor and trustee William H. Scheide and his wife, Gertrude. The Scheide family is also memorialized with buildings on the campuses of Princeton University and Westminster Choir College. The highly valued choir rehearsal and recital room is named for Sarah Belk Gambrell, seminary trustee emerita, who was the only daughter of Belk department store founder W. H. Belk Sr.

FFMG sited the rectangular building with a long west facade and entry to face a campus green and the south facade to face the chapel. They placed a meditative garden between the two buildings screened by a low stone wall. The wall forms an edge of a path that connects Miller Chapel and Scheide Hall with Alexander Hall to the north and Brown Hall to the south. The south facade features a full-height window wall that overlooks the garden and chapel from the choir rehearsal room.

The Gambrell Room occupies most of the second floor and receives daylight from the window wall and also from a clerestory that is set back from the two-story stone exterior wall and capped with a pitched slate roof. The stone-clad gable ends of the pitched roof extend well above the roofline. Together the clerestory, roof, and gable are strong design elements of the building's exterior. Inside the choir rehearsal and recital room the architect expressed the steel "scissor" trusses that support the roof and frame the clerestory.

The architect chose buff-colored sandstone as the primary cladding material, reminiscent of local Stockton sandstone used on colonial-era buildings in Princeton, but now only excavated from quarries in New York and Pennsylvania. The color contrasts with the darker masonry of nineteenth-century buildings on the campus green but forms a transition to the white-painted Miller Chapel. The architect used cast stone for heads and sills of the smaller office windows on the first floor and metal "eyebrows" for the larger second-floor windows. The windows are composed of small panes framed with white painted mullions similar to the Greek Revival design of the adjacent chapel.

118 Stuart Hall
William A. Potter, 1876; Renovation: Ewing Cole Cherry Parsky, 1980s

For Stuart Hall, William A. Potter, the architect of Princeton University's Chancellor Green Library, designed a splendid Venetian Gothic classroom facility that fronts Alexander Street. Walking or riding from the train station to the seminary, one would have seen Stuart's gabled tower topped by finials through the canopy of trees. It was an impressive signpost, leading to the front door of Stuart and the seminary campus. Citing structural concerns, the seminary removed the tower in the 1950s. As the campus developed, the main entrance to the building moved to the campus side and the ceremonial campus entrance moved to Mercer Street.

When it was built Stuart Hall was celebrated for workmanship and the use of masonry building materials. Contemporary critics found it "massive, beautiful and imposing." A century later a 1980s restoration corrected years of neglect and scrubbed off generations of grime, rediscovering for a new generation the former luster of Stuart Hall, which embodies the familiar traits of Victorian architecture: ornament, color, and order within an exuberant variety. The windows of each story follow one architectural style and shape, yet the aesthetic varies from floor to floor. The carved floral motifs at the west entrance are lush to the point of appearing tropical. There is a love of natural light expressed in the ample glazing that punctuates the brownstone masonry, which renders the stone almost lacy. And there is a composition of different materials, from the encaustic tile floor of the street-side entry porch to the limestone-edged windows to the polished marble pillars that support the entry arches.

Stuart Hall

All this exuberance might deceive the contemporary viewer into believing that ornamentation was the primary motive guiding the Victorian architect's hand. This was seldom the case and certainly not true of Potter, who adeptly designed mechanical systems—ventilation, natural lighting, and fireproofing—in consideration of both functional and aesthetic interests. The entry hall is bracketed by a pair of wooden staircases that lead to the upper floors, positioned in the middle of the building to pull fresh air through, up, and out of the towers. High ceilings in the lecture rooms and large operable windows amplify the effect.

An interesting footnote to the history of Stuart Hall is that the donors, brothers Alexander and Robert Stuart—who gave Prospect House to the college for President McCosh's use—made their gift conditional on the seminary honoring in perpetuity several points of Presbyterian doctrine. If any Stuart heir were to catch the seminary in some theological lapse, every tile, finial, and polychrome arch would revert to the family.

119 Brown Hall
J. B. Huber, 1865; Renovation: Ford Farewell Mills and Gatsch, 1994

South of Stuart Hall fronting College Road is Brown Hall, designed by architect J. B. Huber of Newark, New Jersey. It was the first single-use dormitory on the seminary campus, constructed to house an influx of students before the Civil War. The four-story elevation is basically Georgian Revival, while the cupola and deep white portico that shelters the front entrance are Greek Revival. The exterior walls are built of local stone laid in random ashlar with corners emphasized by quoins of darker stone. These details identify Brown Hall as a building of the mid-nineteenth century.

Brown Hall

Brown Hall is named for the donor, Mrs. George Brown of Baltimore. A few years after it opened, the building was equipped with gas heat for which the students each paid ten dollars a session. In 1880 bathrooms were installed. More recent upgrades included central air-conditioning and cable wiring, as well as internet access. The New Jersey Historical Commission awarded first prize to the careful exterior renovation that was completed in 1994.

120 Administration Building
John Notman, 1847; Addition and renovation: Ewing Cole Cherry Parsky, 1981

Opposite the south side of Alexander Hall and facing an expansive lawn is the Administration Building. Over time the seminary constructed buildings to the east, west, and south of the building, creating green courtyards with the building as a defining edge. The building has served many uses in the time since it was built.

Administration Building

John Notman originally designed the modest single-story stone building to house the seminary's refectory and infirmary. After the kitchen closed in 1899 the building was used as a dormitory. A decade later the students were moved out and it was transformed into a gymnasium. After the seminary had purchased the nearby Hun School property in 1945, which had a more modern gym, the building became the seminary's administration building, housing offices of the president and the academic dean. Both Notman's original building and the 1981 addition on the south side are simple structures that can easily accommodate these significant transformations.

121 Mackay Campus Center
George T. Licht, 1952

Mackay Campus Center closes off the west side of the informal quad formed by the Administration Building, and Stuart and Brown Halls. Since the original refectory had closed at the end of the nineteenth century, the seminary was desperate for a centrally located facility in which students could eat and socialize. Seminary students reacted the same way as Princeton University students who established eating clubs. And, like the university, the seminary's administration was concerned that the eating clubs worked against a sense of community. Mackay met the need by providing communal dining space and meeting space for students and groups. Moreover, the construction project proved to be a welcome sign of new energy: after a hiatus of nearly sixty years, the seminary was building again. The building also contains an auditorium and other facilities open to the public.

A parking structure for staff and seminary-related vehicles was completed in 2003 on nearby College Road.

Mackay Campus Center's design alludes modestly to the Georgian tradition of Alexander Hall. It honorably memorializes prominent seminary graduates whose ultimate sacrifice continues to bear witness to their faith: Elijah Parish Lovejoy (Class of 1834) died protecting his printing press from mob attack; James Reeb (Class of 1953) was fatally beaten in Selma, Alabama; and the seminary's third president, Rev. John A. Mackay (1936–59), was the center's namesake and most ardent advocate.

122 Hodge Hall
Robert Henderson Robertson, 1893

Hodge Hall occupies a site that originally housed Langdonic Hall, a wooden gymnasium that the students built for themselves in 1859. As the last of the major nineteenth-century buildings on the original campus, Hodge Hall has a footprint that looks like an enormous stone L, with a round tower joining the two uneven wings like a great masonry hinge. The shape is yet another creative example of how late nineteenth-century architects addressed concerns of daylight and ventilation before electrical and mechanical systems were readily available. In this instance the architect was aided by an enlightened donor who stipulated that every room should have sunlight at some point in the day. As for ventilation, the high ceilings of the rooms, the French doors at the ends of the halls, the operable transoms over the first-floor windows, and the central staircase within the tower all contributed to a constant supply of fresh air.

The design of Hodge Hall is more restrained than its Victorian predecessor, Stuart Hall, yet it retains some of the variety of form and materials. There is a central tower with its crown of windows. The rounded arches of the windows of the top story, the windows at the chamfered corners of the wings, and the paired grouping of windows all manifest a late nineteenth-century affection for extracting order out of picturesque complexity. Early photographs reveal that some of the variety has been removed, including large chimneys—no doubt to prevent fire once central heating had been installed—and decorative arches at the roofline of the side entrances.

The rusticated granite and brownstone materials of the exterior reveal the Victorian heart and soul of Hodge Hall. This is a building that celebrates the craftsmanship of the mason: from the irregularly sized pink-granite blocks that play against the regular brownstone quoins to the horizontal bands of darker stone that deflect rainwater from the wall (and offer a visual clue to the division between the floors); and from the brownstone spandrel panels between the windows of the top two floors to the brownstone cornice under the eaves of the green-slate roof.

Originally a dormitory for men after the Second World War, Princeton Seminary suddenly saw a large increase in married students as the GIs came home.

Hodge Hall

While the seminary had some married student housing on the newly acquired former Hun School campus, it was not adequate, and the Hodge Hall suites were temporarily turned into married student housing. Within a year there were many babies born to these young couples and it was then that the structure obtained the name "the fertile crescent." The building was remodeled in 1980, providing facilities for about seventy students in single rooms and three-room suites. Yet another remodeling in 1989, this time of the first floor, resulted in offices for faculty members. Recent work on the exterior is a textbook case of late twentieth-century technology and scientific restoration. The mortar between the stones, for example, was not simply replaced; it was chemically analyzed to reveal its original color when built; when replaced, the mortar was applied in such a way as to reproduce the original rounded, or "bullnose," effect.

The building honors the memory of one eloquent nineteenth-century Calvinist theologian, Charles Hodge. His brand of conservative theology is perhaps best summarized in his own words: "I am not afraid to say that a new idea never originated in the Seminary....The Bible is the word of God. That is to be assumed or proved. If granted; then it follows, that what the Bible says, God says. That ends the matter."

123 Templeton Hall
Ewing Cole Cherry Parsky, 1989

Like Mackay Campus Center, Templeton Hall also harkens back to an eighteenth-century colonial past. In addition to providing classrooms, faculty offices, and administrative offices, it also houses a state-of-the-art communications and media center. Yet nothing about the exterior offers a clue to the sophisticated business occurring inside.

Templeton Hall

Templeton shows greater agility, if not imagination, than Mackay in reviving colonial forms through the warm colors of the square masonry and the gabled entry pavilion, which is a more compelling front door than the rounded arches of Mackay's shadowy porch. Even the cupola looks as if it were designed especially for this roof, compared to the seemingly off-the-shelf one perched atop Mackay. As one approaches from the east, Templeton appears to be a relatively modest three-story structure, but the site drops away sharply and the entrance is bridge-like at the second floor.

124 Springdale
Attributed to John Notman, 1846

A short walk from Templeton leads to Springdale at 86 Mercer Street. Since 1903 it has been the official residence of the president of the seminary. Springdale was built in 1846 for Richard Stockton, the eldest son of Commodore Robert F. Stockton. Although there is no definitive evidence, the architect is thought to have

Springdale

been John Notman. Springdale is a transitional building at the intersection of several contemporary currents: the elevations of the individual pieces come close to the proportions of a Greek Revival temple; yet the deep eaves with their prominent brackets read more like the Italianate architecture for which Notman was famous; and the crenellated parapets on the bays, the diamond-shaped mullions, and the decorative molding over the windows are characteristically Gothic Revival details. It is a picturesque composition. The client clearly commissioned a residence that would ingratiate rather than overwhelm. It is just the sort of house an English vicar and his daughters might inhabit in Jane Austen's world.

125 Library
EYP and Rayford Law with EwingCole, 2013

North Wing
The Hillier Group, 1994; Renovation: EYP and Rayford Law, 2014

The Princeton Theological Seminary Library is recognized as the one of the world's preeminent libraries for Christian theological scholarship. Expanding and modern-izing the library was the seminary's highest priority in its Bicentennial Campaign in 2012. The new library—yet to be named at the time of this edition—is the most recent in a succession of five library buildings the seminary constructed since the first, in 1842. Three of these buildings—two of which were funded by former semi-nary trustee James Lenox and one of which was designed by Richard Morris Hunt in 1879—no longer exist. Community opposition to the demolition of the nineteenth-century buildings to make way for Speer Library (1956) arose again in 2008 when the seminary announced plans to demolish Speer. By then the neighboring commu-nity was organized into the Mercer Hill Historic District Association and the former Borough of Princeton had instituted a Historic Preservation Review Committee to advise the Regional Planning Board. Over a two-year public approvals process the seminary demonstrated that the Speer Library building was obsolete and the cost of renovation would be comparable to the cost of a new building. The library's growing collections—over one million volumes in print and microfilm—and the adoption of digital technology could no longer be accommodated in Speer due to its relatively low floor-to-ceiling height, which limited the introduction of advanced mechanical and electrical systems; floor construction that precluded use of compact shelving; and other impediments. In the end the Planning Board noted that the seminary "deserves a building that matches the quality of its collections."

The new building, designed by EYP and Rayford Law, forms an L that wraps around an internal core of the collections. It shares a four-story atrium with the North Wing, designed by the Hillier Group and opened as an addition to Speer in 1994. The building entry that faces Mercer Street is marked by a stone-clad tower featuring a Gothic arch flanking a columned arcade at the ground level. Embedded in the tower above the arch are twelve stone seals salvaged from Speer Library, calling to mind basic Christian teachings and the history of the Christian church. The so-called scholar's tower—a stone-clad square set at a forty-five-degree angle to the previously exterior south wall of the north wing—rises in the new atrium to provide historical and functional continuity between the new building and the north wing. The preexisting north wing entry is oriented toward Lenox House and Stockton Street. While the new building contains almost 50 percent more floor area than Speer, the addition is taller, occupies a smaller footprint, and is set back farther from Mercer Street than Speer. The setback allows for generous green space and gradual grade changes that help relate the library site to the main campus entry and historic Alexander Hall on the opposite side of Mercer Street.

The building's elevations are clad in a buff-colored sandstone reminiscent of local Stockton sandstone but excavated from quarries in Pennsylvania and New

Library tower with twelve seals

York. The architect punctuated the stone facade with tall chevron-shaped bay windows on the south and alternating flush and recessed windows on the east side. The clear glass windows are framed in prepatinated copper, a material also used to create a strong roofline in the horizontal plane around the perimeter of the building. These design features, combined with the L-shaped massing, relegate the north wing to be a background element of the Mercer Street composition.

The architect planned the interior based on a simple parti: occupant spaces adjacent to exterior walls, books and media shelving in the interior bays, and all floors open to a

Library

four-story atrium. The occupant spaces include open seating for readers, carrels for graduate students, offices for visiting scholars, and workrooms for library staff. The architect added common spaces, including a cafe, an assembly room, an alumni meeting room, and lounges on the second and third floors that overlook the main campus across Mercer Street. To maximize the number of books and microfilm available on-site, the architect designed the structure of all four floors to support compact shelving and high-density microfilm cabinets. The renovated north wing contains rare books, manuscripts, and missionary artifacts stored in a secure, temperature- and humidity-controlled environment. The atrium features a stone floor; a delightful neon sculpture, *Unending Love* by Hyong Nam Ahn; clerestory daylighting; interior balconies and monumental stair with glass railings and window walls; and the aforementioned scholar's tower. The atrium ceiling features astral-inspired punched skylights and pendant light fixtures in the abstracted form of scrolls. The reference reading room, adjacent to the atrium in a semidetached hexagonal pavilion, rises three stories with tall windows that provide abundant daylight and views into a secluded rain garden that collects and filters storm-water runoff between the pavilion and the north wing.

126 Lenox House
Richard Morris Hunt, 1878

This house, at the corner of Library Place and Stockton Street, is another example of James Lenox's generosity to the seminary. At one point it belonged to a set of two houses that faced Stockton Street, one of which was replaced by a parking lot.

Lenox House

Lenox House combines European Arts and Crafts elements with the American Stick Style, whose forms tend toward the simpler articulation of masses that would become popular toward the end of the century. The hipped eaves and dormers, porches, and painted brick are characteristic details. Whereas the seminary has carefully preserved the exterior of the house, the inside has been subdivided to house the offices of various research efforts, such as the Dead Sea Scrolls Project.

127 Carriage House
Attributed to Charles Steadman, ca. 1826; Renovation: Baker & Dallet, 1909; Renovation: architect unknown, 1967

The Carriage House began its life as a stable for Thompson Hall, a great house likely designed by Charles Steadman that had been located at 50 Stockton Street. The Thompson family heirs bequeathed the carriage house to the Borough of Princeton in 1906. It was transported to its present location on Mercer Street between the seminary library and the Trinity Church parking lot in 1909. Baker & Dallet, a Philadelphia architectural firm, renovated the building for use as municipal offices. The seminary bought the building in 1967 and extensively remodeled the interior to house faculty offices.

Because architecture belongs both to the era of its inception, and to its dialogue with time, one of the most resounding voices can be that of enlightened stewardship. In this regard the architectural history of the seminary is today adding

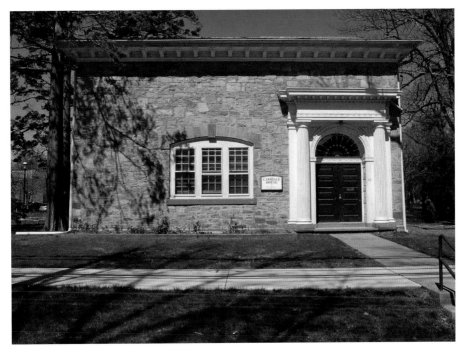

Carriage House

new chapters that, although subtle and not always immediately visible to the casual passerby, are a record of outstanding achievement. The painstaking technologies of modern historic preservation have been applied by the seminary to protect a precious and irreplaceable heritage. This attitude of stewardship, which is also shown in the care of the parklike landscaping that enriches the historic precinct, is evidence of an admirable commitment to pass intact to future generations a legacy that will not only continue to teach, but also continue to delight.

COLLEGE ROAD

DICKINSON PLACE

ALEXANDER STREET

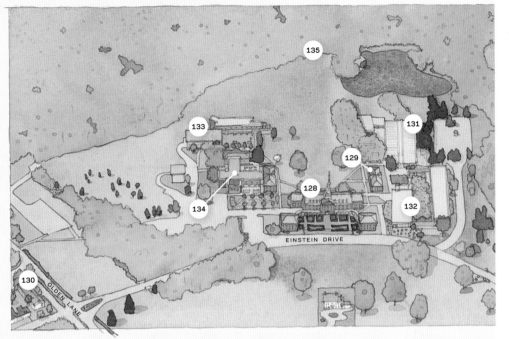

Institute for Advanced Study

AN ENGINE OF INNOVATION

Before and long after its founding on May 20, 1930, timing has played an important role in the meteoric ascent of the Institute for Advanced Study, the first institution of its kind in the United States. While schools and centers devoted to theoretical research abound at leading universities across America in the twenty-first century, such a place in 1930 represented a significant step forward in the name of innovation. The enlightened philanthropy of the Institute's benefactors, Louis Bamberger and his sister, Caroline Bamberger Fuld, was made possible by the fortuitous sale of their retail business to R. H. Macy & Company just weeks before the 1929 stock market crash. Bamberger and Fuld had intended to support a new medical school in Newark and sought guidance from Abraham Flexner, an international authority on medical education. Flexner, however, sixty-four years old and looking for new challenges, responded by convincing them to support a very different kind of project—a model center for postdoctoral research and the art of teaching, rather than a medical school. The Institute first used space in Fine Hall (now Jones Hall) and other buildings on the Princeton University campus and in Princeton. Flexner, while not initially convinced of the necessity for a separate campus, was eventually persuaded and shared this with the founders, who then set their sights on a new campus slightly to the south and west of the university.

The 350-acre farm tract on which the Institute was eventually built was intended to offer scholars and teachers a retreat from the distractions of the world. But the world was not so easily ignored in the late 1920s and 1930s. The

Institute Woods and pond across meadow

rise of Fascism and Nazism propelled many of Europe's most distinguished scientists and educators to come to America. For them, the Institute became a safe haven for what soon became an outstanding faculty. Albert Einstein, one of the early Institute faculty, had an office in Fine Hall, leading to the popular misconception that he was a member of the university's faculty.

Flexner and his associates understood that the Institute's architecture, more than simply housing faculty and administration, should express the Institute's intellectual ideals, financial viability, and confidence in the future. These same principles guided Dean West twenty years before when he conceived Princeton University's Graduate College, the first institution of its kind in this country. But whereas Dean West looked back to what he viewed as a nobler tradition, Flexner looked to the present and future:

> A university like all other human institutions—like the church, like governments, like philanthropic organizations—is not outside but inside the general social fabric of a given era… It is…an expression of the age, as well as an influence operating on both present and future.

The International Style, a form of modern architecture, expressed the age in which the Institute was founded. To modernists pure geometric forms and straight lines were as honest as they were rational; they celebrated the machine aesthetic. Flexner's commitment to utilitarian modernism was reinforced by a paradox of American higher education: Princeton and other universities often housed underpaid faculty members in splendid facilities. He spoke out against institutions that emphasized bricks over salaries: "Glorious buildings, gothic, neo-gothic, colonial, concrete stadia…student buildings of elaborate design, constructed while the college or university is pleading its inability to pay decent salaries." Such institutions had their priorities backward.

As Flexner saw it an enlightened educational institution pursued an architectural program that focused on function, amenity, and cost. The faculty's needs would always be uppermost. His views ultimately guided his successors to build in a way different from the university or seminary. The Institute's history, as revealed through the work of the leading architects of the second half of the twentieth century, shows a continuing commitment to reexamine new building projects within the constraints set forth by Flexner. The Institute has evolved over time into a stylistically heterogeneous campus creating an educational community that continues to be as Flexner intended: "an expression of the age, as well as an influence operating on both present and future." It is a place where scholars and nature are collaborators. If one stands at the edge of the Institute Woods quietly looking north toward Fuld Hall across the lake that occupies the middle distance, one can hear a dialogue between the campus and the natural setting. It is a conversation between fast and slow time, change and permanence, the theories of humankind, and the practice of nature on this gentle site.

Fuld Hall

128 Fuld Hall
Jens Frederick Larson, 1939; Landscape: Patrick Chassé, 2007

When the *New York Times* first carried the story of the proposed new Institute for Advanced Study, leading architects wasted no time contacting Director Flexner (1930–39). This was, after all, the Depression. Letters poured in from traditionalists and modernists alike. By turning to Jens Frederick Larson for its first building, the Institute chose one of the leading contemporary designers of collegiate architecture. He was largely self-taught and began his career designing college buildings at Dartmouth in 1919 as architect in residence. Larson also had a major impact on the architecture and the campus plans of Colby College, Bucknell, Lafayette, and Wake Forest.

The Georgian Revival style of Fuld Hall, perhaps a traditional approach in contrast to the Institute's modernist vision, stemmed from Flexner's immediate concern: the Institute needed instant credibility. Flexner believed that potential donors, as well as faculty and students, were more likely to sign on to a school designed in a familiar, traditional idiom. Larson gave the Institute the impression of historical roots. He also implied a prestige in its relationship to Princeton University by recalling the Georgian outlines of Nassau Hall. An additional impulse peculiar to the years just before the Second World War was a renewed interest in America's colonial past, reflected in the re-creation of Colonial Williamsburg in Virginia. When the building opened it was named in honor of Felix Fuld, business partner of Bamberger and husband of Caroline Bamberger.

Larson's approach to design would be called contextual if he were practicing today. "One should not copy an old existing building and adapt life to that building," he wrote, "but…should envisage the contemporary problem and clothe it in traditional architecture." In other words, the way a building works internally should be a state-of-the-art response to the life inside, whether that activity is a lecture on Kant or a scientific experiment for cloning sheep. But the container for this activity should be covered, according to Larson, in a design that communicates the idea of a college—in the same way a steeple communicates the idea of a church. This is a challenge that modernists faced on campus: they had to create a new language that also communicated a traditional idea.

Fuld Hall's colonnaded porch, leading to a pair of symmetrical two-story brick pavilions, recalls Benjamin Latrobe's 1802 siting of Philosophical and Geological Halls on either side of Princeton's Nassau Hall. Larson also imposed a formal order on the rolling farmland by lining up the director's house (the eighteenth-century country home of the Olden family) as the northern terminus of a north–south axis running through Fuld Hall's cupola. The cupola's three-part massing—square base, rectangular shaft, and circular capped lantern—echoes the cupola atop Independence Hall in Philadelphia, including the wooden urns and clock.

The Institute replenished the foreground to the building's colonnaded porch in 2007 with a design by landscape architect Patrick Chassé. He added symmetrical ramps to provide access to the first floor but maintained the Georgian Revival formality of the courtyard. Four new Japanese ornamental trees grace the planting beds, which were refreshed with new hedges, ground cover, and seasonal bulbs. Chassé also developed a planting program to renew the meadows with native grasses and wildflowers.

Like the first buildings at the university (Nassau Hall) and the seminary (Alexander Hall), Fuld Hall was an all-purpose facility. It originally housed the Institute's administrative functions, seminar rooms, lounges, a library, and dining rooms. Today it contains administrative and faculty offices, visiting scholar offices, and the common room, as well as the Mathematics–Natural Sciences Library. Unlike Nassau and Alexander Halls, Fuld did not have living quarters. The Institute provided assistance to faculty (permanent residents) to purchase nearby homes or construct new homes on Institute property. For members (visiting fellows) the Institute first purchased prefabricated housing from the Federal government and erected thirty-eight units on campus in 1947. Ten years later the Institute started building custom-designed housing for members.

129 Buildings C, D, and E
Jens Frederick Larson (Buildings C and D) with Matthew C. Fleming (Building E), 1948–54

The outbreak of the Second World War put all construction on hold. After the war scarce materials, craftsmen, and institutional funds permitted only basic maintenance and a modest building program. In 1948 Jens Frederick Larson designed a pair of two-story Colonial Revival structures a short distance from the rear of Fuld. Called Buildings C (at the southeast corner) and D (at the southwest), these two mirror-image rectangular blocks extended Larson's formal plan and suggested the beginnings of a large open quadrangle. In 1953 Princeton architect Matthew C. Fleming added a third Colonial Revival brick structure, Building E, located south and east of Building C. Building E was rotated ninety degrees from the north–south orientation of Buildings C and D and placed considerably to the east of the prevailing grid; it remains unclear whether the siting was a matter of convenience or if a future Building F was intended to face Building E.

130 Member Housing

Marcel Breuer, 1957; Addition and renovation: Michael Landau Associates, 2000

As early as 1945 the Institute had asked Alfred H. Barr Jr., the influential director of New York's Museum of Modern Art, for recommendations of modernist architects for Member Housing. Among those he named (for what Barr characterized as a "rather uninteresting problem") were the young Philip Johnson and Louis Kahn. Twelve years passed before the project advanced from discussion to actual construction. But when ground was at last broken in 1956 Marcel Breuer had been chosen to design the housing. Breuer's personal history—a European intellectual who emigrated to America to escape political and artistic repression— resonated with the histories of many of the Institute's early faculty. His credentials as a pioneer and practitioner of modern architecture ensured that his design for

Member Housing

Member Housing would represent a clean break from the revivalist design of previous Institute buildings.

As originally designed, the twenty buildings of Breuer's housing complex constitute a fascinating amalgam of quintessentially 1950s American and European impulses. Here is the European affection for balconies and communal living wedded to the American preference for patios and breezeways. Indeed, the most prominent feature of the front elevation is not the high strip windows (for privacy), but the icon of suburbia—the large carport. The carports serve triple duty to shelter the car, break up the facade to provide vistas through the building, and function as second-story roof decks.

The one- and two-story grouped housing recites a minimalist modern vocabulary, with orange-brick end walls and painted tongue-and-groove cedar siding. Open exterior stairways, roof overhangs, and sunshades vary the exterior surface texture on the street and court facades. Breuer creatively manipulated light, shadow, and air circulation for the benefit of the residents inside. The buildings sit atop concrete pads, as the need for basements was eliminated by a central heating plant and a community laundry room. Although the automobile plays a dominant role in the design and life of Member Housing, the complex is oriented inward rather than out to the public street. The buildings are clustered to define loose courts or quadrangles. These clusters are sited around a central grassy open space, which serves as a village green.

Breuer oriented the kitchen, dining, and living rooms to face the courts. Windows (including the single-pane glass door opening to a small flagstone patio) are appropriately generous to allow views of outside activity. Bedrooms and study areas tend to be grouped toward the street on the front. The parklike setting of mature trees and grass is pleasant, but there is little evidence to suggest that the services of a landscape architect were engaged. Breuer offered the members and their families five floor plans. The rooms of each unit were situated on one level and each unit had a fireplace. The word *kitchenette* provides a glimpse of how the space was used in the years before the kitchen became the social gathering place of most American houses.

An enthusiastic contemporary profile of the project in *Architectural Record* (March 1958) reported that a variety of building shapes was considered during design. But when, as here, the basic form is replicated twenty times, and the veneer is low cost (stock brick and wood paneling), the result is really a more thoughtful version of a suburban garden apartment. In 2000, after two earlier additions and renovations, the Institute engaged architect Michael Landau to expand and renovate the entire housing complex. Internal modifications include everything from new wiring for accommodating contemporary information technologies to a complete reworking of the tight kitchenettes. These were expanded into breakfast rooms that break through the plane of Breuer's original rear elevation and step modestly into the courts as square bays. The architect also re-created Breuer's flat roofs that had been incongruously rebuilt with sloped roofs.

131 Historical Studies-Social Science Library
Wallace K. Harrison, 1965

Nearly a decade passed after the construction of Member Housing before the Institute built again. The Breuer design had set a precedent that was brilliantly confirmed with the construction of a new library. After turning initially to Breuer, the Institute's trustees rejected the proposal he offered and Director J. Robert Oppenheimer (1947-66) contacted architect Wallace K. Harrison. The modernist firm of Harrison and Abramovitz is best known for its work on the United Nations and Lincoln Center developments, both in New York City. For these, Harrison had been indispensable for holding together dynamic consortiums of star architects. Harrison's reputation was that of a manager who could get things done. But as the Institute's library makes clear, his talents were not limited to orchestrating the work of others; Harrison was quite capable of performing on his own and, in fact, received the AIA Gold Medal in 1967.

The library exhibits characteristics of the International Style: the geometry is rectilinear; the walls are great expanses of glass; the coffered eaves are deep and overhanging; and the roof appears flat. Fully appreciative of the natural beauty on all sides, especially the small pond to the south, Harrison gently eased the building into the shoulder of the westward sloping site. On the east side it appears to be a relatively modest single-story structure that hugs the ground. The south and west elevations reveal that the library is two stories. The fieldstone base, the wood panels on the upper story, and the cantilevered white cornices help the building blend in with the setting. The intended transparency of the expansive glass surfaces is somewhat compromised, however, by the ultraviolet film installed on the inside surface of the glass as one of the means by which the books are stored under the proper environmental conditions.

Historical Studies–Social Science Library

The most striking design gesture is initially invisible, located on the roof. Standing outside during daylight hours, one is aware of a soft ambient light that bathes the inside of the library. Once inside, it becomes evident that the roof is a parallel series of east–west coves, the north sides of which are faced by clear glass. The effect is like standing at the bottom of a pool of water looking up through breaking waves. The challenge of protecting paper-based collections from direct sunlight without cutting off the outside world is here solved in a beautiful way.

132 Simons Hall and West Building

Geddes Brecher Qualls Cunningham; Landscape: Zion and Breen Associates, 1972

The Institute is organized as a collection of schools. There are currently four: historical studies, mathematics, natural sciences, and social science. As new schools were founded and as existing ones grew and changed, new facilities were constructed. In 1968 the Philadelphia firm of Geddes Brecher Qualls Cunningham (GBQC) prepared a master plan for the Institute, which identified proposed sites for the next generation of facilities and outlined four guidelines for future growth: respect for the existing landscape, development of courtyards and quadrangles, implementation of rational circulation patterns, and creation of new facilities in scale with existing buildings. The GBQC plan specifically laid out the rationale for a new Dining Hall (now Simons Hall) and facilities for the School of Social Science (West Building), both of which were to be sited west of Fuld Hall and north of the library. After considering Breuer and other renowned modern architects—Kevin Roche, Edward Larrabee Barnes, Richard Neutra, and Louis Kahn—the Institute selected Robert Geddes, the dean of Princeton University's School of Architecture and principal of GBQC, for the commission. The complex he designed solved two

West Building

different yet complementary issues: the West Building provided spacious offices and classroom space for the Schools of Historical Studies and Social Science, while Simons Hall gave the Institute a much-needed social and conference center.

Several faculty members opposed the plan to build the new academic and social complex west of Fuld Hall. The existing open landscaped space was seen as a great amenity that would be forsaken. Geddes's solution was to recast the challenge to accommodate both. With landscape architects Zion and Breen Associates, Geddes ensured his design would incorporate and celebrate the natural beauty of the site. So integral was the landscape that Geddes called it a clearing in the forest.

Like the library, their neighbor to the south, Simons Hall and West Building make inspired use of the natural westward slope of the site. The slope allowed Geddes to design a larger building than is first apparent from the south facade. Because of the slope, the east parapet of the three-story building is level with the eave lines of the existing buildings. This has the further advantage of deferring to Fuld Hall, which remains the focus of the campus.

Simons Hall and West Building are connected around garden courtyards onto which the main dining hall, lounge, and smaller dining/meeting room open. The exteriors of both buildings are predictably rectilinear and constructed of white trim, wood sash and panels, and exposed concrete to reflect the texture, joints, and fasteners of the wooden forms.

Interior spaces work because of the way in which the architect maximized the dramatic potential of the sloping site. Framed horizontal and vertical vistas are visible throughout the complex due to the multistoried columns, massive concrete open stairways, balconies, ledges, and great expanses of glass. The need for privacy as well as social interaction is deftly accommodated. The architect consciously intended the modular planning to permit future adaptation. The project received an Honor Award from the AIA Central New Jersey Chapter in 1973 for the artful collaboration of the building's architect and the landscape architect.

133 Simonyi Hall and Wolfensohn Hall
Cesar Pelli and Associates, 1994; Courtyard: Balmori Associates, 1994

The completion of West Building and Simons Hall defined the western wall of the emerging south campus. The next logical site for development was to the east, south of the C and E buildings. The 1968 development plan identified this as the location for a facility that would ultimately house the School of Mathematics. Like the West Building–Simons Hall complex, the result is two buildings, which anchor the southeast corner of the lower campus.

The program for these buildings addressed two issues: the need to gather mathematicians under one roof where they could interact, and the need for a large auditorium that could serve the Institute and also be a venue for the Princeton community. The architect, Cesar Pelli, exceeded expectations. The Mathematics Building (now Simonyi Hall) includes forty-eight offices and space for eighty-five

Wolfensohn Hall (left) and Simonyi Hall (right); Courtyard with blackboard and fountain

scholars; Wolfensohn Hall provides a 230-seat theater. The excellent acoustics make Wolfensohn a first-class concert hall for individual performers and small ensembles. Renowned violinist Isaac Stern performed the inaugural concert.

Landscape architect Diana Balmori, working with Pelli, created a loose courtyard defined on three sides by the new buildings and Building E. The courtyard features a lawn edged with cherry trees on the open side and containing a fountain and a chalkboard. The fountain is composed of two identical standing, rectangular, copper-clad slabs placed at a right angle. In warm weather water cascades down the faces of the slabs into a moat at ground level. The chalkboard—a single slab aligned with the fountain and faced on both sides with slate—defines the place as the preserve of mathematicians, who often communicate through the medium of chalk.

The mathematicians had listed few, but very specific, wishes regarding the interior: comfort, no distractions, opportunities for interaction with colleagues, and chalkboards. In response to the request for a peaceful environment with a minimum of visual or auditory distractions, the architect specified fabrics with muted tones and blonde oak throughout. To accommodate opportunities for interaction, Pelli designed wide, well-lit halls and stairways where the faculty and members could pause for easy conversation. The chalkboards are natural slate, recycled from old school buildings.

Pelli also used a sloping site to accommodate buildings that are larger than they first appear. The colonnade in front of Simonyi Hall and the arched truss in front of Wolfensohn offer abstract allusions to a classical design tradition. The front entrance of Wolfensohn is sheltered by a wooden arched truss that rests at each edge on round columns. The precedent seems to be a temple, with the truss serving as the tympanum. The entrance is appropriately dramatic for a performance space. Inside the auditorium the clean space features curving wall panels of red cherry wood, which ensures rich and resonant sound. This care for the quality of the acoustics is carried up to the ceiling, which continues the pattern of the arched wood trusses first seen outside.

134 Bloomberg Hall
Robert Geddes and Kehrt Shatken Sharon Architects, 2002; Addition: Pelli Clarke Pelli, 2007

By its seventieth anniversary, in 2000, the Institute could claim state-of-the-art facilities for three of its four schools, in addition to the original multipurpose building and later library, social center, and performance-assembly hall. To provide a home for the School of Natural Sciences, whose faculty and members were inadequately housed in Building D, the Institute linked existing freestanding Buildings C and E with an L-shaped addition. Together these buildings are named Bloomberg Hall. The brick addition features a common room with floor-to-ceiling glass on both the north and south elevations, and is topped by a copper roof.

Bloomberg Hall addition with "Slate Oasis" (foreground)

In 2007 Pelli Clarke Pelli added a wing to the east side of Bloomberg Hall to house the Simons Center for Systems Biology. Systems biology research occurs at the interface of molecular biology and the physical sciences. The three-story addition contains offices and meeting rooms on the upper two floors and central computing facilities and staff on the ground floor. Rafael Pelli, son of Cesar Pelli, expressed this programmatic split by cantilevering the top two floors over the base and projecting an aluminum-framed, glass-enclosed meeting room bay from a corner of the top floor. The primary cladding material is terra-cotta tiles framed with exposed aluminum members. The materials and details relate to the existing brick and grid of Bloomberg Hall. Pelli placed a new entrance on the east side of the addition, emphasized by a two-story recess. The wood entrance doors relate to the wood framing of the adjacent Wolfensohn Hall designed by Cesar Pelli fifteen years earlier. At the intersection of Bloomberg Hall and the new wing, Pelli designed a south-facing courtyard overlooked by a third-floor terrace. The courtyard features a site-specific sculpture, *Slate Oasis*, by Richard Long.

135 Institute Woods

South of the built campus lies an open meadow and pond with trailheads leading into the Institute Woods. Of the eight hundred acres of land owned by the Institute, almost 75 percent is permanently conserved meadows, woodlands, and wetlands. Stony Brook, which flows into Lake Carnegie farther east, borders the woods on the south and is part of the Atlantic Flyway for migrating birds. The woods, containing approximately forty-five species of trees, serve as a habitat for birds and other wildlife as well as a tranquil environment for Institute members and the public. Public access to the woods is from a trailhead in the adjacent Princeton Battlefield State Park.

Walking trails crisscross the woods offering many different experiences of the flora and fauna. Predominant tree species, including beech, tulip, black gum, hickory, pine, sweet gum, birch, oak, dogwood, and maple, are identified by plaques and a map available on the Institute's website (www.ias.edu/files/pdfs/ias-woods.pdf). Founders' Walk, named for Bamberger and Fuld, leads to a swing bridge over Stony Brook and the nearby Charles H. Rogers Wildlife Refuge. George Dyson, former director's visitor (2002–3), said it best: "No one will ever know how many problems in mathematics, physics, history, astronomy, economics, political science, social science, computing and biology have been brought one step closer to a solution by a shared conversation or a solitary walk in the Institute Woods."

WALK THIRTEEN

Downtown Princeton

136 Bainbridge House
137 Lower Pyne
138 Palmer Square
139 Princeton Public Library
140 Paul Robeson Center for the Arts
141 Westminster Choir College of Rider University
142 Nassau Presbyterian Church
143 Palmer House
144 Mercer Hill Historic District

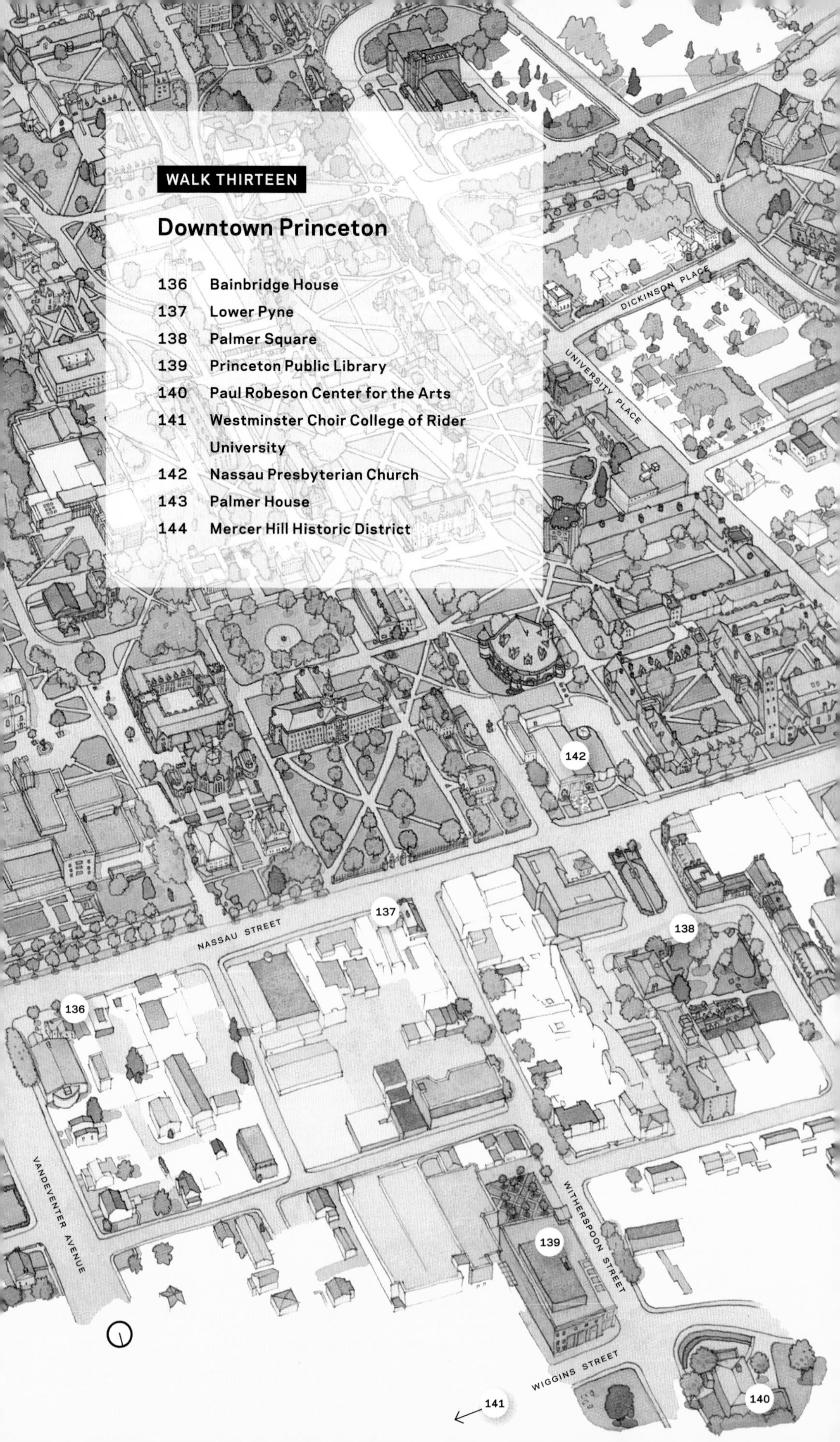
DICKINSON PLACE
UNIVERSITY PLACE
142
137
138
NASSAU STREET
136
VANDEVENTER AVENUE
WITHERSPOON STREET
139
WIGGINS STREET
141
140

Downtown Princeton

> Princeton is a wonderful little spot, a quaint and ceremonious village.
> —Albert Einstein, November 20, 1933

A SHARED EVOLUTION: A COMMUNITY AND A UNIVERSITY

In 1896 when the College of New Jersey became Princeton University, it chose to honor the community in which it resided. Several colonial colleges changed their names in their rise to university status, but not to the name of their location: King's College became Columbia University; Queen's College became Rutgers University; and the College of Rhode Island became Brown University. In spite of occasional misunderstandings and even battles, the town and university have prospered and continued to draw strength from one other. The shared name underscores that shared evolution. The colonial Prince-Town—where the College of New Jersey built its permanent campus—became the Borough of Princeton in 1813. A separate Princeton Township surrounding the borough was formed in 1838 as the countryside was developed. The municipal boundary bisected the campus. In 2013 the borough and the township merged into one municipality, Princeton. This Downtown Princeton Walk is within the former Borough of Princeton.

Palmer Square monument

Evidence of the tie between the university and town appears in the buildings of the community. Architects such as Charles Steadman, John Notman, Raleigh C. Gildersleeve, Ralph Adams Cram, and the members of Cope and Stewardson worked in both. Alumni such as Moses Taylor Pyne and Edgar Palmer used their money and influence to shape the town in ways they believed would enhance the university. Local materials of brick and stone reinforce the visual continuity between the campus and town. There are likewise similar architectural styles, from Georgian to modern, which bring an authentic variety and enviable liveliness to the university and the town.

Nassau Street, the main street of Princeton, has two sides. It is a permeable byway that adheres town and gown dialogue and continues to shape both. And so this guide ends where the university put down roots—in the town that has been its home for more than 250 years. This walk along Nassau Street and around the adjoining neighborhoods provides an introduction to today's Princeton, but there is much more to explore beyond the contours of Princeton's downtown.

Bainbridge House

136 Bainbridge House, 158 Nassau Street
ca. 1766

Bainbridge House is one of the oldest buildings on the north side of Nassau Street and for many years was the headquarters of the Historical Society of Princeton. (The Historical Society planned to move to Updike Farmstead within the Princeton Battlefield/Stony Brook Settlement Historic District in 2015.) Built by a wealthy tanner, Job Stockton, the house honors the memory of early resident Commodore William Bainbridge, the commander of Old Ironsides during the War of 1812. It is one of few remaining eighteenth-century houses in Princeton and presents obvious stylistic affinities to the university's Maclean House on the south side of Nassau Street. Both were among the first structures in Princeton to use brick as a facing material. What distinguishes Bainbridge House from Maclean House is a greater fidelity to the original Georgian design. The crisp articulation of the design elements of Bainbridge, for example, is lost when the brick is painted as it is on Maclean. Also, the roof of Maclean was raised and a porch added; one can look to Bainbridge to understand how Maclean looked when it was first built. Some of Bainbridge's historic interior is intact, including the original paneled walls in the second-floor main room, the staircase, and a treasured collection of town artifacts. The university owns Bainbridge House.

137 Lower Pyne, 92 Nassau Street

Raleigh C. Gildersleeve, 1896

To the west on the north side of Nassau Street is the half-timbered Tudor Revival landmark called Lower Pyne, the surviving twin of a pair of undergraduate dormitories commissioned by Moses Taylor Pyne (Class of 1877). This structure was built in 1896, the university's Sesquicentennial, when Princeton's trustees mandated Collegiate Gothic as the official style. Pyne was perhaps the most vociferous advocate. Inspired by the same spirit transforming the university, Pyne sought

Lower Pyne

to recast the north side of Nassau Street as a more appropriate setting for the "Oxbridge" institution taking shape to the south, or, as he put it, "to bring a touch of English living to a growing college town." If the university were to be America's new Cambridge, Nassau would be an English "High Street." Indeed, Pyne sent a college employee to study the residence-over-commercial buildings in Oxford and Cambridge, and then gave the information and commission to Gildersleeve, his favorite architect. The upper floors of both dormitories, which Pyne gave to the university, housed twenty students each, while the ground floor was rented out to commercial tenants. A recent careful restoration reveals a handsome structure that contributes to the visual variety of the street. Upper Pyne, originally located on the block west of Lower Pyne, was demolished in 1963 and Lower Pyne was sold in 1985 to a British-owned real estate company. Undergraduate students have long since been housed in dormitories on the other side of FitzRandolph Gate.

138 Palmer Square

Thomas Stapleton, 1936–39; Charles K. Agle, 1963–64

Edgar Palmer (Class of 1903), another influential Princeton alumnus and the ambitious heir to a zinc fortune, also tried his hand at redesigning Nassau Street. As he saw it, the town lacked a municipal focus: had Princeton been the seat of government, it might have been organized around a legislative hall; had religion played a central role, as it did in many New England colonies, Princeton might have grown around a church and a commons; instead, the town's design was dictated by the fact that it was a stop along the well-traveled Kings Highway, the principal north–south route between New York City and Philadelphia. And Nassau Street was the focus. Whereas Pyne had dressed the street in English garb, Palmer set out to create a municipal center in the heart of town.

The need for such a center had been anticipated by the work of Princeton Municipal Improvement Inc., a semi-independent association founded by Palmer and

Palmer Square green

committed to preserving "Princeton's character as an attractive place of residence." The group raised money as early as 1924 to hire a professional town planner and in 1925 recommended the building of a plaza that would eventually be Palmer Square, but the Depression intervened. When the project was revived in the mid-1930s it reflected the then-contemporary celebration of Americana, which ranged from the re-creation of Colonial Williamsburg to an influence on painting, movies, and music of the period.

Thomas Stapleton created Palmer Square by inserting a village green in the existing grid with small-scale Colonial Revival buildings to the west. Nassau Inn, rather than a church or a government building, anchored the green. In the course of the transfer of the business from its longtime location on Nassau Street to Palmer Square, the inn was rechristened as a much more historical "tavern" but reverted to an inn in the late 1950s. Ironically, Stapleton's plan implemented through the displacement of a number of Princeton's historic houses as well as poor and minority families who occupied the site. The Second World War interrupted the full realization of Stapleton's plan, and when work resumed in the 1960s on the east side, it was animated by a different spirit.

The new architect, Charles K. Agle, abandoned Stapleton's Colonial Revival plan and substituted a single five-story (six stories at the back), L-shaped brick structure with a hip roof. Sacrificed in the process was Upper Pyne, the other half of Gildersleeve's Tudor Revival project on Nassau Street, as well as other structures. Agle's large brick box on the east side of Palmer Square makes the obvious point that it is usually less expensive to build and maintain one plain structure with open-plan interiors than a series of domestically scaled and styled structures.

For the pedestrian the Palmer Square of the 1930s is more pleasing than
Agle's office building. The Colonial Revival ambiance of Palmer Square West is
admittedly ersatz, but it is preferable to the midcentury modern office building and
plaza on the other side, which are out of scale due to the application of traditional
features (the hipped roof and projecting eaves). The economics of real estate are
evident in the office building, but charm, character, and human scale emanate from
the buildings to the west.

139 Princeton Public Library
The Hillier Group, 2004

The Princeton Public Library celebrated its centennial in 2010. Since 1966 the
library had occupied a building on the corner of Witherspoon and Wiggins Streets in
downtown Princeton, surrounded by streets, surface parking lots, and an electrical
substation. When the library built a replacement in 2004—the fifty-eight-thousand-
square-foot George and Estelle Sands building—it hoped that the municipality
would redevelop the surrounding sites. A private-public partnership subsequently
developed a parking structure, mixed-use building (residential condominiums and
street-level retail), and plaza fronting the library and the mixed-use building. The
library's main entrance opens onto Albert E. Hinds plaza, named for an African-
American resident of the nearby neighborhood. Hinds, who died in 2006 at 104
years of age, chronicled much of Princeton's twentieth-century growth and articulated concerns of long-term downtown residents pressured by commercial and
institutional redevelopment projects.

The Hillier Group's design for the building responds to the library's objectives
of perimeter transparency and internal flexibility. The perimeter bays framed by

Public Library and Hinds Plaza

round, brick-clad structural columns are infilled with aluminum-and-glass curtain walls, allowing library patrons views of street life, and views of the library's activities to passersby on the street. A glass-enclosed stair tower in the middle of the long Witherspoon Street frontage dramatizes these activities. To screen patrons and materials from the afternoon sun, the architect set back the second floor from the perimeter wall and created a shaded terrace overlooking the street on the third floor. Internally there are no load-bearing walls, and few permanent partitions outside the service core, to allow reorganization of functions when needs change. The wisdom of this strategy became apparent when the library eliminated all but a few shelves of reference material—which had been digitized or become available online—and placed public computer workstations where the shelves had been.

On the street level the library welcomes the public with a cafe operated by a local restaurateur and a mural titled *Happy World*, which consists of three thousand individual, three-by-three-inch tiles made by artist Ik-Joong Kang from objects donated by the community. Hinds Plaza functions in part as an extension of the library. A multipurpose room in which the library schedules community events opens onto the plaza, where the library hosts an annual children's book fair.

140   Paul Robeson Center for the Arts
Michael Graves and Associates, 2008

At the corner of Witherspoon Street and Paul Robeson Place is the home of the Arts Council of Princeton, whose mission is "building community through the arts." Michael Graves renovated the Arts Council's 1932 Works Progress Administration-era building and designed a prominent addition to anchor the corner opposite the

Paul Robeson Center

new Public Library. The building is named for Paul Robeson, an African-American actor, athlete, author, and activist who lived in the adjacent neighborhood as a child.

The Arts Council provides classes, workshops, and camps in the building's visual arts and dance studios; hosts performances and events in a 120-seat flexible space; mounts exhibitions in an art gallery; and provides a suite for visiting artists. The entrance rotunda welcomes visitors and serves as a portal to the various activities in the three-story building. Above the rotunda Graves placed a Communiversity Room for events and meetings in a glass-enclosed space that overlooks downtown Princeton. *Communiversity* refers to the collaborative relationship in the arts between the Princeton community and Princeton University, which is celebrated by an annual arts festival.

Graves's preference for multicolored materials is evident on the building's exterior. Orange brick continues the prevalent material of the older building and is accented by blue glazed tiles and red-painted window frames. A two-story freestanding column supports a canopy over the main entrance, where a bust of Paul Robeson sits atop a pedestal.

141 Westminster Choir College of Rider University
Sherley W. Morgan, 1934

Scheide Student Center
J. Robert Hillier, 1975

Marion Buckelew Cullen Center
KSS Architects, 2014

On Hamilton Avenue several blocks east from the Robeson Center and Public Library lies the campus of Westminster Choir College. (The name of the street connecting these three cultural institutions changes from Paul Robeson Place to Wiggins Street to Hamilton Avenue.) The original campus quadrangle is sited on the plateau of a hill that ascends from the intersection of Hamilton Avenue and Chestnut Street. John Finley Williamson founded the choir and school at the Westminster Presbyterian Church in Dayton, Ohio, in the 1920s. In 1932 Sophia Strong Taylor provided funds for the Choir College to purchase ten acres in Princeton, and the college commissioned Sherley W. Morgan (Princeton University Class of 1913), director of the university's School of Architecture, to design four buildings. To commemorate the opening of the campus buildings in 1934, the choirs of Westminster and Princeton University joined the Philadelphia Orchestra in a performance of Johann Sebastian Bach's *Mass in B-minor* in the Princeton University Chapel.

The centerpiece of the four original buildings is Williamson Hall, a four-story Georgian Revival design with a raised, pedimented portico facing Hamilton Avenue and a clock tower on the campus quadrangle side. Morgan designed two dormitories

Westminster Choir College original quadrangle; Marion Buckelew Cullen Center rendering

flanking Williamson Hall in a similar style using red brick, white-painted wood trim, pitched slate roofs with dormers, and chimneys on the gable ends. On the side of the quadrangle opposite Williamson Hall, Morgan designed Bristol Chapel, which features a recital hall and chapel on the upper floor and instructional space and offices on the lower floor. The recital hall features an Aeolian-Skinner organ and is the setting for memorable holiday concerts when the white walls and tall multipaned windows are adorned with seasonal decorations. Perimeter brick walkways and low site walls define the grass quadrangle, which is off-limits to pedestrians and is dedicated to "Professor & Mrs. Sherley W. Morgan in grateful recognition of their many and varied contributions to the college."

Over the years the college acquired an additional thirteen acres to the north and downhill from the original campus. On this land the college built additional dormitories and instructional and rehearsal space, none of which rise to the level

of Morgan's site and building designs. In 1975, however, J. Robert Hillier reversed
this trend with his design of a student center facing the original quadrangle.
The center is named for William H. Scheide, whose gifts funded construction of
buildings at Westminster, as well as at Princeton University and the Princeton
Theological Seminary.

Continuing in the college's tradition of hiring local architects, KSS Architects
designed the Marion Buckelew Cullen Center, an addition to the Playhouse. The
Playhouse, affectionately known as the "Quonset hut," is an all-purpose building for
productions, rehearsals, classes, and special events. The new building, designed in
the spirit of Morgan's original four buildings, houses the Hillman Performance Hall,
a lobby and other audience amenities, a green room, and three flexible classrooms.
KSS configured the Cullen Center and Playhouse complex to form a courtyard
suitable for informal gatherings and for student and alumni events.

142   Nassau Presbyterian Church (formerly First Presbyterian Church)
Thomas U. Walter, 1835; Addition: Short and Ford, 1988

Across from Palmer Square on the south side of Nassau Street stands the dignified
Greek Revival facade of Nassau Presbyterian Church, designed by Thomas U.
Walter. Charles Steadman, architect-builder of the Princeton Theological Seminary's
Miller Chapel, had commissioned Walter to design the building's facade. Steadman
was also the project's chief underwriter and interior planner, and was responsible
for the excellent construction.

Although the facade is an early work by Walter, it conveys the confidence
of a knowledgeable craftsman and foretells the skill that would be applied later in
his best-known design, the great cast-iron dome of the U.S. Capitol. The absence

Nassau Presbyterian Church

of windows at the front draws the eye to the overscaled, recessed porch, an effect that is augmented by two massive Ionic columns that frame the line of sight of passersby. At once delicate and strong, open and screened off, the entrance irresistibly draws those on the street into a realm intended to be separate from the bustle of university and town. Walter's refined Greek Revival design widely influenced American church architecture throughout the nineteenth century. Until the construction of Alexander Hall in 1892, most of the college's commencement exercises were held here.

Over the years the church (with the permission of the university, which owns the surrounding property) has built a series of five major additions, which are all documented in a drawing by Princeton firm Short and Ford that hangs in the hall outside the sanctuary. The most recent addition was designed by Short and Ford in 1988. In theory it should have been virtually impossible to accommodate any additions to Walter's tight classical form; yet in practice the church congregation has been careful to commission work that has never compromised the powerful presence Walter's design continues to exert on Nassau Street.

143 Palmer House, Nassau Street and Bayard Lane
Charles Steadman, 1823; Renovation: HMR, 2000

Charles Steadman was one of a number of builders whose engaging Greek Revival buildings lined the streets of nineteenth-century Princeton. Although hardly innovative, his residential designs were distinguished by consistent quality. In 1823 Commodore Robert F. Stockton commissioned Steadman to design a house for his wife, Harriet Marie Potter. Steadman's design combined Federal elements (e.g., an arched fanlight over the entry and a roof edge balustrade) with the newer taste for Greek Revival (e.g., exterior columns and pilasters, and higher ceilings). The

Palmer House

original two-story house is square in plan with a one-story portico facing Nassau Street. The brick exterior walls were painted, white at first and now yellow.

In 1923 Edgar Palmer purchased the property, and in 1968 his widow donated it to the university. Known today as Palmer House, the university uses it to accommodate events and overnight guests. The original building contains public rooms on the main floor (parlor, library, and dining room) and guest rooms on the upper floor. Over time the building has been enlarged and renovated to serve the changing needs of its occupants. The addition to the rear (north) contains a sunroom, used for meetings and informal dining, a kitchen, and other service facilities. Guests arriving by car enter the property from Bayard Lane and proceed to a motor court on the east side of the enlarged house. Most recently the architect HMR created a new entrance adjacent to the motor court to receive guests and provide access for persons with disabilities.

144 Mercer Hill Historic District

Public Plaza (Stockton and Mercer Streets)
Landscape: Louise Schiller, 1997

Princeton Battle Monument
Architect: Carrère and Hastings; Sculptor: Frederick William MacMonnies, 1922

155 Stockton Street, Morven, ca. 1750

32 Edgehill Street, The Barracks, ca. 1696

112 Mercer Street, Albert Einstein house

43 Mercer Street, Ivy Hall
John Notman, 1846

33 Mercer Street, Trinity Church
Richard Upjohn, 1868; Renovation: Cram and Ferguson, 1915

10 Mercer Street, Bonner Foundation, moved 1868

The former Borough of Princeton created the Mercer Hill Historic District in 1985 to recognize and protect the character of the neighborhood and certain buildings located therein. Listed in the National Register of Historic Places and the New Jersey Register of Historic Places, the district is bounded by properties abutting Stockton Street on the north, Edgehill Street on the west, Mercer Street on the south, and University Place to Dickinson Place on the east. Several historic

Plaza at Stockton and Mercer Streets

buildings featured elsewhere in this book and belonging to the Princeton Theological Seminary (e.g., Alexander Hall and Springdale) and Princeton University (e.g., Palmer House) are within the district's boundaries. In addition to the notable buildings described here, the neighborhood contains houses and streetscapes reminiscent of nineteenth-century Princeton.

At the intersection of Stockton and Mercer Streets—and the offset convergence of Bayard Lane, Nassau Street, and University Place—lies a small, urbane plaza reclaimed from a traffic island. The plaza, designed by landscape architect Louise Schiller in 1997, features stone pavers, benches, planters, and a trellis, and is the site of a seasonal flower market. This walk through the historic district begins and ends at this plaza and moves counterclockwise along Stockton, Edgehill, and Mercer Streets.

Princeton Battle Monument (Stockton Street and Bayard Lane), which commemorates the January 3, 1777, Battle of Princeton, depicts Liberty inspiring General Washington as he leads his troops into battle, and the death of General Hugh Mercer. In 2007 the then Borough of Princeton undertook a conservation project to provide permanent illumination of the monument and a landscaped walkway that leads to it.

Morven (155 Stockton Street) was the home of Richard Stockton, a signer of the Declaration of Independence, and is now a National Historic Landmark. The building currently houses a history museum. Morven was substantially rebuilt after suffering damage from fires in 1758 and 1821.

Princeton Battle Monument

The stone Barracks (32 Edgehill Street), on property once owned by the Stockton family, quartered soldiers during the French and Indian Wars (1755–60) and reportedly hosted delegates to the Continental Congress when it met in Princeton in 1783. A nineteenth-century fire destroyed most of the building and most of the existing stonework was erected in the twentieth century. As evidenced in Morven and the Barracks, it is difficult to discern the original structure in many historic buildings in this district and elsewhere due to additions and alterations following fires, changes in use, and stylistic preferences.

Albert Einstein lived in the two-story clapboard house at 112 Mercer Street from 1936 to 1955 when he was on the faculty of the Institute for Advanced Study. The house is now a National Historic Landmark.

The stone Ivy Hall (43 Mercer Street) was originally built to house a law school for Princeton University (then the College of New Jersey). After the initiative

Morven, 155 Stockton Street; Trinity Church, 33 Mercer Street

failed, the building served diverse functions, including a college eating club, a canal company's office, and now a choir rehearsal hall.

The stone Gothic Revival Trinity Church (33 Mercer Street) was built in 1868 to replace an earlier wood Greek Revival church. It was substantially enlarged in 1915 and interior renovations were completed in 1967 following a fire and liturgical innovations.

The wood Greek Revival house at 10 Mercer Street was moved by barge from Northampton, Massachusetts, in 1868 and currently houses the Bonner Foundation.

A walk along Alexander Street to Dickinson Place and University Place features many white clapboard Greek Revival houses from the mid-nineteenth century. After returning to the plaza from Mercer Street or University Place, one can go back to the shops and restaurants of Palmer Square and the FitzRandolph Gate entrance to the historic campus of Princeton University by walking east on Nassau Street.

As an avid reader—and now author and photographer—of the Campus Guide series, I thank Princeton Architectural Press for creating, expanding, and renewing this series, which now includes twenty-five titles. I am grateful to Publisher Kevin Lippert and series editor Jan Cigliano Hartman, for their support and guidance during the editorial and production processes of this book. As this is a revised and expanded version of the 1999 edition, I am beholden to the original author, Raymond P. Rhinehart, and photographer, Walter Smalling Jr. I am grateful to President Emerita Shirley M. Tilghman (2001–13)—during whose tenure many significant improvements to the Princeton University campus were accomplished—and President Christopher L. Eisgruber (2013–present) for supporting the revised and expanded edition. I am indebted to many others at the university and neighboring institutions who contributed their time and expertise to making this book and list them in the following paragraphs.

At the university my colleague and friend Natalie Shivers (associate university architect) served as the point person for collecting documents and, most importantly, as in-house editor. Others at the university who reviewed drafts of the text include Robert Durkee (vice president and secretary), Ron McCoy (university architect), Daniel Linke (university archivist), Laurel Cantor (university creative director, communications), Karin Dienst (managing editor, communications), and Daniel Casey (coordinating architect). Jon Hlafter (university architect emeritus), who mentored me as a member of his staff, contributed his forty years of institutional knowledge. Former colleagues within the facilities department who provided documents and insights include James Wallace, Jane Curry, Mark Wilson, David Howell, Ted Borer, Eric Witter, Joshua Linkov, and Alex Karels; as well as Chris Lillja, who contributed photographs. For the Princeton University Art Museum, Curtis Scott (associate director for publishing and communications) wrote the museum collections tour (Walk Six) and Lisa Arcomano (manager of campus collections) provided text from the website she created for Campus Art at Princeton. Additional resources that informed my understanding of the campus include the 2008 Campus Plan, developed by a team of consultants led by Beyer Blinder Belle, and W. Barksdale Maynard's recent history *Princeton: America's Campus*.

The following people from neighboring institutions generously provided documents and insights: at Princeton Theological Seminary, Barbara Chaapel (director of communications and external relations), German Martinez (director of facilities and construction), and Kenneth Henke (curator, special collections); at the Institute for Advanced Study, Christine Ferrara (communications); Westminster Choir College of Rider University, Anne Sears (director of external affairs); and at Princeton Public Library, Leslie Berger (librarian). For downtown Princeton, Wanda Gunning of the Historical Society of Princeton reviewed and provided comments on the text and Kristin Appelget (director

Old Frick wisteria

of community and regional affairs at Princeton University) provided contacts and insights.

At Princeton Architectural Press—under the direction of series editor Jan Cigliano Hartman—the project editor Meredith Baber, designer Benjamin English, digital prepress manager Andrea Chlad, and others helped to produce the book. Artwork was provided by Tom Gastel, who created the rendered campus map; Robert Rock and Tim Kirby at Michael Van Valkenburgh Associates, who created the four Landscape Walks plans; and architectural firms, including Steven Holl Architects, Tod Williams and Billie Tsien, and KPMB, that contributed renderings of featured buildings not yet completed at press time.

Finally I am grateful to those leaders, planners, designers, and builders who created, preserved, and continue to improve the environs, buildings, and landscapes that constitute Princeton University and its neighboring institutions.

Baker, Paul R. *Richard Morris Hunt.* Cambridge, MA, and London: MIT Press, 1980.

Balmori, Diana, Diane Kostial McGuire, and Eleanor M. McPeck. *Beatrix Farrand's American Landscapes: Her Gardens & Campuses.* Sagaponack, NY: Sagapress, 1985.

Barnett, Robert S. "Hindsight-Foresight: From the Founding to the Future of Five Ivy League Campuses." SCUP *Planning for Higher Education Journal* 41, no. 1 (October–December 2012).

Breese, Gerald. *Princeton University Land: 1752–1984.* Princeton: Princeton University Press, 1986.

Brownlee, David B., David G. DeLong, and Kathryn B. Hiesinger. *Out of the Ordinary: Robert Venturi, Denise Scott Brown and Associates.* Philadelphia: Philadelphia Museum of Art, 2001.

Campus: Guide to Princeton University. Princeton: Princeton University Office of Communications, 1997.

Cotton, Dale. *Princeton Modern.* Princeton: Princeton University Office of Communications, 2010.

Evans, William K. *Princeton: A Picture Postcard History of Princeton and Princeton University.* Vestal, NY: Almar Press, 1993.

Gambee, Robert. *Princeton.* New York: W. W. Norton, 1998.

Greiff, Constance M., Mary W. Gibbons, and Elizabeth G. C. Menzies. *Princeton Architecture: A Pictorial History of Town and Campus.* Princeton: Princeton University Press, 1967.

Kusserow, Karl, ed. *Inner Sanctum: Memory and Meaning in Princeton's Faculty Room at Nassau Hall.* Princeton: Princeton University Art Museum, 2010.

Lane, Wheaton J., ed. *Pictorial History of Princeton.* Princeton: Princeton University Press, 1947.

Larson, Jens Fredrick. *Architectural Planning of the American College.* New York: McGraw-Hill, 1933.

Leitch, Alexander. *A Princeton Companion.* Princeton: Princeton University Press, 1978.

Maynard, W. Barksdale. *Princeton: America's Campus.* University Park, PA: Pennsylvania State University Press, 2012.

McGuire, Diane Kostial, and Lois Fern, eds. *Beatrix Jones Farrand (1872–1959): Fifty Years of American Landscape Architecture.* Washington, D.C.: Dumbarton Oaks, Trustees for Harvard University, 1982. Eighth Dumbarton Oaks Colloquium on the History of Landscape Architecture, Washington, D.C., 1980.

Oberdorfer, Don. *Princeton University: The First 250 Years.* Princeton: Princeton University Press, 1995.

Princeton University. "Princeton University: An Interactive Campus History 1746–1996." http://etcweb.princeton.edu/campus/Campus.

Rudolph, Frederick. *The American College and University: A History.* New York, NY: Knopf, 1962. Reprint, Athens, GA: University of Georgia Press, 1990.

Seasonwein, Johanna G. *Princeton and the Gothic Revival: 1870–1930.* Princeton: Princeton University Art Museum.

Selden, William K. *Club Life at Princeton.* Princeton: Princeton Prospect Foundation, 1994.

———. *The Legacy of John Cleve Green.* Princeton: Princeton University, 1988.

———. *Nassau Hall.* Princeton: Princeton University, 1995.

———. *Princeton Theological Seminary: A Narrative History 1812–1992.* Princeton: Princeton University Press, 1992.

Shand-Tucci, Douglass. *Boston Bohemia: 1881–1900.* Amherst, MA: University of Massachusetts Press, 1995.

Short, William H., and Constance M. Greiff. "Small Town, Distinguished Architects, Parts 1 and 2." *Princeton History, The Journal of the Historical Society of Princeton*, no. 8 (1989) and no. 9 (1990).

Thorp, Willard, Minor Myers Jr., and Jeremiah Stanton Finch. *The Princeton Graduate School: A History.* Princeton: Princeton University Press, 1978.

Turner, Paul Venable. *Campus: An American Planning Tradition.* Cambridge, MA: MIT Press, 1990.

Wertenbaker, Thomas Jefferson. *Princeton: 1746–1896.* Princeton: Princeton University Press, 1996. Preface by John M. Murrin.

Index

Image Credits

Cover: Holder Hall courtyard and tower
Robert Spencer Barnett: cover, 2, 4,
8, 21, 24, 25, 27, 40, 42, 43, 44, 45, 47,
58 (top), 62, 63, 64, 65, 73 (top), 73
(bottom), 74, 76, 78, 90, 92, 98 (top
and bottom), 101 (top), 103 (top), 104
(top), 104 (bottom), 114, 116, 118, 124
(bottom), 126, 129, 131, 133 (top), 134,
135, 136, 137, 139, 140, 144, 145, 149, 156,
157, 158 (top), 158 (bottom), 161, 162
(top), 162 (bottom), 164 (bottom),
165, 167 (top), 167 (bottom), 169 (top),
170, 173, 175, 202 (left and right), 203,
204, 205, 207, 208 (bottom), 219, 220
(bottom), 222, 227 (bottom), 229,
232, 233, 234, 235 (top and bottom),
244, 245, 247, 248, 251 (top), 253, 254
(top and bottom), 258, 259, 260 (top
and bottom), 263, 264, 278, 279, 280,
282 (bottom), 292, 300, 301, 302, 303,
306, 316, 320, 324, 325, 326, 328 (top),
332, 336
Dale Cotton: 150, 220 (top)
Elizabeth Felicella: 10, 225
Graphic Arts Collections, Rare Books
and Special Collections, Princeton
University Library: 33, 36, 52, 53, 54
(top), 82
Graphic Arts Collections, Rare Books
and Special Collections, Princeton
University Library. Bequest of Mrs.
Luther P. Eisenhart: 282 (top)
Historical Society of Princeton: 68
Courtesy of KPMB Architects: 127, 128
Courtesy of Michael Van Valkenburgh
Associates: 29, 199, 237 (top)
Courtesy of Pei Cobb Freed & Partners:
216
Courtesy of Rick Joy Architects: 213
Courtesy of Steven Holl Architects: 211
Courtesy of Studio Ma: 239
Courtesy of *The Office of Clarke and
Rapuano, Inc: Consulting Engineers
and Landscape Architects* (1972): 146
(top)
Courtesy of Tod Williams Billie Tsien
Architects: 146 (bottom) and 148
Courtesy of Princeton Theological
Seminary: 290, 298
Princeton University Archives,
Princeton University Library: 23, 34
(top and bottom), 49, 56, 58 (bottom),
75 (top), 84, 86, 89, 94, 85, 102, 103
(bottom), 106, 123, 133 (bottom), 147,
154, 201, 208 (top), 210, 242, 268, 270,
282 (top)
Princeton University Art Museum: 192
Princeton University Grounds and
Buildings Maintenance: 69
Princeton University Office of
Communications: Denise

Applewhite: 111; Laurel Cantor: 48
Princeton University Office of the
University Architect: Dan Casey:
107; Jon Hlafter: 223; Alex Karels:
141, 169 (bottom), 224, 322, 329, 333,
334 (top and bottom); Josh Linkov:
250
Princeton University Office of the Vice
President for Facilities: Christopher
Lillja: 3, 37, 39, 61, 70, 75 (bottom), 88,
95, 96 (bottom), 101 (bottom), 190,
110, 124 (top), 142, 159, 164 (top), 168,
172 (top and bottom), 178, 200, 218,
230, 237 (bottom), 251 (bottom), 256,
257, 262, 273
Princeton University Services: 59, 66,
330
Walter Smalling Jr.: 13, 16, 93, 96 (top),
206, 227 (top), 275, 281, 288, 289, 293,
294, 295, 297, 299, 308, 310, 312, 313,
315 (top), 323
Beatrix Jones Farrand Collection,
Environmental Design Archives,
University of California, Berkeley:
99, 272
Photo by Thomas Uphill, Courtesy of
the Institute for Advanced Study:
315 (bottom)
Courtesy of Westminster Choir
College: 328 (bottom)
Bruce M. White: 54 (bottom)
Photo by Bruce M. White, courtesy of
Princeton University Art Museum:
180, 181 (left and right), 183 (left and
right), 184 (left and right), 185, 186,
187, 188, 189, 190, 193, 194, 195
Source unknown: 179, 192